Starting Your
Tropical Aquarium

Dr. Herbert R. Axelrod

Title Page:
A spawning pair of *Trichogaster leeri*, the gorgeous pearl gourami. This fish is not always available, but it is one of the most spectacular fishes that the beginner can not only keep but spawn in his tank. Photo by R. Zukal.

ISBN 0-86622-105-0

© 1986 by T.F.H. Publications, Inc. Distributed in the UNITED STATES by T.F.H. Publications, Inc., 211 West Sylvania Avenue, Neptune City, NJ 07753; in CANADA by H & L Pet Supplies Inc., 27 Kingston Crescent, Kitchener, Ontario N2B 2T6; Rolf C. Hagen Ltd., 3225 Sartelon Street, Montreal 382 Quebec; in CANADA to the Book Trade by Macmillan of Canada (A Division of Canada Publishing Corporation), 164 Commander Boulevard, Agincourt, Ontario M1S 3C7; in ENGLAND by T.F.H. Publications Limited 4 Kier Park, Ascot, Berkshire SL5 7DS; in AUSTRALIA AND THE SOUTH PACIFIC by T.F.H. (Australia) Pty. Ltd., Box 149, Brookvale 2100 N.S.W., Australia; in NEW ZEALAND by Ross Haines & Son, Ltd., 18 Monmouth Street, Grey Lynn, Auckland 2 New Zealand; in SINGAPORE AND MALAYSIA by MPH Distributors (S) Pte., Ltd., 601 Sim Drive, #03/07/21, Singapore 1438; in the PHILIPPINES by Bio-Research, 5 Lippa Street, San Lorenzo Village, Makati Rizal; in SOUTH AFRICA by Multipet Pty. Ltd., 30 Turners Avenue, Durban 4001. Published by T.F.H. Publications, Inc. Manufactured in the United States of America by T.F.H. Publications, Inc.

Table of Contents

Preface... **7**
Foreword to the 1969 Edition **9**
Foreword to the 1986 Edition **11**

Chapter 1: Rules for a Healthy Aquarium **14**
Preparations for a New Aquarium, 20; Water,
22; Handling Tropical Fish, 25; General Types
of Fish, 26
Chapter 2: Livebearers......................... **28**
Guppy (*Poecilia reticulata*), 32; Swordtail
(*Xiphophorus helleri*), 35; Platy or Moonfish
(*Xiphophorus maculatus*), 37; Mollies (*Poecilia*),
41; Gambusias, 45; Least Killifish, *Heterandria
formosa*, 47; Halfbeaks, *Dermogenys pusillus*, 49
Chapter 3: Egglayers **50**
Siamese Fighting Fish (*Betta splendens*), 51;
The Libby Betta, 54; Paradise Fish (*Macro-
podus opercularis*), 54; Dwarf Banded Gourami
(*Colisa lalia*), 55; Three-spot Gourami (*Tricho-
gaster trichopterus*), 56; Kissing Gourami
(*Helostoma temmincki*), 57; Pearl Gourami
(*Trichogaster leeri*), 58; Cichlids, 59; Festivum
(*Cichlasoma festivum*), 66; Ports (*Aequidens
portalegrensis*), 74; Jewel Fish (*Hemichromis
bimaculatus*), 75; *Cichlasoma cyanoguttatum*, 78;
Cichlasoma meeki, 78; *Cichlasoma octofasciatum*,

79; *Cichlasoma severum,* 79; *Etroplus maculatus,* 82; *Aequidens maronii,* 82; *Astronotus ocellatus,* 83; Red Devils (*Cichlasoma labiatum* and *Cichlasoma dovii*), 83; Egyptian Mouthbrooder (*Pseudocrenilabrus multicolor*), 86; The Malawi Cichlids—Mbunas (*Pseudotropheus, Melanochromis,* and *Labeotropheus* species), 90; The Golden Nyasa (Malawi) Cichlid (*Melanochromis auratus*), 90; The Zebra Nyasa (Malawi) Cichlid (*Pseudotropheus zebra*), 90; The Trewavas Nyasa (Malawi) Cichlid (*Labeotropheus trewavasae*), 91; The Compressed Cichlid (*Lamprologus compressiceps*), 91; The Lemon Cichlid (*Lamprologus leleupi*), 91; Other Malawi and Tanganyika Cichlids, 94; Angelfish (*Pterophyllum scalare*), 94; Discus (*Symphysodon* species), 99; Dwarf Cichlids, 102; The Ram, *Microgeophagus ramirezi,* 103

Chapter 4: Other Egglayers **106**
Characins (tetras), 106; Other Tetras, 110; Danios, 111; Barbs, 113; Tiger Barb (*Capoeta tetrazona*), 114; Medaka (*Oryzias latipes*), 116; White Cloud Mountain Minnow (*Tanichthys albonubes*), 117; Rasboras, 117

Chapter 5: Scavengers **119**
Catfish, 119; *Corydoras paleatus,* 120; Glass Catfish (*Kryptopterus bicirrhis*), 122; Other Scavengers, 122; Japanese Livebearing Snail, 125; Red Ramshorn Snail (*Planorbis corneus*), 126; Mystery Snail (*Pomacea bridgesi*), 126; Pond Snails (*Lymnaea, Physa*), 127

Chapter 6: The Annual Fishes **128**
Chapter 7: Plants **135**
Anacharis, Elodea (*Elodea canadensis*), 155; Milfoil (*Myriophyllum spicatum*), 158; Fanwort (*Cabomba caroliniana*), 159; Tape Grass, Val

(*Vallisneria americana*), 159; Sagittaria (*Sagittaria graminea*), 161; Hygrophila (*Hygrophila polysperma*), 161; Nitella, 162; Amazon Sword Plants (*Echinodorus* species), 162; Ludwigia, 163; Cryptocoryne (*Cryptocoryne* species), 163; Floating Plants, 163

Chapter 8: How to Keep Fish Healthy **165**
Aquarium Conditions, 165; Feeding, 169; Live Food, 170; Prepared Foods and Formulas, 176; Gordon's Formula, 177

Chapter 9: Appliances—Use and Repair **178**
Thermometers, 178; Thermostats, 180; Heaters, 181; Air Pumps, 183; Filters, 185; Power Filters, 186; Water Changers, 187; Siphoning Tubes, 188; Fish Nets, 188; pH Test Kits, 189; Planting Tongs and Snips, 190; Other Gadgets, 190

Chapter 10: Aquarium Genetics,
by Dr. Myron Gordon **192**
Mendelian Laws of Inheritance in Aquarium Fish, 192; Inheritance of Gray in the Platy, 193; Inheritance of Black (Nigra) in the Platy, 199; Problem Suggested for the Reader, 202; Answer to Problem, 202; Further Examples of How Fish Inherit, 203; One-spot Twin-spot x Crescent Moon Platy, 204; Discovery of the Gold Platy, 206; The First Gold Platy, 208; The First Link: The Ruber to Golden Ruber, 210; The Second Link: Golden Ruber to Gold Platy, 212; Black Lace for the Gold Platy, 213; Back to Their Ancestors, 217; Reversions in Plants and Animals, 217; Reversion at the Aquarium, 218; The Golden Swordtail, 219; Pink-eyed Albinos, 220; Wild Equals Golden Plus Albino, 221; Use for the Albinos, 221; Conclusions, 223

Chapter 11: The Balanced Aquarium Myth,
by James W. Atz **224**
Chapter 12: How the Cardinal Tetra
Got Its Name **239**
How the Cardinal Tetra Got Its Name, 246;
Two New Brazilian Fresh-water Fishes, by
Myers and Weitzman, 250; Opinion 485:
International Commission on Zoological Nomen-
clature, 254; Back to the Rio Negro, 272; My
Most Successful Expedition—Cardinals in
Colombia (1965), 275
Index **284**

Preface

The ever-increasing popularity of tropical fish as a hobby has given people a desire to learn more about these fascinating creatures. As we watch them through the glass walls of their aquarium home, marveling at their color and grace of movement, we naturally wonder about their native habitat, their food, their breeding habits, their temperament, and so on. It is the purpose of this book to give beginners all the information they need to maintain a healthy aquarium and to make their hobby more enjoyable.

The owner of a home aquarium takes on his responsibility with the pride and passion one would have toward a family of children. Actually, tropical fish require little care, but the few basic rules of care and feeding are essential to their existence. Those rules are presented here in simple terms, and can be applied to the scores of tropical fish described and illustrated in the book.

The author's experience as a teacher in the Department of Science Education, New York University, leads him to believe that this book may serve still another purpose—as a reference text for teachers and students of biology.

But whatever its use, the author will feel that his work has been repaid if the book helps to advance the interest of the hobbyist and of the student in tropical fish. There is no more absorbing hobby and no more enlightening example of the laws of nature and natural history.

Herbert R. Axelrod, Ph.D

FOREWORD TO THE 1969 EDITION

In the seventeen years since I wrote the first edition of this book, the aquarium hobby has achieved substantial growth. From an almost "exotic" hobby in the late forties, aquarium keeping is now the second largest hobby in America, with 22,000,000 households participating.

This rapid growth in the hobby has enabled me to travel widely over most of the jungles of the world, and in the past fifteen years I have brought back almost 300 species new to science.

Along with the greater assortment of aquarium fishes, hobbyists have available to them, through pet shops, hundreds of new aquarium accessories at much reduced prices. Stainless steel, slate-bottomed aquaria are less expensive today than they were fifteen years ago! Heaters, pumps, filters, and colored gravel look nothing like those available at the time the first edition was written.

Perhaps the greatest invention of all was the undergravel filter. This filter enabled *anyone* to maintain a crystal-clear aquarium without the disadvantage of having an outside filter box. It brought the hobby to the masses with its simple message: "You never need change water again!" Freeze-dried fishfoods also helped make the hobby more popular, for you no longer need live worms for your fishes; the freeze-dried tubifex worms are safer and much less expensive.

Since the writing of the first edition, my teacher, Dr. Myron Gordon, passed away. I loved Myron as a friend and counselor, for he shaped my life and led me into tropical fishes as a means of livelihood and happiness. This new edition would not have been possible without him; nor would the first.

FOREWORD TO THE
1986 EDITION

It really is a coincidence that the second edition (1969) was written exactly 17 years after the first edition (1952)...and it is also a coincidence that the third edition (1986) is being written 17 years after the second edition. But what is really interesting for me is the total change in the aquarium hobby during these past 34 years.

First, the most significant change is the absence from the market of the stainless steel framed aquarium. In the late 1940's and early 1950's, when the first edition of this book appeared, tanks had frames made of galvanized sheet metal painted black and marbleized with white streaks of paint. They were referred to as "marble tanks." Later in the 1950's, stainless steel framed tanks made their entrance and shared the market with the marble tanks until the price of stainless dropped and marble tanks went out of style. In both styles of tanks, gray slate bottoms were in vogue and the aquarium industry used most of the slate produced in Pennsylvania.

Then, with the advent of silastic adhesive from Dow-Corning, glass could be glued to glass and frames on aquaria were no longer necessary. The major aquarium manufacturers went out of the aquarium business, and new faces on the scene began producing aquaria made entirely of glass.

Another change was the result of one of my patents. Since I was the first to develop the freeze-dried methods, the U.S. Patent Office granted me a patent for freeze-drying tubifex worms and other fish foods. This has revolutionized the fish food industry, and today freeze-dried fish foods represent about 25% of the total market (in terms of money, not units).

In the fish world, other changes have been wrought that reflect upon my years of fish collecting. In the early 1950's, my expeditions were mainly in South America and it was the new South American fish that kept the business so vitally interesting. *TFH* Magazine, now the world's largest, started with stories of expeditions and to this day still carries color photos of new fish.

Then I began collecting in Africa and brought back hundreds of previously unknown fishes from Lakes Malawi (then called Nyasa), Tanganyika, and Victoria. These hundreds of species are now well-established with tank-bred populations available from just about every aquarium shop. None were available in 1952; less than a dozen were available in 1969. Some 350 are available now, 1986.

But the most exciting change has been in the literature. The first edition of this book contained one color photograph. Look, now, at this present edition. The same is true of the *Dr. Axelrod's Atlas....* Its first edition in 1985 contained about 3,500 color photos. The 1986 edition of the international "reference" book that I am writing now will contain almost 5,000 color photographs, as will the saltwater volume.

Such investments in color photographs, color separations, and color printing may reach over $1,000,000, and T.F.H. Publications, the company I started in 1947, will be responsible for pet shop sales of books in the range of $25 million. T.F.H. sells almost 5 million books and magazines each year, making it the largest publisher of pet books in the world.

All of this has been made possible because of the growth in aquarium keeping; the growth in aquarium keeping has resulted from the many products that make aquarium keeping easier and safer (in terms of fish losses). Jet airplanes now bring fishes from Africa to New York in the same time it took for a flight from New York to San Francisco in 1952, thus bringing down the cost of aquarium fish to the point that aquarium fish today cost less than they did in 1952!

I hope I'm around in another 17 years to see what progress has been wrought in the tropical fish world!

Chapter 1
Rules for a Healthy Aquarium

The first thing to consider in starting a collection of tropical fish is the type of aquarium you intend to maintain. Several factors enter into its selection: the cost, the types of fish you are interested in, the number and size of fish for the space available, and the reason for keeping fish (commercial, decorative, or as a hobby).

The question of how large an aquarium to get is easily answered: Get the largest size practical. The larger the tank, the safer it is for the fish, because there will be less variation of temperature in a larger body of water. Large fluctuations in temperature over a short period of time are dangerous to fish; in their native habitat, which you should try to imitate as closely as possible, there is relatively little temperature change. The easiest method to maintain the correct temperature is with a thermostatically controlled heater. Another reason a large tank is best is that there is less chance of the fish suffocating. Most people believe that the term "balanced aquarium" refers to a balance between the plants and the fish in regard to the production of respiratory gases. They are incorrect. The essential exchange of gases occurs with the atmosphere through the surface of the water, even when aquatic vegetation is present. Therefore, the size of the tank, and consequently the amount of water surface, is of vital importance.

There are many types of aquaria on the market. Only buy an aquarium where tropical fish are sold since "cellar manufacturers" use thin window glass and bathtub variety silicone cement. Aquarium shops won't sell these tanks because they know their business depends upon your success...and a tank that ruptures because the glass is too thin is hardly a successful experience for anyone.

Pet shops have standard size aquaria. The sizes of these aquaria have evolved so that one tank could nest inside another tank. This makes shipping less costly than shipping "air" when tanks are sent without another tank inside them. Reflectors and stands were made for these standardized aquaria, and basically the sizes haven't changed over the years.

After you have decided upon the location of the aquarium and how much space you have available, visit your pet shop dealer and see what standard sizes he has that will fit the space. Of course custom sizes are available to fit exactly into almost any corner (a triangular tank) or any other type of niche.

By the way, there is a difference in the meaning and use of the word for the plural of "aquarium." The word "aquaria" is the plural of the fish tank, aquarium. The word "aquariums" is used for the plural of the buildings which house the aquaria. For example: "I have 23 aquaria in my home, and I have visited the aquariums in Boston and San Francisco. These are public aquariums and each contains hundreds of aquaria." I hope the plural of "aquarium" is clear now.

There has also been a distinction in the plural of the word "fish." If you have a plurality of a single fish species, you may call them "fish." If you have two species or more, then you should use the term "fishes." For example, "I have 100 guppies in my tank. They are beautiful fish. I also have a community tank with swordtails, platies, and mollies, a total of 11 fishes in all." In most cases, this distinction is ignored since the meaning is usually clear.

A good size aquarium to start with is a 10-gallon. This offers plenty of room for a dozen or more small tropical fish and gives the novice a chance to learn all the intricacies of fish care without going into the hobby too expensively. The tank should be equipped with a thermostatically controlled heater, a reflector, scavengers, and some sort of vegetation. These are the basic essentials for an aquarium. Remember that you are trying to imitate the native surroundings of the fish. The more successfully you do this, the more successful you will be with your aquarium.

A cover should always be provided for your aquarium. This should be a piece of plastic or glass—ordinary windowpane will do—cut to fit the tank. This will keep the fish from jumping out, will help control evaporation, and will protect the water from soot, dust, and other kinds of dirt. Moreover, it will serve to discourage prying creatures, be they cats or people! Do not worry about suffocating your fish; even the tightest fit of glass laid on the tank will still admit sufficient air. It is permissible to cut off one small corner of the glass for convenience in feeding.

The next consideration is light. As plants must have strong light in order to remain healthy and to grow, the aquarium should be placed near a window, if possible, so that it can get a minimum of two hours' direct sunlight daily. However, light from an ordinary light bulb serves as well as sunlight, and reflectors for this purpose are made to fit all standard aquaria. Fluorescent lights are equally effective.

Scavengers are a necessity with every tank for they eat the food that is left uneaten by the other fish and thus prevent it from decaying and contaminating the water. Since the starting aquarist may overfeed his stock, a few scavengers will give him some leeway on overfeeding. Scavengers also help keep down unwanted algae that may grow on the sides of the tank. Some of the best types of scavengers are snails and catfish, although there are many other types.

The three hazards that most tropical fish face are **overcrowding, overfeeding,** and **temperature change.** Overcrowding exists when there are more fish in the tank than it can support. It has been found that there is hardly ever a shortage of oxygen dissolved in aquarium water but that there may develop an excess of suffocating carbon dioxide. When fish are too crowded, the concentration of this gas reaches lethal proportions. The safest formula for spacing your fish, therefore, is to allow 1 gallon of water for every inch of fish. If you have ten small fish that average one-half inch in length, then you can safely keep them in a 5-gallon tank.

The water gives off carbon dioxide to the atmosphere at its surface; thus the surface area of the tank is another important factor in determining the number of fish that you may safely maintain in your aquarium. The larger the surface area, the more chance for the carbon dioxide to escape into the atmosphere. One of the dangers of a spherical or globe type of tank is that it has a small neck and not much carbon dioxide can be discharged by the water. To be safe, figure on a minimum of 10 square inches of surface area for every inch of fish. Using a proper filter and air pump can greatly enhance the capacity of your aquarium. While 10 square inches of surface for every inch of fish is acceptable for un-aerated aquaria, sufficient aeration and water changing on a regular basis can easily allow you to have four times that many fish. But don't overcrowd! Instead, buy a larger aquarium...or smaller fish.

Then, too, there are other considerations about the density of fish in a given aquarium. Many fish, especially cichlids, are extremely territorial and they may fight off any fish that comes into what they consider their territory. African Great Lake cichlids are almost always territorial and not more than one pair of adults can be kept for any length of time in any tank under 10 gallons...and even that is a bit small.

These precautions should be taken into consideration *before* you buy your tank.

A good understanding of the needs of your fish is important. When an aquarium is well prepared, it requires little attention—if you care to go on a vacation for a week or so there is no danger of leaving the fish behind without food; they can get along on the microscopic bodies that are to be found in every aquarium. You should by no means dump a whole week's supply of food into the tank and imagine that the fish will eat only as much as they need and leave the rest for the next day. Fish do not know how to ration their food; their code of survival is "catch as catch can," and they eat all that they find. Even if they did leave some over, the food would get stale and contaminate the water. Many more fish die from overfeeding than from underfeeding, so be very careful.

The best rule to remember is: *Feed your adult fish once a day and only as much as they can consume in five minutes.* As well as the quantity, the regularity of feeding is important for the health of your fish.

There is quite a selection of food that is offered by many concerns. A rotation of three or four standard foods, using a different kind every four days, is successful. The live food that is prevalent in the fish's natural environment is also necessary as a part of their ration for a high standard of health.

Another important environmental variable is the temperature of the water in your aquarium. Fish are cold-blooded, and with very few exceptions their body temperature is nearly the same as that of the water they live in. Tropical fish are accustomed to live in water that rarely goes below 70°F. and so they usually get along at the ordinary house temperature of 72°F. However, as the different species are accustomed to different temperatures, each fish must be considered individually. Seventy degrees is only a minimum. If the fish are expected to reproduce, some mechanical means must be used to raise the temperature of the water to the optimum temperature for breeding. To keep the temperature of the water as constant as possible at night, when the room temperature drops, and also to raise the temperature for the treatment of ich (white spot disease), a thermostatically controlled heater is used. In North American pet shops, a single tube thermostatically controlled heater practically dominates the market. Some are completely submersible, but most hang from the edge of the aquarium. A few are built into the filter where the warm water is circulated by the pressure of the pump, but these units are rare. In England, Australia, and most of the rest of Europe and Asia a thermostat is available with outlets for several individual heaters. Each system has its advantages and drawbacks. A thermostat that controls many heaters may malfunction and destroy the fishes in several tanks. At least that's the main argument pet shop personnel give for not carrying separate heaters and thermostats.

Preparations for a New Aquarium

One of the first steps in preparing a new aquarium before introducing your fish into it is to clean it thoroughly. Many tropical fish hobbyists use a rock-salt solution to wash out the inside of the tank. This preparation is simple and inexpensive. First, fill the tank with fresh water at about the temperature of the water that you expect to keep in it. Do not use hot water, as it may crack the glass. Then check to see whether the tank is leaking—even if it was tested in the shop, there is every likelihood that it was jarred in the transportation to your home. Do not try to move the tank when it is full of water—a cubic foot of water weighs over 60 pounds. If you find there are no leaks, scoop out the water, leaving about 1 inch on the bottom. Take some rock salt and dissolve it in the water. Then run a small piece of cloth over all the surfaces of the tank. After every surface has been in contact with the salt solution, again fill the tank with water and let it stand for a few hours, leaving the salt solution in also. Then scoop out all the water and run fresh water into the tank for ten or fifteen minutes. Scoop this fresh water out and dry the tank, making sure that no large crystals of rock salt have remained undissolved. Although a trace of salt in the water is more beneficial than detrimental to the tank, too much salt has a toxic effect on the fish and plants. Salt acts to kill fungi and certain other disease-producing organisms and so aids in the protection of the fish. Do not use any other type of disinfectant in the tank; most of the others are poisonous to the fish. Play safe and use salt. If rock salt is not available, any type of table salt will do. Your pet shop may have a suitable substitute.

The next step in preparing your aquarium is to get material in which to plant the vegetation. Pebbles, shells, marbles, and large rocks are not advisable, except for spawning purposes. They may have some soluble salts in them that would be dangerous for the fish and they will create spots that the fish and snails cannot reach, and thus provide a lodging place in which food may decay. A good rule to follow is not to have any place in the aquarium that the snails and fish are unable to reach should a piece of food fall in that spot. The plainer the tank, the better it is for the fish. Fancy designs in rock and clay have little value, though such rocks as granite, sandstone, quartz, and slate are not harmful and tend to give the tank a natural setting. Coarse white gravel is the best material to use for your base. Do not use fine sand as it packs too tightly and the roots of the plants may not be able to penetrate it. Although, in general, enough gravel to cover the floor of the aquarium about 1 inch deep will be sufficient, some rooted plants need a bed of sand from 2 to 3 inches deep to provide proper anchorage and root space. The best arrangement for sand distribution is to start your sand deeper in the rear of the tank and let it run shallower toward the front of the tank. This serves two purposes: first, all the debris and uneaten food will tend to roll to the front of the tank where it can easily be seen and siphoned out; and second, the gravel in the rear, where most of the vegetation will be planted, needs more depth than the front of the tank, which should be left rather free of any growth. Actually, the best plan for plant distribution is the horseshoe type, where the planted vegetation is around the three borders of the tank, leaving the front and center free for a swimming and display area. The tank should never be cluttered with plants. Fish should have at least one-third of the tank to swim around in freely.

All gravel must be thoroughly cleansed before being used. The best and easiest method of doing this is to put it in a large pot, letting fresh hot water run over it constantly for ten or fifteen minutes. Make sure that the water is running in under some pressure so it will wash all surfaces and depths of the gravel. After the gravel has been thoroughly washed, pour off some of the water, leaving just enough to cover the gravel. Put the pot on the stove and boil the gravel and water for twenty minutes. Then pour off the boiling water and wash the gravel again. After it is thus sterilized, it may be placed in the bottom of the tank.

Water

Your next consideration will be the water that goes into your new aquarium. Water looks the same regardless of what temperature it is, what colorless salts or gases may be dissolved in it, or where it comes from, but chemically it may be very different, and the difference is very important to the fish that must live in it.

As an extreme concentration of chlorine is fatal to all fish, the chlorine used in many districts to disinfect the water supply may be a danger. However, the health authorities will not pump water that is too highly chlorinated, and therefore water that is obtained from the faucet will usually be satisfactory in this respect, though even tap water is toxic to some delicate fish. (The more dangerous chloramines are now present in the waters of many cities.) But to be safe, allow the water to stand for a day in the fresh air and in contact with the direct rays of the sun. Before putting it in the tank, scoop out a glassful at a time and pour it back into the container so that the chlorine or other gases dissolved in the water will have another opportunity to escape.

Many aquarists prefer to use pond water, but it has been found that there are many organisms in pond water that are detrimental to the health of certain fish. The safest water for the beginner to use is tap water that has been aerated by the method previously mentioned, or with an air pump, filter, and aerator.

The proper way to introduce this water into the aquarium so as not to disturb the gravel is to place a piece of paper over the gravel and pour the water slowly until the tank is about one-third full. Then take the paper out and anchor the plants in the gravel. Planting is much easier with this method than when the tank is full of water.

Before entering plants of almost all kinds into your tank, however, sterilize them thoroughly in a concentrated solution of salt and potassium permanganate (purple crystals). This will destroy any harmful organisms that might otherwise gain entrance to a healthy tank. Do not keep plants in this solution for more than a few hours or they may be destroyed. When the vegetation is properly anchored, fill the tank up to about one inch from the top, then check again to see if the plants are still firmly in place. Some of the plants are very buoyant and are apt to pull loose from the sand.

Remember an earlier precaution: *Before putting any water into the tank, make sure the tank is placed where it is to be located permanently.* Water weighs about 8-1/3 pounds per gallon and, besides being quite a load to carry, the sides of the aquarium might be loosened if you move the tank from place to place. Many a time has the bottom fallen out of a large tank when someone tried to lift it off a table. Do not let this happen to you!

Now that the tank is set up and you have all your equipment in place, you are ready for the thermostatically controlled heater. Caution: Be sure to test the heater first in a plain glass container (such as a bottle) with a thermometer to ascertain that the thermostat is set at the desired temperature. If you put it into the tank with fish before checking you may later find that the fish have either boiled or frozen to death.

Before you bring your new fishes home you should have ascertained the temperature at which they were maintained in the tropical fish store. Most dealers keep their aquaria at about 78°F., but this may vary. In any case, 78°F. is a fine temperature with which to start your aquarium. First, then, you must bring your aquarium to that temperature BEFORE any fish are placed in it. This is done by adjusting the thermostat on your heater. There are many ways to do this. One easy way is to put the thermostat into the dealer's tank and allow him to adjust it to the temperature of that tank. He does this by putting the thermostat into the tank and allowing it about 10 minutes to adjust to the tank's temperature. Then he turns the adjustment knob on the thermostat until the light just goes on or just goes off, depending upon the initial setting of the thermostat. This setting then is the same as the setting in his tank and is ideal for fish coming from that tank.

Now take the thermostatically controlled heater and place it in your own aquarium. Once it is in place, plug it in and wait to see what happens. In a very short time the light will go on indicating that the heater is working. This means that the water in your tank was colder than the water in the dealer's tank. It is possible but unlikely that the water in your tank is warmer than that in the dealer's tank, but should this be the case, then the heater will not go on until the tank cools down. A thermometer will tell you the temperature of your aquarium. A good thermostatically controlled heater will be able to maintain the temperature to within 2° of the control point at all times unless the heat fails in the room and the room temperature is extremely cold.

Handling Tropical Fish

A word or two about nets and handling fish are always helpful to the beginning aquarist. The fact that aquarium stores sell many sizes of nets, with varying sizes of mesh, should be indicative that different nets are used for different sized fish. In general, use a net at least 1 inch longer than the fish itself. Never use a dry net on a fish; let it soak for a few seconds. Sometimes a dirty net will become stiff when dry, which, if used in this condition, can cause serious damage to the scales of the fish and thus leave the fish open to fungus infection.

Fish can always jump out of small nets and fall onto the floor. This is usually not a fatal accident and, with proper handling by the aquarist the fish may be replaced in the tank. There are several methods for picking up a fish from the floor. The easiest is to throw a wet net over the fish and hope that it will stick to the net when the net is inverted. Another way is to place a stiff, thin card under the fish and get him into the wet net that way. Don't be foolish enough to grab the fish and squeeze. If you use your hands, it is better to get him by the tail fin between your nails—at least he can grow another fin!

It should be mentioned that fish can sometimes fall from relatively great heights and not be killed. Sometimes they are just stunned and when replaced in the aquarium they "come back to life." This is probably the explanation for a lot of stories about fish which were found "dead" on the living-room floor and came back to "life" after being placed in the aquarium.

Sick fish should be handled with a special net, and the net should be sterilized in boiling water before being used again. Diseases may be spread from one tank to another if these precautions are not taken.

General Types of Fish

The task of classifying tropical fish into categories has fallen into the hands of those zoologists who deal with fish, the ichthyologists. They are responsible for the technical tongue twisters given as names to the fish. The reasons behind the scientific system of naming animals and plants are logical but somewhat complicated.

It is not too advisable for the beginning aquarist to sit down and learn all the names of these different categories for each family of fish, as they are mostly either Latin or Greek and may not mean much at first. But with later enthusiasm, and after hearing the names mentioned over and over at the different stores that deal with tropical fish, they will gradually become familiar and can easily be memorized. The Latin or Greek words are descriptive and give a clue to the type of fish. Some fish are named after the discoverer of their species. For example, take the common Mexican swordtail. Its technical name is a combination of both Greek words and the name of the discoverer. The name given it by the ichthyologists is *Xiphophorus helleri*. *Xiphophorus* means "bearing a sword," and Carl Heller, the discoverer of the species, had the honor of having the species named after him. The family name is Poeciliidae, meaning "many colors, variegated, and changing." From the original description of the fish we know that what the scientist who named it had in mind when he called it a "sword-bearer" was not the long swordlike tail of the male fish, but rather its smaller, sticklike belly fin, known as a "gonopodium."

One advantage of knowing the scientific name of your fish is in ordering by catalogue; using the scientific name ensures greater accuracy in the filling of your order. There are about 3,000 different types of tropical fish available, and the only way a large wholesaler or breeder can keep his fish straight is to use the scientific name; also, a common name in one section of the country might mean nothing in another section. Most retailers and hobbyists use the common names; this may be the easier way out, but it may also cause confusion through improper use. If you learn the technical names of your favorite fish, the rest will come easily.

To make differentiation easy, fish will be classified here in the following groups: (1) livebearers: those fish that deliver their young alive; (2) egglayers: those tropical fish that lay eggs and are usually the more colorful; (3) labyrinth fish: those tropical fish that have a labyrinth-like structure above the gills enabling them to take air from above the surface of the water as well as from the water itself (also called "bubble-nest builders" because the male of the species builds his nest on the top of the water, composed of bubbles in which he deposits the eggs of the female); and (4) scavengers: those aquatic animals that are kept mostly for the purpose of keeping the aquarium free of excess food and algae.

This grouping is by no means a completely arbitrary one. It is a grouping of convenience and will help the new hobbyist in his selection of the type of fish he may desire to keep. Each of these categories will be broken down further and fully discussed.

Chapter 2
Livebearers

For the beginning aquarist, the livebearers are the most interesting fish to breed. With no particular trouble they may be propagated easily and rapidly. As is implicit in their title, these fish bear their young alive, the eggs having been fertilized within the female by the male. It was once believed that livebearing fish are not truly viviparous (Latin for "livebearing"), but that they simply carry their eggs inside until they hatch. Careful studies have revealed that some female livebearers contribute to the growth of their offspring in a way quite similar to that of higher, warm-blooded mothers, and that her young receive nourishment and other vital assistance from her during their period of prenatal life. Unlike mammalian mothers, however, the female livebearer carries her developing young in the ovary, the same organ that produces the eggs from which they arise. There is no uterus in tropical fish. Another peculiar feature of practically all the livebearing fish found in aquaria is that they can have several broods after a single contact with a male. For example, female guppies have had as many as eight broods while being kept isolated from all males. This is made possible by the storage of the male sperm in the female's ovary.

One distinctive characteristic of most livebearers—and a number of other fish, too—is their habit of eating their own young if the young are not separated from the parents as soon as they are dropped from the mother fish. The breeding trap is a helpful device to keep the mother away from her brood as she drops them. This is a small container constructed to fit inside the tank and into which the gravid female is placed. When the young are dropped from the mother fish, they fall right through the slotted bottom of the breeding trap and swim away into the rest of the tank. Some aquarists believe that these traps are rather dangerous to use, however, and that natural dense foliage (such as *Nitella*) better serves the same purpose.

There is no difficulty in getting viviparous fish to mate. All that seems necessary is to have one of each sex in the same tank and they will multiply. The sexes are easily distinguished in this type of fish: the female has a fully developed anal fin, while the male has a cylindrical, pointed gonopodium with which he fertilizes the female. Most of the viviparous young are matured and able to reproduce two to four months after birth.

If we attempted to set down over-all rules for breeding livebearers, we would be making generalizations that would be very limited and not at all helpful to the beginning aquarist. So we shall discuss here only a few considerations that must be taken into account. It must be kept in mind, however, that they are only general and that a more thorough understanding for raising each species of fish is necessary.

It is best to choose the fish that you want to raise according to their physical characteristics: size, color, and vigor. Choose only those fish with the best color. If you are going to take the trouble to raise fish, you might just as well raise good fish with color and stature that you will admire and which will be admired by your friends. There is a feeling of satisfaction and success that comes from raising your own fish, so add to this pleasure by raising fish that you will be more than proud to display.

When fish show signs of being "loaded" with young (a dark area, the gravid spot, in the anal region), they should be separated from the rest of the fish if possible. This separation has a dual purpose. First, it prevents the mother fish from being molested by the males that are around the tank; and second, it prevents the newborn young from being eaten by the other fish. The delivery tank need not be larger than one gallon, for as soon as the mother fish drops her young, she should be removed—or she will eat her young herself. The mother fish should be kept well fed while she is waiting to drop. It is a good idea to have the delivery tank heavily planted. Dense *Elodea* and *Vallisneria*, with some *Cabomba* floating around the surface, will greatly aid the young fish in hiding from their parent, if necessary. Remember to take all precautions when shifting the mother fish from one tank to another. If possible, take the gallon of water from her original tank; if not, make sure that the water in the new tank is not more than 2°F. above or below the temperature of the original tank and that the pH in both is the same. The temperature should be checked with a thermometer, and the pH may be checked with a pH testing kit.

After the baby fish are born, the mother should be removed immediately and placed back either in the original aquarium or in a tank by herself. If she is put in the community tank, it is a good idea to have more than one female in with her, as a female is usually weak after she has given birth and is easily annoyed by male fish chasing her (especially in the case of the guppy).

The baby fish should be left by themselves in their own tank for as long a period as possible, preferably until they are mature. If they are put into the community tank too early, they are liable either to be eaten by the other fish or else they will have a hard time competing with the older fish for food. After they are three or four weeks old, they should be transferred to a tank with rooted plants in it.

Baby fish should be fed finely powdered food. This food is prepared commercially and is very reasonable. As the fish get older, they can eat coarser foods. Daphnia and freshly hatched brine shrimp are also excellent foods for newborn fish.

If you are having difficulty breeding livebearers, there are several possible causes of trouble that should be checked. If you have bred too often from the same fish, she may stop producing for a while. Sometimes the fish are undernourished. In this case, the best remedy is to feed them some live food and several varieties of dried food. Fine particles of chopped fresh meat (no fat!) are good. You should feed it to them a little at a time, because if you pour a large quantity into the tank all at once some may get hidden in the crevices and start to decay. Another cause of breeding interference could be stale water or water with an improper pH. Checks should be made on the pH as well as the temperature. If all these causes are eliminated and the fish still fail to breed, then, in all probability, they are either too young to breed and may still need a few weeks to mature or are too old. Old fish may frequently be recognized by the hump on their back. Compare them to young fish and you will recognize this physical characteristic easily. As mentioned earlier, the average livebearer matures at about two to four months.

Guppy
(Poecilia reticulata)

These are the fish to which the entire population of tropicals owes its popularity. They have a long recorded history, and there is evidence that they have been bred in this country for at least eighty years. Today they are the least expensive and most plentiful of all tropical fish.

It is easy to see just how prolific the guppy is by the following figures. If one pair of guppies raises a brood and they all live, and then this generation raises a brood and they all live, and this process goes on for two years, there will be close to three million guppies. Of course the guppy mortality rate is high. Parents sometimes eat their young before they realize that they are dropping them. Larger fish consider guppies as tasty morsels. Besides all these natural enemies, improper environment, such as temperature and food, and other types of improper care are also responsible for a large percentage of young guppy mortality. But these fish produce such a large brood—every 28 days when at their peak—that if only two or three thrive out of every brood, the proportion is not too bad.

Many experts in the field, even Dr. Myron Gordon himself, started with a pair or two of guppies and recommended them as the first fish for beginners. They are best for the uninitiated for the following reasons: first, there is more material and advice available on these fish; second, they are the most inexpensive fish that are obtainable; third, the males of the species are among the most colorful (many people call them "rainbow fish"); and fourth, they are hardy, and with proper environmental conditions they will live actively and breed often. Do not think that because they are inexpensive they should not be taken seriously. The information and techniques that you will acquire by taking care of guppies properly will be invaluable when you decide on more expensive fish.

The males of the guppy are the individuals of the lot. There seem to be no two males colored alike, and there are few, if any, colors that do not appear in one or another of them. So beautiful are these fish that many have proclaimed them the most desirable fish to have in one's aquarium. They are timid, peaceful fish, but when a male guppy dances in front of a female, displaying his magnificently colored fins, he is a sight to behold. The female guppy is more stereotyped and less colorful than the male, usually a dull, silvery gray-green that blends perfectly with her natural habitat. She is heavier and longer than the male, running to about one and a half inches in length, while the males, though a few larger varieties are now produced, are seldom longer than an inch. There are many variations of the guppy, the main differences lying in the shape of the tail—some tails have two or three nodes, while others are square or fan shaped. But a guppy is a guppy, in spite of the strains that have been developed. Some people believe that those guppies with the sword-like tail came from a cross with the *Xiphophorus helleri,* the fish commonly called the swordtail, but since such a cross has never been shown to be possible, it is more logical to surmise that this was just a chance development of the tail. Guppies have, however, been crossed with mollies.

Guppies have an average litter of ten to 50 at a time—the largest brood on record, however, contained 126. These young fish, if properly cared for, will mature in eight (sometimes just two to four) months and be able to reproduce themselves.

An indication that a female guppy is ready to drop her young is the black gravid spot on the abdomen. When this spot gets darker and darker, you may be sure that the time for birth is approaching. The spot is easily recognized, for the female guppy is lightly colored in that region of her body. When the guppy mother shows signs of being ready to drop, she should be very carefully removed to a tank in which there are no other fish and in which there is plenty of vegetation. The vegetation offers a sheltering place for the young if they should need to hide from the parent who, if allowed to remain in the tank with them, invariably tries to eat them. If the beginning aquarist has gone to the expense of a breeding trap, he may use that; it will save him many young. But the guppy breeds so quickly that a few fish lost can be made up for in the next month's delivery. When the mother fish has dropped all her young, she should immediately be removed to another tank, preferably by herself so she will not be bothered by the male fish. Prominent scientists have made thorough studies of the sex life of the guppy and have found that a male fish will try to fertilize a female fish even if she is placed in a jar separated from the rest of the fish in the tank, or even if she should be anesthetized and allowed to drop to the bottom. A freshly dead female in a similar position, however, would either be eaten or totally disregarded.

The young should be left in a tank of their own. They are pretty hardy at birth and can eat semicoarse food immediately, but it is more advisable to start them on newly hatched brine shrimp and gradually give them coarser food as they get older.

The proper temperature for the guppy is about 75°F., though it may run as low as 65°F. and as high as 80°F. without doing any serious damage. Extreme temperatures are tolerable to the guppy only as long as there are not large fluctuations over a short period of time; that is, do not let the temperature drop more than a few degrees per hour. The optimum temperature for breeding the guppy is 75°F. This temperature may be maintained by the use of the thermostatic heater.

There is no narrow selection of food that guppies will eat, but they are vegetarians to some degree and like fresh greens. The best thing to do for this green appetite is to give them some finely chopped lettuce. If there are plenty of green plants in the aquarium there is nothing to worry about, as they will take their own as they need it. These green plants grow so quickly that they do not miss a little nibble here or there. Guppies also eat the standard dried fish foods. The ordinary freeze-dried tropical fish foods are best and will keep your fish healthy and active. Along with a variety of these prepared foods, the guppies should be offered some live food, too; any type is suitable as long as it is not too large. A little fresh meat chopped into fine particles will act as a fair substitute for live food when the latter is not available.

Swordtail
(Xiphophorus helleri)

The fish next to *Poecilia reticulata* (guppy) in popularity is undoubtedly the swordtail, *Xiphophorus helleri*. Wild swordtails reach lengths of about six inches, but aquarium breeding has developed a smaller fish that is more suitable to the home tank. In the male swordtail, the lower part of the caudal fin develops into a long sword-like tail that serves as a positive identification for the sex of this fish. Since it is native to waters in and near Mexico, this fish is sometimes called the "Mexican swordtail."

The swordtail is subject to the same care and treatment as all livebearers, and as its temperament is much like that of the guppy, it is an ideal fish for the community tank. The swordtail has another feature that adds to its desirability, that is, its ability to be used in hybridization experiments. (Dr. Myron Gordon and the author used them extensively in cancer research as well as in hybridization work.) *X. helleri* has been successfully crossed with the platies, or "moons" as they are commonly called. The platies (also *Xiphophorus*) are hardy fish and are also very desirable for the community tank. One of the many different hybrids that has been developed is the "red Helleri," the final result of a cross between a reddish moon and a swordtail.

It is remarkable how these fish react to their environment. One case is known where a female swordtail was kept in a small tank with several betta females—the bettas are a rather ferocious bunch, although the female is less so than the male. The bettas immediately chased the swordtail around, and for a few days it looked as though they would kill her. Then, suddenly, they left her alone, and they got along very well. After a month of this rough environment the female was put into a tank with a male swordtail to mate. The female immediately started for the male and in 20 minutes she had killed him. After a few days another male swordtail was put into the tank and the same thing took place. The female never accepted a mate.

Two lessons about fish can be derived from this case: first, they are quick to respond to their environment; and second, they have potentially many different behavior patterns. Together with a group of swordtails, this female would probably have been all right, but by placing her in a rough-and-tumble environment she lost all her timid traits and the more savage instincts in her were brought out. Many fish of a timid family get very savage in a savage environment, and the reverse statement is also true. So keep an eye on all new fish that are introduced to the community aquarium.

The *X. helleri* is an interesting fish to watch, especially when the male is "driving" the female. He will swim in front of her and then, with his sword-like tail erect, swim backward in a quivering courtship display. The male constantly swims back and forth about a female, always eager to mate. An interesting fact about the female is that at an old age she may lose her female characteristics and develop the secondary characteristics of the male, growing a sword-like tail and sometimes trying to court other females. This process of sex reversal occurs regularly in certain species of fish. In the swordtail, however, it is apparently an abnormal occurrence, and the vast majority of such transformed females is infertile. By injecting hormones into normal female swordtails, scientists have been able to change them to look and act like males, but these, too, are never functional.

Platy or Moonfish
(*Xiphophorus maculatus*)

Xiphophorus maculatus or the platy is the color king of the livebearers. These eye-appealing fish are more than just beautiful; they are peaceful, hardy, and prolific, and deserve a place in every community tank. Also called a platy is *Xiphophorus variatus*, the "platy variatus."

The first platies to be exported from Mexico, the homeland of several beautiful tropical fish, went to Germany in 1907. Three years later they are said to have been brought to the United States. In the years that have elapsed since they arrived in the United States, more than a dozen popular varieties have been developed through selective breeding—each more beautiful than the other. This process of selective breeding is long and laborious, but with the proper knowledge you can develop your own strain, provided you have the time and the space. Your reward in developing such a strain will be in the satisfaction that you have started something new. You may even have contributed something to science. Gregor Mendel will be remembered as the first one to realize, through his work with peas, that species carry certain characteristics from one generation to the other through submicroscopic, discrete particles, later called "genes." The laws that Mendel formulated are applicable to tropical fish as well as to peas and humans. If you are interested, look up a text on fish genetics and see if you would have the patience and fortitude to go through the same painstaking steps as he did.

The platy has been developed in many unusual colors and finnages; the gold-colored ones are often called "moonfish" because of the crescent-shaped spot at the base of their tails. For example, your fish dealer may say "gold platy," while calling the colored platies "red moonfish," "blue moonfish," "black moonfish," etc.

In the early 1960's platies were developed from hifin swordtails as basic stock, which had huge dorsal fins. These platies were called by various names such as "sailfin platy," "topsail platy," and "hifin platy." Nearly every color variety of *maculatus* and *variatus* platy has been bred with the huge dorsal fin.

Breeding the sailfin platy is simple, though many of the offspring usually do not show the huge dorsal of their parents. A good strain might breed 50 per cent true and an amazing strain might breed 90 per cent true, but to date there is no strain that breeds 100 per cent true.

The prices of these beautiful platies are considerably higher than the normal platy, but they are well worth it, especially if you intend breeding them.

In 1965 I was able to bring back from Hawaii the first albino *variatus* platies. In 1966 I found the first albino *maculatus* platies in Hungary. These strains were bred in Florida where they were able to propagate thousands of these delicate platies for distribution to pet shops all over the world. Eventually, the strains were lost.

Sex differentiation in the platy is not a perplexing problem. There is a marked difference between the physical characteristics of the male and female platy that enables identification; the male is shorter and of lighter build than the female; also the anal fin is an indication of sex. In the female, the anal fin is fanlike and kept spread out, while in the male the anal fin is rodlike and is kept close to the body. This is the organ the male uses to fertilize the female and it is characteristic of almost all the livebearing fish kept in aquaria. If you feel doubtful identifying the sexes, ask the fish dealer to give you two or three pairs and trust that his judgment is better than yours. However, do not worry as there is no danger of having either too many males or too many females.

Raising platies is not too great a problem. The main obstacle is keeping the temperature constant, as the platy is very sensitive to change. A thermostatically controlled heater is the best way to do this and it is indispensable with the platies. A temperature of at least 72°F. is desirable, and 75°F. is the best for breeding, but whatever the temperature is, make sure that it stays the same.

The best way to breed these fish is to give them an aquarium of their own. The platy will rarely eat its young, and therefore one of the biggest headaches of the amateur aquarist takes care of itself. Most of the other fish will eat any young fish that swims and is small enough to be gobbled up, as well as their own young, so play safe and keep the platies all alone in a large tank.

Females can have broods every four weeks and, depending upon size, health, and breeding conditions, may drop from two to 200 at one time, though they usually average about 20. Care should be exercised with the female platy, as she is as soft and delicate as she looks; when the time is near for her to drop, she must not be excited or moved. If you move her at all, you should do it well in advance of her expected dropping or you will lose her and the brood as well.

Food for the platies is no problem as they will eat anything that they find. They will get along very well on the regular prepared dried food, with a little daphnia or some worms now and then. Gordon's formula is excellent. They are partly vegetarian and enjoy eating algae.

All the different types of platies can be crossbred, and the results of the crossbreedings are often remarkable. The colors will, in a sense, mix, and if the fish retain the correct gene combination, this color mixture will breed true. Of course this is sometimes a difficult thing to accomplish, but it is worth the effort.

Platies have frequently been crossed with swordtails, and most of the swordtails and platies that are purchased are more or less remote descendants from such a cross. A purebred swordtail or platy is much more the exception than the rule. If you desire to try this cross, make sure that you have a large tank with plenty of foliage for the young to hide in, as the female swordtail, as well as the male, will eat the young.

Platies and their close relatives the swordtails, and the hybrids between them, have become regular aquatic guinea pigs for students of genetics. They are used in medical research because some of the excessively black hybrids, resulting from the cross of black-spotted platies with ordinary swordtails, develop pigmented cancers called "melanomas." This type of cancer is found in many kinds of fish and in birds and mammals, including man. No one knows what causes it in other animals, but in platy and swordtail hybrids it is known to be inherited. That is one of the reasons scientists are so interested in these fish. As a by-product of his investigations in this field, Dr. Myron Gordon and the author have produced some beautifully colored normal strains of fish.

Young platies are hard to distinguish from the young of other types of livebearing fish. They are one of the most delicate types and are susceptible to all the evils of bad tank management. They will grow swiftly and be healthy if kept in the proper type of tank, with lots of room, a constant temperature, a normal pH, and plenty of vegetation. They will mature in about eight months (less in some aquarium situations). The following example will illustrate the importance of having optimum conditions for the growth of these young fish.

A typical brood of 22 was divided into two groups of 11 each. One group was put into a 15-gallon tank, which they had all to themselves—plenty of room, constant temperature, and live food every other day. The other group was left to their own devices in a tank of the same size but with many other fish. Of the 11 in their own tank, nine matured and reproduced in eight months; the group in the crowded tank took ten months to mature, and only two were alive at the end of that period.

Of course, separating all the young fish is a prohibitive task for the beginning enthusiast, but the idea should be kept in mind that it is better to have ten healthy fish than 20 unhealthy ones.

The varieties of *Xiphophorus* need the same general care as the common variety.

Mollies *(Poecilia)* (previously known as *Mollienesia*)

We now come to the fish that are dear to the hearts of many people, mainly because they are found in many of the waters of the southeastern and southern parts of the United States—for example, the waters around the Gulf of Mexico are infested with them. These "mudpussers," as they are affectionately called by the Floridians, are truly the fish for the amateur who is advanced enough to play with more interesting fish.

The reason for the complexity of the care of these fish is that they must be maintained in water that is slightly alkaline or somewhat salty. It is impossible to maintain the pH of the water at a certain level because regardless of how careful you are, there will be a certain amount of fluctuation. It is easier, and most frequently done, to maintain the pH if the fish are kept in a tank of their own to which some sea salt has been added (1 teaspoon per gallon). The reason for keeping mollies alone is that there are not many other types of fish that get along well with them and that can survive this radical pH. Since the mollies do not usually eat their own young if they are properly fed, the young can be left in the same tank as their parents; it is not too much trouble to keep them in a tank by themselves. Also, they do best in old water, so it is recommended never to change their water unless there is a good reason. As mollies come in many varieties (differing in color, shape or dorsal fin, etc.) and are often beautiful species, a separate tankful of different mollies is just as interesting as any community tank and is the best way to keep these fish healthy.

The male and female of this species are very nearly alike; the male has slightly more hue than the female, and since they are livebearers, the anal fin of the male is modified into an intromittent organ. Mollies of the same type are very nearly identical, not varying from one another as do the guppies.

The mollies like to eat algae, and algae are an important part of their diet. If there is not enough light for a profusion of algae, they should be fed finely chopped greens, lettuce probably being the best.

There is no trick to breeding the mollies; they breed frequently, like the majority of livebearers. Since mollies have the ability to control to some extent the time they will drop their young, there is no set schedule that they follow, and the female should not be disturbed or removed to another tank to have her young. The temperature of the water has something to do with it: 73°F. gives the best results. Broods of mollies run up to 100, depending on the type of the molly. The young are free-swimming and will take small brine shrimp or daphnia immediately.

A few singular types are worth individual mention.

The sailfin, *Poecilia latipinna,* is really the true Florida molly that earned the name "mudpusser." It is the most common type of molly and usually the most inexpensive. This fish has a large dorsal fin (uppermost fin on the top of the back) that is sometimes as large as the body of the fish itself. It is a greenish color with black dots, closely resembling a striped bass. Sailfins breed more profusely than any other type of molly.

The sailfin has been interbred with many other types of mollies. The large dorsal fin seems to be a dominant characteristic because, in interbreeding the sailfin with other types of mollies, it has been found to breed true, while other characteristics of the original have disappeared. Successful crossbreeding between the guppy and the molly has also been reported.

Another popular type of molly is the black molly or midnight molly. This fish gets its name from its velvety black color and may belong to the previously mentioned species, the sailfin, or to the following one, since black strains of both these species are known.

A fish of increasing popularity is *Poecilia sphenops*. As their name, *sphenops,* implies, these fish have wedge-shaped faces and look quite pugnacious. The true *sphenops* is sometimes hard to distinguish from the other species of the genus. Color is no indication, as their color range is quite extensive, nor can they be recognized by their size and disposition, as these are also varied. (It is quite common for the commercial fish dealer to sell certain types of odd-sized or colored mollies for true *sphenops*.) About the easiest way to differentiate between the *sphenops* and the *latipinna* is by the location of the dorsal fin. The dorsal fin in *sphenops* is set toward the rear of the hump in the back, while in *latipinna* the dorsal fin is set in front of the hump. The *sphenops* are usually very good jumpers, but it has been the author's experience that they are not so desirable as the more peaceful members of their family. They have a nervous, tense disposition.

Since its development by Yam Ming in Singapore in 1954, the lyretail molly has become an established strain in every country of the world. Lyretail mollies are available in marble, green, black, chocolate, and albino varieties, and they certainly seem to be a dominant enough characteristic to be able to show themselves in early crossings with any established strain.

In Florida, where mollies are raised in huge dirt-bottomed pools, most major growers have found that they do well by dedicating a few dozen pools to the raising of various strains of lyretail mollies since the throwbacks are normal mollies in the particular strain to which that pool is entrusted. That means that a pool of black lyretail mollies will have throwbacks which will be black normal mollies, certainly a fish which can be sold and which will not harm the basic strain. Were the case that black lyretail mollies threw green babies as throwbacks, it would contaminate the basic strain.

As lyretail mollies grow older, they begin to lose the lyretail in many strains with which I have experimented. It seems that the tail is most lyre-shaped when the fish is less than one year old. As the fish gets older, the tail gets fuller and the top and bottom extensions seem to atrophy and finally disappear.

There seems to be extensive sex reversal among lyre-tail mollies, more so than among normal blacks and greens.

Many hobbyists write to me and inquire about red mollies. To date there is no such strain known. There are albino mollies with red eyes, but there are no red mollies in the same sense as red swordtails or red plat-ies. There is no reason why a sport might not appear that will be red and might be crossed back into a normal strain to produce reds in future generations, but at the present writing it does not seem that any reds have ap-peared as mutants or sports among the many millions of mollies raised in Florida, Singapore, and Hong Kong every year.

Feeding mollies in captivity is a great art and requires constant attention. If you feed your mollies a normal diet of the typical fish foods available at a variety store, you'll be doomed to stunted mollies. Mollies must have certain foods in their diet if they are to grow at a maxi-mum rate.

Most mollies require algae, preferably *Chlorella* algae, which are soft and very digestible with an extremely high vegetable protein content, along with crustaceans such as daphnia and brine shrimp, and fleshy meat such as tubifex worms. Though this sounds like a difficult diet to obtain, there are a variety of foods available at your pet shop that supply these requirements.

Other Livebearers:

Gambusias

The gambusia or mosquitofish has been collected all over the southern United States. In appearance it resem-bles the guppy, but in disposition they are as unlike as day and night. The gambusia is usually pugnacious and is not recommended for the community tank.

Gambusia affinis, the best known of all the gambusias, has established quite a reputation for itself in medical and public health circles. Because it has proved to be such an efficient destroyer of mosquito larvae, it has been introduced into no less than 70 different countries to help control these pests. Since mosquitoes carry such dreadful diseases as malaria and yellow fever, spreading them as they bite and suck blood, the gambusia is undoubtedly the most important fish in preventive medicine. It is both hardy and prolific and will live in lakes, ponds, ditches, streams, mudholes, in fact almost any body of fresh water. There are numerous gambusia spread throughout the United States, Mexico, the West Indies, and Central America. Although it is a warm-water fish, special cold-resistant strains have been established as far north as Chicago.

Some gambusia are black spotted, but there is generally so little difference between species that it would serve little value to discuss the distinguishing features of these fish here.

In breeding, they follow the general rules of live-bearers. The optimum temperature for their breeding is about 75°F., but they fare well at 5 or 10 degrees above or below. These fish have a rather fond taste for their own young, so if it is at all possible, separate the female before she is ready to drop her young. Fortunately, the young grow very rapidly, and after the first week or so they are too large for the parent to eat, so the best practice has been to leave them alone with her in a large tank that is densely vegetated and hope that they will last the week. Keep plenty of live food in the tank, also, when there are young fish there.

Feeding the gambusia is no problem at all. They have

an appetite for almost any live food and they also do very well on the standard prepared foods. Gordon's formula is recommended.

As mentioned before, these fish are very hardy and prolific. They are not known to be particularly susceptible to any disease and, barring their ferocious nature, can be classified as very desirable fish, especially for outdoor pools.

In large lakes they are extremely valuable. Their prolificness tends to keep the larger game fish well stocked with live food, while they themselves tend to eat all the undesirable beetles, larvae, and what-have-you that are usually found in most lakes.

A Cuban species of gambusia, *G. punctata,* is quite different from the types described above. They are more susceptible to discomfort from temperature change and not so prolific as their relatives.

Least Killifish
Heterandria formosa

Another American fish worth mentioning and recommended for the home aquarium is *Heterandria formosa*. It is outstanding in many ways. One of its distinctions is that it is undoubtedly the smallest of all livebearers. The mature male is only half an inch long and is distinguished from the female by its telltale anal fin; the female may be an eighth to a quarter of an inch longer than the male. This fish has been given the name "mosquito fish," perhaps because of its size, but mainly because of its importance as one of the three types (along with the guppy and the gambusia) of fish that are used for mosquito-larvae destruction.

The life cycle of the mosquito is an interesting one. The larvae and pupae of the mosquito are aquatic and wriggle around in the water. After a certain length of time, the larvae change to pupae that metamorphose and fly away as full-grown mosquitoes. Once the insects have left the water, there is no practical means of disposing of them in great numbers, but while they are in the aquatic stage there are several techniques. One is to pour oil on the water so that when they come to the surface to breathe atmospheric oxygen, the oil slick will suffocate them. This method has its drawbacks, as it presents a fire hazard, frequently destroys other wildlife besides mosquitoes, is unsightly, and also must be done several times a season. An alternative method is spraying with chemicals, but this method also has its disadvantages. The third method (there undoubtedly are more, but they are all variations of these three) is to infest the water with fish that will eat the young mosquitoes. This need be done only once, as the fish, instead of becoming less effective like the chemical measures, multiply and become more effective. The fish can eat their weight in mosquito larvae daily. Many aquarists actually bring mosquito pupae into their homes and feed them to the fish. But the problem of how to become rid of the adult mosquitoes once they have transformed is another story.

The breeding habits of *H. formosa* are quite remarkable. The female drops a few fish every day and this feat may go on for a few weeks at a time. If there are quite a few females in the tank, you will probably find two or three new offspring every day. Sufficient vegetation should be provided in which the young can hide.

The optimum temperature for the breeding of these fish is about 70°F., and, as is true of the majority of fish, they fare better when kept only with members of their own family.

Halfbeaks
Dermogenys pusillus

The halfbeak is an interesting little livebearing species from the East Indies. It generally occurs in semi-brackish waters, and the addition of a teaspoonful of salt to each gallon of the water is distinctly beneficial. Males have a constant "chip-on-the-shoulder" attitude and are fond of staging battles, which seldom end in injury. The lower jaw is immovable, and the fish usually feeds by taking food from the water's surface and clamping down the upper jaw on it. Dry foods are not taken with any great relish, but small insects such as wingless fruitflies are gobbled greedily.

Females give birth to about 25 young, with the pregnancy lasting 28 to 30 days. They should be given a separate tank that is heavily planted when their time comes, because many of the youngsters are otherwise eaten.

The main difficulty in keeping halfbeaks is providing them with a proper diet. In their home waters they get most of their nourishment by snapping at insects at or near the water's surface, and their tank must be kept covered at all times. They should be provided with small insects if possible, and wingless fruitflies are a good item here. Some breeders get very good results providing their halfbeaks with newly hatched anabantoids such as paradise fish, blue gouramis, etc.

Chapter 3
Egglayers

The fish just discussed are viviparous like human beings; that is, they reproduce by bearing live young. Chickens typify another kind of reproduction, in which the female lays eggs which have been fertilized by the male by physical contact with the hen before they are laid; the hen then incubates the eggs until they hatch. There are relatively few fish that reproduce in this latter manner, that is, by laying fertile eggs that have come in contact with the milt, or male element, while still inside the female.

In the vast majority of fish, other than the livebearers, fertilization takes place outside in the water surrounding the parents. The female either freely drops her eggs or carefully deposits them on some object such as a stone or the leaves of underwater plants. The male follows her, dropping his milt on the eggs, fertilizing them. Those who are familiar with the blood spots in chicken eggs can realize the difference between fertilized and unfertilized eggs. An unfertilized egg can never hatch.

Siamese Fighting Fish
(Betta splendens)

Let us examine closely the actual reproductive process of one of the most famous fish of the aquarium, the Siamese fighting fish or betta *(Betta splendens)*.

The betta is probably the most beautiful fish that ever adorned an aquarium, and one of the fiercest. It has been bred in many different colors and, owing to its popularity, will probably continue to be the subject of much experimental breeding. The male, as in most vertebrates, is the more gaily colored and pugnacious. He is distinguishable from the female of the species by his long-flowing, deeply colored fins that sometimes reach well over an inch in length. The female is seldom as colorful as the male and never has fins that can be compared in size or beauty with those of the male.

The reproductive habits of the betta are *most* interesting. As is true of most egglayers, the bettas, both male and female, must be conditioned for their orgy of reproduction. This conditioning process is a very old one, having long been used by hobbyists with many types of birds, fish, and reptiles. It is as follows: The male and female are put in the same tank, being separated only by a glass partition (many aquarists make their own tanks of this type, but betta tanks arranged just for this purpose are on the market). The male tries vigorously to reach the female, and the courting begins. The more frustrated he gets, the more beautiful and deep his colors become; he really defies description. His dance is one to behold; with his gills expanded and the look of a killer on his face, he dashes madly against the glass, trying vainly to get to the female.

Fortunately enough, after hours or sometimes days he stops this mad capering and starts to build a bubble-nest. This bubble-nest is a work of art. First, the male betta gulps air from the surface of the water, "chews" on it for a second, and then blows out a mucous bubble. This process is repeated hundreds of times until a nest about an inch and a half in diameter is constructed. The nest may be high enough to be raised out of the water and sometimes reaches a thickness of about a half inch. After the nest is complete, it is time for the glass partition to be removed. But first you must be sure the female is ready for the male. This is not easy for the amateur to decide, as it must be ascertained that the female has eggs to be fertilized. It will be noted that if the female is ready she will seem a lot heavier and fuller than before the seasoning process, owing to the many eggs that she is about to drop. When you are sure that it is time, the partition should be lifted out very carefully so as not to destroy the bubble-nest, and the male and female should be allowed to have their romance. This is by no means the end of the story.

When the male sees the female, he will make a headlong dive for her, maybe ripping off a piece of her tail or dorsal fin in his clumsy attempts. The female will probably hide in the foliage that must be provided on one end of the breeding tank just for this purpose. The rest of the tank must be free from any other material, including gravel.

After a few hours of what looks like a rough fight, with the male chasing the female all around the tank, ripping her scales and fins to shreds, they will finally settle down. Fertilization requires that the genital pores of the male and female betta be close together during spawning, as the male fertilizes the eggs as they are dropped. The male will wrap his body around the female and squeeze her until some eggs drop out, then he will quickly release her and go down for the eggs and catch them in his mouth. Some females may help the male move the eggs, but many are so stupified from breeding that they just stay in the water without moving. As the eggs that the female drops are very small and sand colored, it is obvious why there must be no sand on the bottom of the breeding tank. If the eggs should reach the bottom before the male has a chance to get them all up, they may be lost.

After the male has a mouthful of eggs, he blows them into his bubble-nest and then returns to his bride for more squeezing, and consequently more eggs. This process may take hours or days, but should never take more than two days, since the fertilized eggs will start to hatch by that time. After the female has given up all her eggs, she must be removed or the male will surely kill her. Then the male can be left alone with the hatching fry for a few days.

One of the functions of the bubble-nest is undoubtedly to keep the fry up near the surface of the water, where it is well aerated. The betta often lives in stagnant water, and it is entirely conceivable that the eggs, which are heavier than water, would otherwise sink toward the bottom where they would smother. Should a fry get too active and fall to the bottom, the father betta is waiting to catch it and blow it back to the top. He may need to continue doing this for as long as ten to twelve days. To prevent his starting to eat the young fry after this period of time, he should be removed after ten days.

When the fry have hatched out, they must be fed infusoria. Infusoria culture may be purchased in special pills which , when placed in water, will dissolve and release millions of microscopic animals—rotifers, paramecia, amoebae, and many others—that swim around the water. Strictly speaking, some of these animals are not infusoria, but nevertheless they are contained in infusoria pills. Other forms of fry food are also available at your pet shop.

The Libby Betta

The most outstanding strain of *Betta splendens* during the 1960's was the Libby Betta bred by Warren and Libby Young of Little Falls, New Jersey. The Youngs concentrated their efforts on developing a strain of Siamese fighting fish that was the best to be found anywhere. They encountered some difficulties that were not insurmountable and arrived at four rules which they considered essential:

1. Use absolutely clean water, especially for young fish. Change the water twice a week whether it looks dirty or not.

2. Don't use unseasoned water. Store in a wooden barrel or some such container for at least three days before using it.

3. Use water that is as close to neutral (pH 7.0) as possible. The Youngs' tap water was 7.8 and had to be corrected before using.

4. Use water as soft as possible. The Youngs used a commercial zeolite softener that brought the water hardness down to 2° or 3°.

By the relentless use of these rules Warren and Libby Young were able to produce fish that were the envy of all who saw them. Contrary to what many believed, they had no "secret" methods. All that they would tell you was to observe their four rules and, most important of all, *keep working at it!*

Paradise Fish
(Macropodus opercularis)

Known to the technical world as *Macropodus opercularis*, this fish has had a lot to do with the increase in the fashion of home aquaria. The paradise fish might be called the "guppy of the egglayers." Its ability to survive dirty water, extremes of temperature, and poor feeding conditions, coupled with its beautiful color during mating time, makes it a very desirable fish. It breeds exactly the same as the betta, but in contrast to the betta a domestic paradise fish is never so vicious and will seldom attack the female after she has spawned.

Many people keep paradise fish in their outdoor pools during the summer months. Temperatures as low as 50°F. and as high as 90°F. seem to have little effect upon their well-being, though temperature and environmental conditions do affect their breeding habits.

Strains of this fish have been noted to breed true once a pure line has been developed. The albino paradise, with its contrasting pink eyes and reddish sides, is a very popular strain.

A caution should be sounded about mixing the paradise fish with goldfish: if they are not in a large pool, keep them separated. The paradise fish seems to be jealous of the goldfish's flowing fins and sees to it that they do not stay flowing very long. They attack most long-finned fishes.

Dwarf Banded Gourami
(Colisa lalia)

Colisa lalia, the dwarf gourami, is another fish that has gained many fans. Since it is one of the smallest of the gouramis, it is very desirable in the smaller aquarium. But this is not the only reason for its popularity. The dwarf gourami is one of the prettiest members of its group. Like the betta, it builds a bubble-nest, but it goes one step further than the betta in nest-building and it weaves in bits of plants as a sort of superstructure. Owing to the added complexity of the work of nest-building, it is rather common for the female to help the male in the construction, though frequently she meets death as her reward during the period following mating. As two strange fish thrown together for mating may not get along too well, it would be wise to observe the same precautions with the *C. lalia* as you would when mating the betta.

The shyness and timidity of *C. lalia* may cause its keeper some concern, but these undesirable characteristics may be overcome by keeping them hungry for awhile and then introducing some friendly fish into the tank. When you throw a little food into the front of the tank, the friendly fish will race for it, while the shy *C. lalia* will stay hungry. After a few days of this treatment, the hunger will help overcome their shyness, and they will eat and mingle easily with the other fish.

The optimum breeding temperature for this gourami, as well as the other species, is about 79°F. At this higher temperature their color is more intense than at lower temperatures.

Other gouramis are popular, too. The striped gourami, *C. fasciata*, is also called the "giant banded gourami," both names being attributed to the physical characteristics of the fish. This species has the general breeding habits of the family, and the female should be removed after spawning. The species is rather peaceful toward other fish, as is the entire group.

The thick-lipped gourami, *C. labiosa*, is halfway between the size of the giant and the dwarf and is not as colorful as either. Though its "lips" are not really very different from the other gouramis, a careful comparison with other types will undoubtedly reveal some contrasts.

Three-spot Gourami
(Trichogaster trichopterus)

The three-spot or blue gourami, *Trichogaster trichopterus,* may be a popularly misnamed species. Actually, the species has only two spots, large and dark, on its body. The third spot is generally considered to be the eye.

The three-spot is not as peaceful as the other gouramis and has been known to attack smaller fish. Though it also builds a bubble-nest, it really does not need it since its eggs are lighter than water and float. The young, too, when they hatch out of the eggs are very light and float on the surface of the water. The three-spot and the blue gourami are identical except that the blue gourami has a hazy coat of whitish blue that does not obscure the spots, however.

The blue and three-spot gouramis, as well as the pearl gourami, which we shall mention presently, are well known for their hydra eating. Hydras are tiny pests with tentacles that contain a potent venom. When a small fish comes into contact with their tentacles it is held fast and paralyzed, and then devoured. Hydras also have an appetite for daphnia, which are more their own size. The writer has observed hydras that have had all their tentacles filled with paralyzed daphnia, awaiting a suitable appetite to ingest the unfortunate victims.

As can be understood, therefore, hydras are not welcome guests in the home aquarium. When they have infested the aquarium, about the only economical way to clear them out is to place a few pearl gouramis in the tank and let them stay hungry until they resort to eating hydras. After a time they get to relish these pests, and your hydra problem is solved.

Kissing Gourami
(*Helostoma temmincki*)

A very interesting gourami is the kissing gourami, *Helostoma temmincki*, so named for the unusual shape of its mouth when eating or sucking debris from the sides of the tank. Kissing gouramis seem to delight in sucking up debris on the bottom of the tank, ingesting whatever digestible matter it may contain. This gourami is reputed to be an excellent algae-eater, though the author is rather skeptical about this claim. Sometimes two kissing gouramis will come together with their puckered lips and actually "kiss" each other. This is probably not an act of love, in the sense that it is not part of a reproductive process or mating technique. In their native habitat they run up to a foot long, though the average aquarium size is usually 5 to 6 inches.

Pearl Gourami
(Trichogaster leeri)

T. leeri, the pearl gourami, is one of the most beautiful of the gourami family. Reaching a length of 3 to 4 inches, it is one of the most peaceful and delightful fish to be added to a community tank. In breeding, the *T. leeri* develops a brilliant red hue. The eggs are lighter than water, and when the female is embraced under the bubble-nest by the male between 35 and a hundred eggs float up into the nest. Spawns sometimes reach into the thousands. The writer has been quite successful in raising *T. leeri* commercially in 100-gallon wooden-frame tanks.

The pearl gourami will spawn continuously during the summer months. If adequately fed, they will not eat their young and eggs. The whole secret in raising gouramis is the feeding of the young. They should be fed four or five times a day at the minimum, with as much as they will take. A close look at their bellies, which should be like miniature balloons, will give ample indication of the success you are going to have. The young fish should be supplied with a profuse infusion. They should also receive egg yolk from the time they are free-swimming. To prepare this food, remove a piece of yolk from a hard-boiled egg. Wrap this piece of yolk in a clean white handkerchief and place it in warm water for a few seconds, then squeeze the yolk through the handkerchief and stir it into the water. Keep doing this until the water is a bright yellow. Feed it to the young fish through an eyedropper. (This egg suspension will keep in the refrigerator for a week, so the whole yolk of an egg may be prepared at one time.) The yolk makes a very desirable food since it does not sink as rapidly as regular dry food. After the first week, the young may be fed very fine, dry, powdered fish food, and after two weeks they should be fed brine shrimp with the egg suspension. Heavier foods may also be tried. The writer has been successful in raising *T. leeri* up to maturity in nine months by a sole diet of egg and dried food.

Adult *T. leeri* relish daphnia and tubifex and are also dependent on floating foods. They should be supplied with these constantly.

Cichlids

Another large group of egg-laying fish is the family Cichlidae. These are characterized by having only a single nostril opening on either side of their heads, between the eye and mouth. The nostrils in most other fish are U-shaped tubes, with two openings to the exterior. (In neither the cichlids nor most other fish do the nostrils communicate with the mouth or throat, being employed only in smelling and not breathing.)

The cichlids vary so, both in appearance and in habits, that they would seem not to belong to the same family. Anyone who has seen the angelfish and the Egyptian mouthbrooder will realize how different cichlids may look, and anyone who has bred these species knows how diverse are their breeding habits.

A discussion of those characteristics common to all but the exceptional few, however, will serve well as a general introduction to the care of the cichlids as a group. The cichlid is the largest type of fish that is normally kept in the home aquarium, but because of its size and temperament it is not too desirable for the community tank; its other characteristics more than make up for this temperament, however.

Breeding pairs of cichlids are very hard to buy satisfactorily. Not only are the fish difficult to mate, but even should a mated pair be purchased from a reputable dealer there is no guarantee that they will breed again in strange surroundings. The best way to breed cichlids is to plan your breeding in advance and prepare your own breeders. Most cichlids are very inexpensive and readily available before they reach sizes over 2 inches. It is wise to purchase six to ten small cichlids and place them in a large community tank to mature. When maturation has been reached, the fish will tend to pair off, one fish (usually the male) chasing after another particular fish (usually the female). When such is the case, it is easy to separate the two fish into a 10-gallon tank of their own and prepare to breed them. This method is probably the best way to breed a certain species of fish but may be unsatisfactory owing to the time wasted in the maturation process. Most people contend that they would rather spend ten dollars for a mated pair of cichlids than spend ten dollars on the live food necessary to bring the fish to a rapid maturation and seasoning. This is fine, except that after you have spent the money for the mated pair there is no reward for you if the fish will not reproduce, and you are stuck with a pair of vicious fish that are valueless for your original purpose. So, if possible, try to obtain a group of small cichlids and bring them to sexual maturation in your own tank. The thrill of knowing that you are entirely responsible for the brood, as well as the fact that you are not gambling with nature, more than makes up for the time consumed in maturation.

The selection of the mate is a serious process. Just as other types of living creatures have definite patterns of mating, so do fish. Birds sometimes fight over a mate, and the male often may attack and damage the female in trying to force his attentions upon her. A male pigeon, for instance, may peck a female's head until it is bloody in his attempt to "win" her. A similar occurrence is to be found with this most intelligent fish, the cichlid. The male cichlid will attack the female cichlid much in the manner that the betta will attack his mate. Plants will be torn up by the roots, and any small ornament is sure to be displaced as the battle between male and female persists. As it is not infrequent that the two fish will lock their strong jaws and roll over and over on the bottom of the tank, it is not advisable to have any sharp rocks or decorations on the floor of the aquarium. With some types of fish this may continue for a few days, but others usually stop after six or eight hours. If the fish have been properly seasoned for this encounter by being separated by a glass partition and being fed live food for a week or so before the mating, they usually proceed to mate and spawn with no trouble. But, should one be in better condition than the other, and should this superiority show in the love duel, then death is sure to be the reward of the weaker one. This may be nature's test for parenthood, but it is always wisest to prevent this mating fight, as the weaker fish invariably loses its life if it is allowed to occur. As is easily seen, then, it is usually best to have the fish of approximately the same size, though cichlids differing by an inch or more in length have been successfully bred.

Should this marriage test fail, that is, should one of

the fish be stronger and start to overcome the other, then the fish should be separated and new mates provided for each after a further seasoning period. This second period should be longer than the first in order to give their wounds a chance to heal.

When a pair has finally been mated, they must be sure to have the proper "rooms" in which to breed. Several considerations must be taken into account in providing a favorable situation.

We know that the smallest breeding size of the average cichlid is about 3 inches. Two of these make 6 inches. Since you anticipate a nice fight, several hundred (more or less) young, and possibly many holes being dug in the gravel on the bottom, the minimum requirement would be a 10-gallon tank. The water should be well aged and at about 78°F.; plants are not necessary and should be omitted, except where mentioned for specific fish.

Prior to mating, the fish usually dig holes in the gravel on the bottom of the tank; they grab a mouthful of gravel and blow it a few inches away, until, by repeating this process many times, they produce a hole. Then they may move to another location and start the process all over again.

Their next step is to find a suitable place to protect their eggs. Since the eggs are adhesive and small, the parents must find a very clean, satisfactory depository. This is usually a flat, smooth stone. Once the stone has been selected, they scrub it with their mouths until every speck of debris or algae has been removed and the rock is spotless. As the cichlids seem to prefer a light-colored stone, a piece of light slate or quartz is suitable. It should be at least 3 inches square, though its edges need not be uniform.

Now everything is in readiness for spawning. The fish develop a tube that projects from the anal region like a nipple; this is a sure signal that they are ready to spawn. The tube gets to be about three-eighths of an inch long in most types of cichlids. It is through this tube that the female drops her eggs and that the male emits his sperm to fertilize the eggs. After spawning, the tube slowly recedes into the body of the adult fish; this usually takes about five days to a week.

Now that the eggs are on the clean rock, fertilized by the male, they are ready to be incubated. This incubation period observed by the cichlids is analogous to that of the pigeon or the chicken. The eggs need oxygen to carry on life processes. If the water in the tank is still and the eggs are very compact (there may be several hundred eggs in a 3-inch square), it is easily seen that they do not receive much oxygen from the water immediately surrounding them. Undoubtedly it is for this reason that one of the parents stays above the eggs and fans them with its fins, gently forcing water over the eggs. It is a good thing that the eggs are sticky or they would be scattered all over the tank by this operation. Fanning the eggs probably has other purposes besides getting oxygen into the batch of eggs; wastes from the young embryos are diluted more quickly into the water, and the temperature is kept rather constant throughout the area by the greater circulation. This is an important part of the reproductive cycle of the cichlids. After carefully fanning the eggs for a few hours, the parents make sure that none have been attacked by fungus. If they spot any that have been attacked, they eat them. Sometimes they eat the rest as well, but such is usually not the case. It has been said that they can exercise judgment as to whether or not their spawn are up to par, and if they are not, they eat them. But as far as the writer knows, there are no scientific data to support this theory.

As soon as the young are about to hatch, after about

five days, the parents take them into their mouths and move them to one of the depressions they have dug in the sand. During the many trips that may be needed to carry them all, one of the parents is always awaiting the arrival of the other at one of the destinations, to make sure that they never lose all their young at one time. After a day or so, the young seem to be moved continually from one hole to the next, in the same careful way, always being guarded by their parents. Should any other fish venture near their hole, the parents either eat their young or fight the aggressor.

So far as can be determined, this daily moving is to provide the young, when they are old enough to eat, with fresh feeding grounds. The holes also provide good protection against possible enemies and are an easy way for the parents to keep their brood concentrated in one small area. Any too venturesome young fish straying beyond the confines of its "nursery" is quickly snapped up by one of the parents and spat back into the hole.

Cichlids, as a whole, are very good parents, and many of them may be left with their growing young. It may be wise, however, to remove the parents as soon as the young are free-swimming, since they are not essential to their young after they reach this size, and one never knows when a temperamental fish will start to eat its own offspring.

Among average aquarists, cichlids are usually unpopular for their size and because they eat small fish with no concern at all. Some of these cichlids get to be very nasty, and for that reason may require a separate tank for themselves. The famed oscar, *Astronotus ocellatus*, which gets to be very large (close to a foot long), must be fed live food constantly in the form of small fish (such as guppies, mollies, etc.), earthworms, chunks of meat, or pieces of shrimp. There are few, if any, small tropical fish that may be kept safely in the same tank as

k Sphenops Molly
cilia sphenops
to by Andre Roth

Green Sailfin Molly
Poecilia latipinna
Photo by Andre Roth

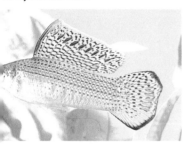

rid Sailfin Molly
cilia velifera X *latipinna*
to by Andre Roth

Albino Lyretail Molly
Poecilia species (hybrid)
Photo by Andre Roth

tail Sailfin Molly
cilia latipinna
to by Dr. Karl Knaack

Black Molly
Poecilia species (hybrid)
Photo by Dr. Herbert R. Axelrod

rter Black Veiltail Guppies
cilia reticulata
to by Andre Roth

Red Bicolor Delta Guppy
Poecilia reticulata
Photo by Andre Roth　　65

Astronotus.

There is one important rule in dealing with cichlids: *Give them plenty of room.* A pair of cichlids should not be kept in a tank smaller than 10 gallons.

The breeding habits of the cichlids, as you have seen, are very interesting. As the foregoing discussion has of necessity been general, we shall now progress to more specific discussions about the popular cichlids, how to breed each group, and their peculiarities.

Certain of the cichlids breed alike, but such fish as the angelfish *(Pterophyllum scalare)*, Egyptian mouth-brooder *(Pseudocrenilabrus multicolor)*, and jewel fish *(Hemichromis bimaculatus)*, though members of the same family, display different breeding habits. There is no reason to expect fish of the same family to breed exactly the same way; fish are classified according to physical characteristics, not according to breeding habits.

Festivum
(Cichlasoma festivum)

The breeding habits of *Cichlasoma festivum* might be well worth investigation and thorough study, as it is unique: it seldom gets larger than 3 1/2 inches in length and is very peaceful for a cichlid.

As mentioned previously, the best way to obtain a mated pair is to allow them to pair off by themselves. When you notice the peculiar antics of a pair of fish, remove them to a tank that has been prepared in advance for them. The tank should be unplanted but contain some type of dense vegetation. Any of the long, stiff-stemmed plants are good; place a rubber band and strip of lead about the bottom of a bunch and just drop it into the tank. Several inches of clean sand should be placed on the bottom of the tank, and a clean, light-colored, flat stone or small flowerpot should be placed on the sand. Next, the fish should be separated, as with the betta, by a glass partition. This separation should continue until both fish are ready for the actual process of spawning. While the fish are thus separated, they must continually be fed freeze-dried food—any of the usual kinds are good, daphnia, tubifex, or brine shrimp probably being about the best—or live foods along with their normal fare.

When both fish show full color—this is a deep gray green with a long band of black running from the mouth, through the eye, across the back toward the tip of the dorsal fin—they may be allowed to get together by a removal of the glass partition. As soon as the partition is removed, the fish will slyly investigate this new condition, hardly paying any attention to each other. This is in direct contrast to the actions of the bettas, which even when separated dash against the glass partition in a vain attempt to reach the other fish.

After making sure that there are no enemies, the fish methodically go about tearing up any planted vegetation, as if making sure that no evil lurks in darkened corners. Next comes a process of much interest. The fish face each other and lock jaws, twisting and turning, rolling and milling, all over the tank. Again, be sure that there are no sharp edges upon which the fish may cut themselves. This test of strength may be repeated several times during a period of a few hours. Everything will be all right if neither fish gets "cold feet" and runs away from the other when approached. Should such be the case, the fish must be separated immediately or the coward might meet its death. You may try to recondition the fish, but the chances of succeeding on the second try are definitely less than on the first. For this reason you must be sure that the fish are ready for mating before you separate them by the glass partition.

Blue Bicolor Delta Guppy
Poecilia reticulata
Photo by Andre Roth

Purple Delta Guppy
Poecilia reticulata
Photo by Andre Roth

Half Black Guppy
Poecilia reticulata
Photo by Andre Roth

Red Wagtail Platies
Xiphophorus maculatus
Photo by Andre Roth

Tuxedo Platy
Xiphophorus maculatus
Photo by H.-J. Richter

Mickey Mouse Platy
Xiphophorus maculatus
Photo by H.-J. Richter

Hi-fin Tuxedo Platy
Xiphophorus maculatus
Photo by H.-J. Richter

Hi-fin Wagtail Platy
Xiphophorus maculatus
Photo by H.-J. Richter

een Swordtail
hophorus helleri
to by H.-J. Richter

Variegated Green Swordtail
Xiphophorus helleri
Photo by H.-J. Richter

ino Lyretail Swordtail
hophorus helleri
to by H.-J. Richter

Red Lyretail Swordtail
Xiphophorus helleri
Photo by Andre Roth

ck Swordtail
hophorus helleri
to by Andre Roth

Hybrid Tuxedo Swordtail
Xiphophorus helleri X maculatus
Photo by Dr. Karl Knaack

d Swordtail
hophorus helleri
to by Andre Roth

Red Wagtail Swordtail
Xiphophorus helleri
Photo by Andre Roth

69

Should this "wrestling" period be consummated successfully, they will then proceed to dig holes in the sand. This interesting process may take several days, the fish gobbling a mouthful of sand and blowing it away from the hole. Next, the fish start chewing and scraping at every surface of the stone you have placed on the sand, to ensure maximum cleanliness. This action reminds one of the molly scraping algae from the sides of the aquarium. The painstaking care with which this rock is prepared for the deposit of the eggs makes human cleanliness and meticulousness seem rather shoddy.

You can be quite sure that the pair will spawn in a very short time when both fish develop a short tube from the anal region. This tube (called an "ovipositor" in the female) reaches a length of about three-eighths of an inch immediately before spawning, though the size is usually proportional to the size of the fish. They usually spawn about a day and a half after the appearance of this tube. During this entire process, the male and female fish stay very close to each other, usually in one of the holes they have previously dug.

When all is in readiness, the female approaches the selected rock and deposits a few eggs on it from her ovipositor; this may be repeated many times until an area of 3 square inches is covered with eggs; the male immediately follows and fertilizes the sticky eggs by squirting his sperm on them. After four or five hours, the fish are usually finished spawning and begin to fan the eggs. Fanning is accomplished by the male or female staying directly above the mass of eggs and moving its pectoral and caudal fins unceasingly. When one fish gets tired, the other takes its place. The reasons for this fanning process may be threefold. First, by constant circulation the temperature of the water is kept rather constant—

80°F. is best—which undoubtedly helps the development of the eggs. Next, the circulation may help prevent bacteria or fungus from lodging on the infertile eggs and "rotting" them. Third, the fanning may keep fresh, oxygenated water constantly over the eggs, avoiding a concentration of carbon dioxide and other wastes.

After four days at 80°F., the eggs start to hatch. At this time the fish start to move the young, mouthful by mouthful, to one of the holes which one fish has dug while the other was fanning the eggs. Sometimes a lazy pair will just use the holes that were dug before actual spawning took place. The transfer of the young is well organized. The rock is protected by one of the fish while the other protects the hole into which the young are being transferred. The rock protector gets a mouthful of young, signals the other fish (how this is done is not known, but they do face each other for a second or so before moving), and they quickly exchange places. The new mouthful of young is deposited with the others in the hole, and the fish repeat the process. This is kept up until all the fish are removed from the rock. Any infertile eggs which have started to rot are eaten by one of the fish. The young are then continually moved from hole to hole, being scrubbed by their trip in the parents' mouth. Do not misinterpret this as an act of eating. Now the young should be left alone with the parents; if the parents are disturbed or too badly frightend by an intruder, they might eat their litter right up.

For a week or so after hatching, the fish may be noticed to possess a yolk sac. This yolk sac contains food for the embryo fish as well as a ration for a short time after it hatches. However, this sac is soon absorbed, and food must be provided for the young. Infusoria are the best. The larger types of paramecia, amoebae, and rotifers are good for the first few weeks; then quantities of

Blue Hi-fin Variatus Platy
Xiphophorus variatus
Photo by H.-J. Richter

Marigold Variatus Platy
Xiphophorus variatus
Photo by H.-J. Richter

Four-eyes
Anableps anableps
Photo by Andre Roth

Pike Livebearer
Belonesox belizanus
Photo by Andre Roth

Caudo
Phalloceros caudimaculatus
Photo by Ruda Zukal

Mosquitofish
Gambusia species
Photo by Andre Roth

Merry Widow
Phallichthys amates
Photo by Dr. Karl Knaack

Humpbacked Limia
Poecilia nigrofasciata
Photo by Dr. Karl Knaack

ardinus
ardinus metallicus
oto by H.-J. Richter

Blue-eyed Livebearer
Priapella intermedia
Photo by Klaus Paysan

ng-finned Spot-tail
eudoxiphophorus bimaculata
oto by H.-J. Richter

Least Killifish
Heterandria formosa
Photo by H.-J. Richter

tterfly Goodeid
eca splendens
oto by H.-J. Richter

Red-tailed Goodeid
Xenotoca eiseni
Photo by H.-J. Richter

layan Halfbeak
rmogenys pusillus
oto by Klaus Paysan

Black-finned Celebes Halfbeak
Nomorhamphus liemi
Photo by H.-J. Richter

73

sifted daphnia or brine shrimp must be supplied. Microworms may also be used.

During this entire breeding process, the older fish must constantly be fed live food. This holds true of all the cichlids except the mouthbrooders.

The parents may be left with their young as long as you wish. During the first few days the young are definitely dependent on their parents, but after a week or so the parents may be moved—at the esthetic expense of not being able to be watched swimming with their brood.

Cichlids may be bred again six weeks after they are removed from their brood, though breeding them too often is not advisable, as they tend to lose interest in their successive broods.

Ports
(Aequidens portalegrensis)

The port is a very popular fish and one that should be able to be successfully bred by whoever tries. It follows the breeding habits of the cichlids, though offering more tolerance to critical conditions. The ports usually can stand overcrowding, disturbances, and poor breeding conditions, while many other cichlids can't.

Aequidens portalegrensis are about 4 inches at breeding size, usually getting larger after a few successful breedings. They are very shy, and when introduced into a new aquarium they usually stay well-hidden in some obscure corner of the tank. Often they will refuse the most enticing foods for a few days, preferring to stay in complete seclusion. Even if they are the sole members of the tank and are left undisturbed, there is little chance that they will be very active for the first few days. But, as always, their hunger pains eventually change their attitude, and they finally realize that their keeper is only interested in their welfare.

Sex may be easily determined by observing the shape of the anal fin, the male's being the more pointed and flowing, while the female's is shorter and rounded. In order to see this difference easily, you must compare the two fish. After a little practice you will be able to distinguish the males from the females easily.

Care should be taken to get fish of approximately the same size if you intend to breed them. When a pair have once spawned, they usually stay mated forever. This was observed under the following conditions: out of a brood of 20 A. *portalegrensis* raised together, six pairs developed. The fish were matured in a community tank all together, but were removed, pair by pair, to spawn in a separate tank. When their spawning was over, they were again placed in the community tank with the other ports. Subsequent spawning always took place with the original mates. Never did any fish try to intercede with another's mate. This is an unusual characteristic for a fish to possess, since in so many cases more than one male is used for mating.

Jewel Fish
(Hemichromis bimaculatus)

The viciousness of certain fish makes them undesirable for the home aquarist. But if the fish has a nearly unparalleled beauty of color, some people will put up with its savage idiosyncrasies. Such is the case with the jewel fish *(Hemichromis bimaculatus)*, which is one of the most savage aquarium fish.

Breeding must be carefully supervised. In addition to the material suggested in the general discussion of the preparation of a tank, some very dense foliage must be

Brunei Beauty
Betta macrostoma
Photo by Dr. Herbert R. Axelrod

Siamese Fighting Fish
Betta splendens
Photo by H.-J. Richter

Red Siamese Fighting Fish
Betta splendens
Photo by Andre Roth

Red Siamese Fighting Fish
Betta splendens
Photo by Andre Roth

Blue Siamese Fighting Fish
Betta splendens
Photo by Dr. Herbert R. Axelrod

Butterfly Siamese Fighting Fish
Betta splendens
Photo by Dr. Herbert R. Axelrod

Paradise Fish
Macropodus opercularis
Photo by Andre Roth

Day's Paradise Fish
Pseudosphromenus cupanus dayi
Photo by H.-J. Richter

ney Gourami
lisa chuna
oto by Klaus Paysan

Sunset Honey Gourami
Colisa chuna
Photo by H.-J. Richter

ick-lipped Gourami
lisa labiosa
oto by Andre Roth

Giant Banded Gourami
Colisa fasciata
Photo by Klaus Paysan

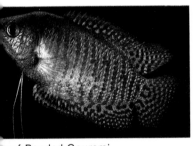

varf Banded Gourami
lisa lalia
oto by Andre Roth

Chocolate Gourami
Sphaerichthys osphromenoides
Photo by Andre Roth

ant Gourami
sphronemus goramy
oto by H.-J. Richter

Kissing Gourami
Helostoma temmincki
Photo by Andre Roth

77

added, the best being large clumps of *Elodea*. The necessity for such foliage is easily seen when you realize that the jewel fish is probably the most active, sexually, of the cichlids during the spawning interlude. Should one of the fish show the slightest signs of weakness, the other would immediately rip it to pieces; such dense foliage will help save the fish from such an end.

The jewel fish are quite beautiful when in breeding colors. They are bred the same way as the *A. portalegrensis*. Some authors suggest the use of the mature eggs of the *Hemichromis* for embryological studies. Solberg and Brinley have done some serious work on the embryological development of the fish and have found that heart action begins about 36 hours after fertilization, and that 48 hours after fertilization the embryo bursts from its containing membrane by a violent swish of its tail and moves away. They state that the yolk is absorbed after seven days, and advise that at this time, when the jaws become movable, the young jewels should be fed protozoa.

Other fish which have the same breeding habits as *A. portalegrensis* and *H. bimaculatus* are as follows:

Cichlasoma cyanoguttatum—commonly called the "Texas cichlid"; in Texas, they call it a "perch." These fish are usually caught and eaten by the poor in and around the Rio Grande. While on a visit to San Antonio, the author saw them swimming in the river which flows right through the heart of town. They run to about 8 inches and are rather pretty, being covered with pearl-like speckles. They should be kept by themselves in a large tank.

Cichlasoma meeki—commonly called the "firemouth cichlid." The firemouth is so named because of the brilliant red color it develops on the underside of its body, from the base of the tail to the mouth. Sex is distinguished by the shape and size of the anal fin. A 10-gallon tank is minimum for firemouths as they sometimes get to be 6 inches long and need room to spawn. They breed very much the same as other fish, except that it is advisable to have a piece of slate for them to spawn on; if you have a slate-bottom tank and do not put in a rock, they will dig through the sand and spawn on the tank bottom. The size of the slate should be about 5 by 10 inches. Thickness is of no consequence.

Cichlasoma octofasciatum—commonly called the "Jack Dempsey" because of its ferociousness. It is a truly beautiful fish, always displaying magnificent colors that tend not to change much and are also permanent. The Jack Dempsey can stand the normal fluctuation of temperature from 60° to 90° F. without any trouble, though the color is at its best around 82° F.

After a year, the fish may reach 4 inches in length, usually getting larger and more colorful as it gets older. It breeds as we would expect any of the cichlids to breed and is an exceptionally good parent, though it must not be disturbed too frequently.

A pair of Dempseys breed best when they are kept in a 20-gallon tank by themselves. They may be kept with their young and usually take excellent care of them.

Cichlasoma severum—This fish grows a little larger than 5 inches long and will get along nicely in a 10- or 20-gallon aquarium. Conditioning before mating is very important, and they should be fed live food or chopped earthworms for a few weeks before trying to spawn them. They will show little color at temperatures below 78° F. Sex may be determined by a comparison of the dorsal and anal fins. As always, the male fins are longer

Three-spot Blue Gourami
Trichogaster trichopterus
Photo by Andre Roth

Cosby Blue Gourami
Trichogaster trichopterus
Photo by Andre Roth

Golden Blue Gourami
Trichogaster trichopterus
Photo by H.-J. Richter

Pearl Gourami
Trichogaster leeri
Photo by Andre Roth

Moonlight Gourami
Trichogaster microlepis
Photo by Andre Roth

Snakeskin Gourami
Trichogaster pectoralis
Photo by Klaus Paysan

Congo Ctenopoma
Ctenopoma congicum
Photo by Ruda Zukal

Combtail
Belontia signata
Photo by Andre Roth

Angelfish
Pterophyllum scalare
Photo by Andre Roth

Silver Veiltail Angelfish
Pterophyllum scalare
Photo by Andre Roth

Brown Discus
Symphysodon aequifasciata axelrodi
Photo by Andre Roth

Blue Discus
Symphysodon aequifasciatus
Photo by Andre Roth

Heckel's Discus
Symphysodon discus
Photo by Andre Roth

Rainbow Cichlid
Herotilapia multispinosa
Photo by Andre Roth

Oscar (juvenile)
Astronotus ocellatus
Photo by Dr. Herbert R. Axelrod

Bronze Red Oscar
Astronotus ocellatus
Photo by Andre Roth

81

and more pointed. The male is also more highly colored, being covered during high color with rows of parallel dots. The female has at times faded vertical bands, though in a matter of seconds if frightened she may lose every bit of color she previously had.

Etroplus maculatus—commonly called the "orange chromide," is sometimes very shy and timid and may refuse to eat several types of dry foods. It is a small fish for a cichlid, seldom getting larger than 3 inches. As sex is rather difficult to distinguish and mated pairs are hard to obtain, the group pairing plan is about the only way to get a decently mated pair. This method is further advantageous in that the orange chromide will breed in a community tank, as long as the other fish are not too large. The mother fish will usually tend the young while the father tries to keep strangers away from them.

The fish will spawn on the top part of the inside of a flowerpot or on the underside of the slate if the slate is laid against the side of the tank rather than being placed flat against the sand. They are a nice fish to keep in the community tank because of their size and breeding habits.

Aequidens maronii—commonly called the "keyhole cichlid" because of the dark region near its lower quarter that takes the shape of a keyhole. The reason for the name *maronii* is simple: the fish was originally found in the Maroni River in Venezuela. Keyhole cichlids are very mild mannered and usually will not attack any smaller fish without provocation. They are fairly timid and lose their color when frightened. Sex is easily determined by a comparison of the anal fins of the male and female, the male's fin being much longer and more pointed.

Keyhole cichlids are good parents and may be bred

easily by the amateur if the proper conditioning precautions are followed. They thrive well on all types of live food.

Astronotus ocellatus—commonly called "oscars." Anyone owning a mated pair of these fish paid over $100 for them, and anyone who believes he can breed them and successfully rear the young knows enough about the fish not to rely upon popular names. They are vicious, large (up to a foot in length), and very difficult to breed. Though in relatively rare instances they have been successfully bred, they probably did their spawning alone in a 100-gallon tank or larger. This will usually put them out of reach of the ordinary fancier. A 100-gallon tank filled with water weighs close to half a ton, and not many homes have floors that can stand such a concentrated weight. However, many aquarists feel that oscars develop a distinct personality. They recognize their keeper and like to be stroked, facts making them very popular with some hobbyists.

A. ocellatus is pugnacious looking, and, in character with its looks, it makes short work of any fish smaller than 3 inches and has been known to attack larger fish. Young are often available, but as they grow they will eat larger and larger fish.

If they do spawn, their eggs must be removed and hatched in a 35-gallon tank by themselves.

Red Devils
(Cichlasoma labiatum and *Cichlasoma dovii)*

Late in 1964 these monsters among aquarium fishes were introduced to hobbyists. Some of them are so big that they even make a grown oscar look small, and if you don't have a tank that's really big, forget about them! Home waters are in several parts of Central

Chocolate Cichlid
Cichlasoma coryphaenoides
Photo by H.-J. Richter

Jack Dempsy
Cichlasoma octofasciatum
Photo by Andre Roth

Firemouth Cichlid
Cichlasoma meeki
Photo by Klaus Paysan

Yellow-belly Cichlid
Cichlasoma salvini
Photo by Dr. Herbert R. Axelrod

Convict Cichlid
Cichlasoma nigrofasciatum
Photo by Dr. S. Frank

Golden Convict Cichlid
Cichlasoma nigrofasciatum
Photo by Andre Roth

Flag Cichlid
Cichlasoma festivum
Photo by Klaus Paysan

Severum
Cichlasoma severum
Photo by Klaus Paysan

Blue Acara
Aequidens pulcher
Photo by Andre Roth

Flag Acara
Aequidens curviceps
Photo by H.-J. Richter

Port Acara
Aequidens portalegrensis
Photo by Klaus Paysan

Ram
Microgeophagus ramirezi
Photo by Andre Roth

Double-banded Dwarf Cichlid
Apistogramma bitaeniata
Photo by Dr. Karl Knaack

Spade-tailed Dwarf Cichlid
Apistogramma agassizi
Photo by Klaus Paysan

Golden Dwarf Cichlid
Nannacara anomala
Photo by H.-J. Richter

Checkerboard Lyretail Cichlid
Crenicara filamentosa
Photo by H.-J. Richter

85

America, Costa Rica and Nicaragua being two of the possibilities mentioned. They vary greatly in color as well as shape, some of them being pure white and others red all over, some with black markings on fins and the mouth. Some have large rubbery lips that come to a point and remind one of some of the salt-water wrasse species.

Egyptian Mouthbrooder
(Pseudocrenilabrus multicolor)

The Egyptian mouthbrooder is truly a fish to catch the eye. Not only is it very neatly colored, but its breeding habits are most unusual. The habits of breeding are similar to those of the other cichlids only in that a hole made by the fish for itself—usually by fanning the sand—is used for depositing the eggs. The male entices the female over the hole and she drops a few eggs into it; they are then quickly fertilized by the male. However, following this the process is quite different. As soon as fertilization takes place, the female swoops down and gathers up the fertile eggs in her mouth. She may continue to do this for some time, but as soon as her mouth is full, she will no longer go near the hole. Sometimes this irritates the male and he will nip at her; the female, with her mouthful of eggs, is helpless to fight back, and unless the merciful intervention of the aquarium manager saves her, she may die with her brood still in her mouth. For this reason it seems wise to remove the male as soon as possible after the female exhibits signs of leaving her position over the hole.

Day after day, the female keeps her eggs in her mouth, sucking water in over them through her mouth and blowing it out of her gills. She will steadily refuse the most tasty morsels offered her, never daring to take anything into her oral cavity. This refusal to eat may last as long as two weeks, during which time the young fish hatch and live off their yolks sacs. The mother may at times allow her brood to swim around her out of her mouth, but at the slightest noise or disturbance she will open her mouth and the young will swim directly in. During this time the female fish may appear to lose all her flesh; she will get very thin and emaciated, and her eyes will seem to bulge from their sockets. So strong is this mother's instinct, however, that, as hungry as she is, she would rather starve to death than eat her own young. After about two weeks, the young are too large to be able to fit into the mouth of their mother, so they take off on their own, searching for the protozoa or other infusoria that should be placed in the tank for them.

One odd thing about the Egyptian mouthbrooders is that they will attack and kill any of the swiftly swimming fish that may be present in their mating tank. This is undoubtedly a precaution they take, fearing that a fast-moving fish might swoop down upon their brood before they get a chance to seek refuge in their mother's mouth.

After she has served her purpose, the mother fish should be put in a small tank alone for a few days so she can regain her health without being bothered by stronger fish attacking her. She should be fed small amounts of daphnia or tubifex at frequent intervals, but not too much at once as she may become ill.

The optimum temperature for the breeding of the young and the mating of the parents is about 78° F. The young should be fed live food as often as possible for quick maturation.

Sex in these fish is easily discernible by the larger head of the female and the more brightly colored anal fin of the male during high color.

Paraguay Mouthbrooder
Geophagus balzani
Photo by Dr. Herbert R. Axelrod

Lifalili Jewel Cichlid
Hemichromis bimaculatus "lifalili"
Photo by H.-J. Richter

Orange Chromide
Etroplus maculatus
Photo by Klaus Paysan

Golden Orange Chromide
Etroplus maculatus
Photo by Dr. Herbert R. Axelrod

Pink Kribensis Cichlid
Pelvicachromis pulcher
Photo by H.-J. Richter

Dwarf Egyptian Mouthbrooder
Pseudocrenilabrus multicolor
Photo by Klaus Paysan

Frontosa
Cyphotilapia frontosa
Photo by Dr. Herbert R. Axelrod

Golden-sided Victoria Hap
Haplochromis brownae
Photo by Andre Roth

Fenestratus Hap
Haplochromis fenestratus
Photo by Dr. Herbert R. Axelrod

Night Peacock Cichlid
Aulonocara "Night"
Photo by G. Meola

Fuelleborn's Lab
Labeotropheus fuelleborni
Photo by Andre Roth

Red-top Trewavasae
Labeotropheus trewavasae
Photo by Andre Roth

Short-bodied Labido
Labidochromis cf. *mathothoi*
Photo by Andre Roth

Brown-lined Labido
Labidochromis exasperatus
Photo by Dr. Warren E. Burgess

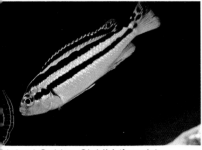

Malawi Golden Cichlid (female)
Melanochromis auratus
Photo by Dr. Karl Knaack

Malawi Golden Cichlid (male)
Melanochromis auratus
Photo by Klaus Paysan

89

The Malawi Cichlids—Mbunas
(Pseudotropheus, Melanochromis, and *Labeotropheus* species)*

Every time the hobbyists of the world become jaded and say that there is nothing new to be seen among fishes, it seems that someone comes along with the news that a new source has been found and there is a new set of tongue-twisting names to learn and fishes to admire. In 1957 the author found a new supply of fishes in Lake Nyasa, now called Lake Malawi, in the eastern part of Africa. A strange thing about many of these African lakes is that they harbor a fish life that is found nowhere else in the world except in that particular lake.

The Golden Nyasa (Malawi) Cichlid
(Melanochromis auratus)

One of the most beautiful of the cichlids from Lake Malawi is this one, which has created a bit of a furor among hobbyists. It was quickly established that this was a mouthbrooding species, but so scrappy in disposition that two males should never be kept together unless the tank is very large and each can lay claim to a certain part of the tank for himself. They spawn like the other mouthbrooding cichlids, the female carrying the eggs in her mouth for two weeks. Unlike the other mouthbrooders, these have been observed to spit out the eggs on occasion and eat a hearty meal. At this time the eggs can be siphoned out and allowed to hatch, and this has been done successfully.

The Zebra Nyasa (Malawi) Cichlid
(Pseudotropheus zebra)

Body color is blue, with a number of color morphs or varieties. The male's anal fin has a group of interesting orange spots that have an intriguing story, as have those on some of the other mouthbrooding species.

The male stands by while the female lays her eggs in a depression in the bottom and then picks them up in her mouth. Then he spreads out his anal fin with those orange spots in front of her. The spots look like eggs to her, and she picks at them vigorously while at the same time the male is emitting sperm, which gets to all the eggs and fertilizes them.

The Trewavas Nyasa (Malawi) Cichlid
(Labeotropheus trewavasae)

So different   are the male and female of this species that it was at first thought they were two different species. The male has a blue body with a number of dark vertical stripes and a bright red dorsal fin, while the female is mottled brown all over, with darker markings and tiny blue spots. Both have an odd, underslung mouth. This is a mouthbrooding species like the others. There are color morphs of this cichlid, too.

The Compressed Cichlid
(Lamprologus compressiceps)

This is one of the many cichlids that the author found in Lake Tanganyika in 1957. They have a very thin body that lets them slip in among the clefts of the rocks. The natives collect them by diving. The dorsal fin spines are very sharp and cause an unpleasant itching if the skin is pierced, so if you ever get to own one, handle it with care!

The Lemon Cichlid
(Lamprologus leleupi)

This little rarity comes from the home of many cichlid species, Lake Tanganyika. It gets to be only 4 inches in length and is not hard to keep if given living foods

Blue Zebra Mbuna
Pseudotropheus zebra
Photo by Klaus Paysan

Tropheops Mbuna
Pseudotropheus tropheops
Photo by Andre Roth

Livingstone's Mbuna
Pseudotropheus livingstoni
Photo by Dr. Warren E. Burgess

Striped Goby Cichlid
Eretmodus cyanostictus
Photo by G. Meola

Lyretail Lamprologus
Lamprologus brichardi
Photo by H.-J. Richter

Lemon Cichlid
Lamprologus leleupi
Photo by H.-J. Richter

Julie
Julidochromis ornatus
Photo by H.-J. Richter

Marlier's Julie
Julidochromis marlieri
Photo by J. Hansen

Cardinal Tetra
Paracheirodon axelrodi
Photo by Dr. Herbert R. Axelrod

Neon Tetra
Paracheirodon innesi
Photo by Andre Roth

False Neon Tetra
Paracheirodon simulans
Photo by H.-J. Richter

Glowlight Tetra
Hemigrammus erythrozonus
Photo by Klaus Paysan

Head and Tail Lights Tetra
Hemigrammus ocellifer
Photo by Dr. Herbert R. Axelrod

Buenos Aires Tetra
Hemigrammus caudovittatus
Photo by Dr. Herbert R. Axelrod

Black-finned Rummy-nose Tetra
Petitella georgiae
Photo by Klaus Paysan

Garnet Tetra
Hemigrammus pulcher
Photo by Andre Roth

93

and water which is definitely alkaline. They have been spawned and breed like the usual cichlid species, using a flowerpot as a substitute cave. The eggs hatch in three days. They are easily raised with the standard procedure.

Other Malawi and Tanganyika Cichlids

So beautiful, interesting, and popular are these colorful cichlids that hundreds of different species have been imported. Most are very easy to induce to spawn, but all require a specially set up aquarium in which there are few, if any, plants and lots of rocks and caves. If you want to spawn these beauties there is little to fear as long as the tank is large enough and you have a pair. It is easiest, as a general rule, to get a 20-gallon aquarium with just some gravel on the bottom. A few flowerpots lying on their sides will provide enough hiding places. The majority of them spawn readily. *Lamprologus* species prefer to spawn in caves. The eggs are taken from the mouths of mouthbrooders for protection and hatch in small jars that are heavily aerated.

To really "get into" these fishes requires a lengthy study, and Dr. Warren E. Burgess and the present author have written a book all about *African Cichlids of Lakes Malawi and Tanganyika;* ISBN 0-87666-541-5; published by TFH as style number PS-703. At this writing it has gone into 10 editions.

Angelfish
(Pterophyllum scalare)

The angelfish bears little resemblance to other cichlids, or, for that matter, to the saltwater angelfish for which it is named.

The angelfish, *Pterophyllum scalare,* has been bred for

more than 50 years after a very slow start. It took almost 20 years of captivity before it became almost a beginner's fish to spawn. Once only the most skilled aquarists could spawn this highly desirable and expensive fish. Then, after constant inbreeding of the first tank-bred strains, the fish now spawns in community tanks! Yet the two wild angelfishes, *Pterophyllum scalare altum* and *Pterophyllum dumerilii*, imported from South America have still never been spawned, though some of the most talented breeders have tried, all over the world! The same was true of discus, *Symphysodon*. Originally they could not be spawned either; now their spawning is commonplace.

The angelfish, timid, temperamental, and delicate as it is, is one of the most popular egglaying fish. The interesting complexities of spawning and the intriguing techniques for rearing the young present a worthy challenge to the advanced aquarist. Many people have successfully bred the angel.

Let us take a close look at a sensible approach to the breeding of the angelfish.

Since in the angelfish the two sexes are practically indistinguishable, the only ways to get a mated pair are to use the group pairing method, allowing the fish to pair off by mutual attraction, or else to purchase a pair that has been successfully bred by another aquarist. Such breeding pairs are rather expensive, while young angels may be selected for less cost. The size of breeding pairs varies from one pair to the next, the usual size being about 3 to 4 inches. The young grow rapidly when reared on live food. Their attractiveness adds greatly to the appearance of the community tank, as they tend to swim in groups when kept in a large tank. They may be safely allowed to grow to breeding size without your having to worry about their attacking any fish larger than a guppy. As there is little food better for the angels

Black Neon Tetra
Hyphessobrycon herbertaxelrodi
Photo by Andre Roth

Flame Tetra
Hyphessobrycon flammeus
Photo by Andre Roth

Black-lined Tetra
Hyphessobrycon scholzei
Photo by Andre Roth

Bleeding Heart Tetra
Hyphessobrycon erythrostigma
Photo by Andre Roth

Red Phantom Tetra
Megalamphodus sweglesi
Photo by Klaus Paysan

Black Tetra
Gymnocorymbus ternetzi
Photo by Andre Roth

Blind Cave Tetra, "Anoptichthys"
Astyanax fasciatus mexicanus
Photo by Andre Roth

Boehlke's Penguin
Thayeria boehlkei
Photo by Dr. Karl Knaack

than the newborn guppy, it is usually a good idea to place them in a tank with a dozen or so guppies so they may benefit from the constant source of live food. When the fish get very temperamental and refuse all types of food, they will usually accept guppies. The same is true for a great many of the cichlids that show signs of being too timid or afraid to eat.

When you have a breeding pair of angels, your next step is to put them into a large, well-planted tank of their own. The reason for the dense foliage is twofold. First, since the angel is, as previously mentioned, very timid and gets disturbed at the slightest provocation, the more vegetation there is, the more secure the fish will feel. The shadows and hiding places offered by the plants seem to instill confidence in the angel. The other important reason is that the plants, especially giant vallisneria, Amazon sword, and giant sagittaria, play a part in the spawning procedure of the angels, the eggs of the fish many times being deposited on the stiff, rather broad leaves of the plants, which offer firm anchorage for the sticky eggs. On other occasions the angels may elect to deposit their eggs either on one side of the tank if it has some sort of paint on the outside, on the glass containing the heater thermostat, or on the face of a piece of slate which has been left tilted against the side of the tank. It is easiest for the aquarist when the slate is used since the eggs can be removed without too much trouble. This removal is sometimes very necessary, because at the slightest provocation or alarm the eggs or newly hatched young may be gobbled down out of the parents' fear for their welfare. It has been claimed many times that the parents eat their brood out of sheer dislike for the responsibility placed upon them, but there is little reason for such a theory. There are many cases known where parents successfully spawned and reared brood after brood of young and then suddenly ate up the next spawning.

Although the parents may be left in with the young for the entire maturation, if the tank is large enough (35 gallons), it is wiser either to remove them, if they have spawned on the plants or glass, or to remove the slate, if they have spawned on that. The slate should be placed in a shallow tank of 4 inches of water, with a drop of methylene blue for each gallon of water to prevent fungus; it should be slightly tilted off the bottom so an aerator may be placed underneath it, allowing the bubbles to flow all around it and hence causing the water to circulate. This takes the place of the parents' usual habit of scrubbing the eggs every once in a while.

The optimum breeding temperature for the angel is about 80° F. Seasoning on live food—daphnia and whiteworms are the best, next to young guppies, of course—is of the utmost importance in preparing the angels for spawning.

The young must have live infusoria on hand for their first meal. After a few days they must be fed sifted daphnia, newly hatched brine shrimp, or microworms. Brine shrimp seem to be the best.

The key factors in working with angels are cleanliness and the pH. The water can never be clean enough for the angels; it is usually wise to have a reserve jug of seasoned water at the proper temperature in case a cloudiness develops in the breeding tank. This cloudiness is often caused by too strong an infusion, that is, too dense a culture of small protozoa, or the rotting of organic matter.

The manner in which parents care for their eggs should they be allowed to remain with them is really impressive. Their actions are generally the same as those of the other cichlids, except that instead of transferring the young from hole to hole—though they may do this, too—in the sand, they usually transfer them from leaf to leaf, by the mouthful. Should one of the young fall free from the leaf, the ever-alert parent will be sure to catch him and return him, in one gentle blow, to his proper place on the leaf.

Angelfish have been produced in several varieties, all from the original *Pterophyllum scalare.* To Ludwig's Aquarium in Detroit goes the credit for being the first to produce an all-black angelfish strain. Good specimens are solid black in color, making a wonderful appearance in a well-planted aquarium.

The veil angelfish was once found as a sport in a batch of normal youngsters by a German breeder. He kept breeding it back to others until he arrived at a pre-ponderance of long-finned beauties. Of course, it had to happen that the blacks and veils were crossed and a magnificent black veil strain was produced.

Discus
(Symphysodon species)

The discus is probably unknown to many beginning aquarists owing to its size, cost and temperament. The fact that young discus cost upward of five dollars each gives an idea of how difficult they are to breed. A mated pair may cost over five hundred dollars. Although the acquisition of a mated pair may guarantee spawning, raising the spawn is another story. Many advanced aquarists have spent fortunes on all types of equipment for fancy techniques to help their spawn to survive, but very few have had success, though as more tank-raised discus become available the fish become easier to spawn.

The breeding of the discus is similar to that of the angelfish, but the discus is much more delicate and temperamental than any fish that has been previously mentioned. About the only foods it will take are tubifex worms, whiteworms, beef, brine shrimp, and daphnia, and these only sparingly. Many a discus has been lost because it simply refused to eat.

The main interest of these fish is their scintillating beauty and nearly perfectly circular shape. They display beautiful colors when spawning, which may be quite frequent when they are in a tank by themselves. They range in size up to 6 inches, and a 25-gallon tank should be their minimum requirement. The tank should be densely planted at both ends, leaving the center free for them to display their natural beauty.

If you can afford to purchase a half dozen of these young and raise them to maturity—this is not too great a feat if they start eating right away—they will pair off by mutual attraction when the time is ripe. This is about the only sure way to get a mated pair from them, as sex is practically indistinguishable.

In the past few years the discus has attained a much more popular position than it held in the days when it was first offered to awe-struck hobbyists and commanded astronomical prices. Since then it was discovered that spawning them, while still not an everyday thing, is not the near impossibility it was once considered to be, and every well-stocked hobbyist nowadays is very likely to have a few.

Dr. Leonard P. Schultz, of the Smithsonian Institution in Washington, D.C., has divided the genus *Symphysodon* into several species and subspecies. At present there are five: *Symphysodon aequifasciata aequifasciata*, the green discus; *Symphysodon aequifasciata axelrodi*, the brown discus; *Symphysodon aequifasciata haraldi*, the blue discus; *Symphysodon discus discus*, the original red discus or pompadour; and *Symphysodon discus willischwartzi*, the pineapple discus recently discovered by the author in the Rio Abacaxi, Brazil.

Breeding of the various discus species is exactly the

same, and the best method to get a well-mated pair is to keep about a half-dozen growing ones together and let them pick their own mates. They should have a large tank, about 50 gallons or more, and when the two are observed to get chummy and claim a portion of the tank as their property, the time has come to give them a tank of their own. This tank should have soft water, a temperature of about 82° F., and have an acidity that measures pH 6.5. Planting should be heavy, to give the pair some retreats where privacy can be attained. As with angelfish, it is a good procedure to lean a slab of slate against one side of the tank. This is generally where the pair will spawn. Some breeders prefer to give them a large flowerpot with the open top down. Preferences by the fish vary, and a little trial is indicated. Just like angelfish, the pair will swim close alongside each other, the female laying the eggs and the male fertilizing them. Then they take turns fanning and mouthing the eggs, which hatch after two days. The youngsters become free-swimming two days later, at which time they attach themselves to the sides of one of the parents and "graze" there until the time comes to change to the other parent. This is the big difference in discus breeding: the youngsters usually do not do at all well unless they get this slime as their first food. An acceptable substitute food has been found, and the eggs can now be hatched artificially as angelfish eggs are, eliminating the danger of being eaten, but raising the young is still complicated.

It is a fascinating sight to watch the parents "trading" the youngsters. The one with the youngsters feeding on the sides will wait for the other to swim up, then with a quick motion the youngsters are left behind to find their new feeding spot. In about two weeks the youngsters can be "weaned" to newly hatched brine shrimp, and when they no longer feed on the parents' slime the parents can be moved to their own tank. Frequently they are ready to spawn again by this time.

Discus are very timid fish and are easily frightened. For this reason, they should not have their tank where there are frequent disturbances. Any fish that must be left with its young as discus are would be very likely to become panicky and eat the eggs and young whenever frightened.

Dwarf Cichlids

With a natural consideration for the aquarist, importers have long been looking for a fish as interesting as the average cichlid but much smaller and more peaceful. The problem was easily solved with the acquisition of the now popular South American and African dwarf cichlids. These cichlids, the *Pelvicachromis*, *Nannacara*, *Microgeophagus*, and *Apistogramma* species, are commonly offered to the aquarist. In this instance the aquarist has been able to help the ichthyologist by relaying to him his observations of the fish, because when the dwarf cichlids were first offered for sale very little was known about their breeding habits.

The main advantage the dwarfs have over their larger relatives is their temperament. No dwarf cichlid will tear up plants or attack the other fish in the community tank. Most of the dwarfs can be spawned in 5-gallon tanks, since they seldom measure more than 3 inches in length. Care of the breeding pair is the same as with the larger cichlids, with the possible exception that both parents should be separated from the eggs as soon as they spawn. The dwarf cichlids are especially fond of eating their eggs. The frequency of spawning depends upon the environment but normally should be at least once a month from April through October.

The Ram
(Microgeophagus ramirezi)

As a characteristic dwarf cichlid, and one of the most beautiful, let us examine *Microgeophagus ramirezi*. Rams measure between 2 and 2 1/2 inches in length. They get rather rounded, a shape that seems to be common to all mature dwarf cichlids. When in color they show all the hues and shades their distant relative the discus possesses. The only drawback is that they are very shy and timid. At the slightest shadow or loud noise, they hide in the vegetation. Breeding color is normally prevalent most of the year, provided the fish are supplied continually with live food. They seem to be especially partial to tubifex, though too much tubifex is too rich a diet for any fish. It is better to feed tubifex two or three times a week, with intermittent feedings of whiteworms, daphnia, and brine shrimp.

You may have either a few inches of sand (deeper than for other cichlids) or no sand at all. On top of the sand, if you use it, there should be placed a few pieces of slate about 2 or 3 inches square. These are the slates on which the fish will deposit their spawn. In one corner of the tank you should have some thick vegetation. If possible, keep the tank covered with paper so that shadows of people walking by will not disturb the fish.

The ram is bred similarly to the other cichlids. A few males (the first three black spines of the dorsal fin are much longer than those of the female) should be placed in a 10-gallon tank with a few females. Natural selection should get at least one pair from three or four fish. As soon as the rams have paired off, you will note that the pair will stay much to themselves in a corner, keeping the other fish away. At this time remove all the unmated fish, leaving the pair to themselves.

If the fish are properly mated, they should show small

white breeding tubes prior to spawning. Plenty of tubifex should be left around the tank with the appearance of these tubes. When the fish have spawned, remove the slates to a tank—from 3 gallons upward, the larger the better—to which has been added one drop of methylene blue per gallon of water. The water need be only the same temperature as that from which the eggs were removed, from 75° to 85° F. The eggs hatch in three days at 80° F. Keep a light on the eggs at all times so the bluish dye will be decomposed—in about five days—and the water will again be transparent. The young fish should be supplied with infusoria the first week. As soon as they are free-swimming, they should be given newly hatched brine shrimp and microworms and should be kept on this live food for four weeks. The young fish mature at six months.

One of the most beautiful cichlids from the African continent is *Pelvicachromis pulcher,* the krib. They do very well on the diet and care recommended for *M. ramirezi,* but seem to go one step further when it comes to hiding their eggs from sight. A very useful thing in the spawning aquarium is an ordinary clay flowerpot with a piece broken out of the rim. This is stood on its open end in such a manner that the fish can swim in and out of the opening. They soon learn to accept this as their "home," but one day you will notice that the male, which is more than twice the size of the little female, is ejected every time he tries to gain entrance. Take him out and put him into another tank when this happens, or you will have a male that may soon be badly beaten up. The female, who of course is guarding eggs, will put in an appearance in about a week's time, herding a brood of fry. This is a good time to take her out as well and leave the youngsters to their own devices. Many breeders prefer to leave the female in for a week or two,

Rams, *Microgeophagus ramirezi*, are commonly available in both a bright yellow color phase and the more varied but still bright colors of the natural form. Males have higher dorsal spines than females and usually have brighter colors. Photo by G. Senfft.

but there is the danger that at any time the young might be eaten.

All the *Nannacara* and *Apistogramma* should be treated the same way as the ram.

Chapter 4
Other Egglayers

Characins (tetras)

The characins may usually be recognized by the possession of an adipose fin, which is located on the back between the dorsal and caudal fins. Breeding of all the characins is quite similar, with a few exceptions (when you have bred one you can usually breed them all). There are several very important points to follow when breeding that apply to all the characins.

1. Remove parents after spawning.
2. Feed plenty of daphnia during the spawning process.
3. Keep temperature at about 80° F.
4. Have tank more or less filled with *Nitella*.
5. Have plenty of infusoria and brine shrimp handy for the young fry.
6. Have no snails in tank with egglayers. Snails eat the eggs.

For the sake of clarity, let us select one characin to be

representative of the whole family and discuss its breeding habits carefully.

Of all the characins, the most beautiful and difficult to breed are the three "neon" tetras called *Paracheirodon*. *P. axelrodi* is the cardinal tetra; *P. innesi* is the neon tetra; and *P. simulans* is a rarely imported fish called the false neon.

The longest a neon will grow is 1 1/2 inches, about the size of a large male guppy but much more colorful than the guppy could ever be expected to be. Even if breeding is difficult, neons deserve a place of honor in every community tank because of their unique beauty. They are rather peaceful and very active, always swimming about at high speeds. (This speed decreases slightly when the fish is preparing to spawn, which is one way you may be able to predict to some extent when the female will be ready to drop eggs.)

The breeding of neons requires complete understanding of the general characteristics of the fish. A long, low, 20-gallon tank should be filled with 15 gallons of water (about three-fourths full). Leaving the center free, the bottom should be lined with an abundance of sterilized dense foliage, *Nitella* being the best. The sides of the tank should also be spread with this *Nitella* to a thickness of about 2 inches. Have no sand on the bottom of the tank, but do have a few pieces of old log or twigs in the open center portion. Arrange the twigs so there is a maximum area of undersurface free for the young to attach themselves.

The water that is placed in the tank must be specially prepared; the entire success of breeding depends upon the preparation of this water. The primary concern is to have the water bacteria-free. The best water to use is distilled water that has been thoroughly aerated. The aeration apparatus must be sterilized by boiling for twenty minutes before insertion into the tank. Remember to keep everything that goes into the tank sterile. The plants (*Nitella*) must be sterilized by a thorough treatment with salt and potassium permanganate. The tank itself should be sterilized by soaking for 48 hours with a very concentrated solution of salt and potassium permanganate. The twigs may be sterilized by boiling in water for 20 minutes. The glass cover plate for the tank must also be sterilized and can be placed in the tank with the sterilizing solution. Allow the glass to dry in the air; if the solution was concentrated enough, there will be a salt deposit left on the glass plate when it has been dried. Next, drain the water out of the tank and refill it with the sterile water (boiled for 20 minutes, then cooled); then aerate it for 24 hours. Add enough peat moss boiled water to have a pH of less than 6.

The optimum temperature for breeding is 78° F. The best way to approach this temperature is with a thermostatically controlled heater that has a pilot light that shows when the heater is working. Sterilize this heater by boiling the part of the heater that will be submerged in the water. Steam the top or wash it with alcohol (after unplugging it of course).

When you have selected a very heavy female—she is easily recognized by her roundness in comparison with the slim male—she may be placed for a minute in a 5% solution of salt and potassium permanganate. If you use a net that has been used for other purposes, make sure it has been sterilized before using it to remove the female from the salt solution. Then put her in the tank when the temperature is about 74° F. (of course, the water in the tank from which she has been taken should be the same temperature).

Next, select the male and place him in a weaker solution of salt (2%) and gradually raise the temperature in this solution to 78° F. At the same time, raise the temperature of the water in the breeding tank to 78° F. and place the male with the female. Then cover the entire tank with a large towel or sheet; this ensures a minimum amount of light and a minimum fluctuation of temperature.

The fish will need some sort of live or freeze-dried food, the best undoubtedly being grown brine shrimp. These brine shrimp are to be raised in a very strong salt solution. If you use a large-mouthed eye dropper, it will be easy to regulate the amount of food you drop in. Care must be taken to feed them enough to satisfy their hunger, but not to feed them more than they will eat. Spawning will take place after a few days when the male chases the female into the vegetation. The eggs are dropped at random while the female swims through the dense foliage; fertilization is haphazard.

As soon as spawning is completed—if the female is very heavy it should not take more than 48 hours—remove the female. The female should be removed before the male, as she is the one that will eat the eggs; the male tries to protect the eggs by constantly chasing the female from them. The eggs are very small and practically colorless. They will hatch out in 36 hours and may be seen clinging to the twigs in the water. The young do not resemble anything at all. They are small and colorless, taking upward of four weeks before they show color. They should be fed on as pure a culture of infusoria, preferably rotifers, as can be prepared; when four weeks old, they will take brine shrimp.

The pH of the water should be kept as close to 6.0 as possible.

The neons may have been an unfortunate selection to illustrate breeding generalities, but if anyone can reproduce them, he can breed any fish. In general, all characins may be bred the same way, with the omission of the sterilization processes.

Other Tetras

The popular name "tetra" is given to many fish that look entirely unlike each other. Tetras are usually classified according to their color. Platinum, silver, and blue are just a few of the prefixes that are added to the equally unorthodox name "tetra."

From the Rio Taquary in Brazil comes *Hyphessobrycon herbertaxelrodi*, the black neon tetra. There is a broad, velvety-black area on the lower half of the sides, topped by a glowing enamel-white stripe above it. The upper half of the eye is bright red.

Spawning this beautiful fish can be accomplished in the same manner as described for neons and it falls into just about the same area as far as difficulty is concerned, though now all black neons are tank-raised and almost no cardinals or neons are tank-raised.

The Congo River in Africa gives us the gorgeous Congo tetra, *Phenacogrammus interruptus*. With the sun shining on its opalescent scales, this fish is really a sight to behold, reflecting shades of blue, green, gold, and purple. A peculiarity of this species is in the middle rays of the tail fin, which become longer than the rest of the tail and resemble feathery appendages, especially in the males.

This species is rather large in size and takes a big tank for spawning. Eggs are laid among the plants near the bottom at a temperature of 77° F. and take six days to hatch. Of course the parents should be removed as soon as spawning is finished. The fry are quite large and able to take newly hatched brine shrimp at once.

The black tetra (*Gymnocorymbus ternetzi*), with its overly developed anal and dorsal fins, looks completely out of balance, with the majority of its mass being in the lower half of its body. The flame tetra (*Hyphessobrycon flammeus*), with its beautiful red color, has a different type of anal and dorsal fins but is similar to those of another type, the yellow tetra (*H. bifasciatus*), except that those of the latter are pale yellow. The yellow tetra looks much like the dawn tetra (*H. eos*). The glow light tetra (*Hemigrammus erythrozonus*) appears to be more closely related to the neon tetra. It is a very colorful fish and easily bred.

Danios

Among the most popular egglayers is the zebra danio (zebra fish) (*Brachydanio rerio*), a good example of the misleading character of popular names. Assuming that the zebra danio was named after the familiar four-legged animal, we would expect to see a fish with numerous vertical stripes, but such is not the case. The zebra has dark stripes running horizontally from the head and through the tail along the body, not at all like the striped "horse." It belongs to the Cyprinidae, the barb family.

The zebra has long been a pet of the aquarium, especially since it is so easily bred (with the help of a little imagination). Its breeding habits do present a problem, however, as you will see from the following description.

The zebra breeds at high speeds, scattering eggs as it travels the length of the aquarium and back in record time. The non-adhesive eggs fall as they may, wherever they happen to be dropped. In the average-size tank, at a water level of 8 inches, the zebras can make two round trips before the light eggs hit the bottom of the tank. Should the parents pass a few falling eggs on their return, they will quickly eat them as they go and then continue dropping, as though it were the most natural thing in the world. The aquarist must therefore find some system for the eggs to be trapped before the parents get a chance to catch them. Several methods have been devised, all being of equal value. One of the easiest to perform is as follows:

Place a long 20-gallon tank near a window; the sunlight will be beneficial for the propagation of algae and infusoria. Fill the tank with no more than 4 inches of water. Put in no sand or plants. Purchase some large marbles, the larger the better (those about an inch in diameter are about the best). Sterilize the marbles by boiling them in water for 20 minutes. After the marbles have cooled—do not cool them by dropping them in cold water as this will crack them—cover the entire bottom of the tank with them to a depth of about 1 inch. Let the tank stay in the direct sunlight for a few hours each day for three days. Then select the female that looks most promising and place her in the tank just prepared. It is easy to recognize the female by her full, rounded body in comparison with the slimness of the male. Also, you can determine the sex if you can spend time watching them by the fact that the males chase the females. You will see that the male fish show amorous attention to the females loaded with eggs and follow them very closely wherever they swim. If there is an empty female in the lot she will be noticed as a straggler. As soon as the female that you have placed in the new tank has become acquainted with her surroundings—it may take a day or two—place in with her three or four of the most active males, those that you have noticed have always been slim and fast. Do not choose a male straggler, as he will probably only eat the eggs instead of helping in their fertilization.

The reason for selecting three or four males is twofold. First, in case there should be any doubt, you want to be sure to have at least one male in the group; and second, assuming you are able to determine the sexes, it is best to have more than one male because if the female is well loaded she may drop more eggs than one male can fertilize.

After spawning, the female will be slimmer than she was before, and all the fish should be removed to their previous home. The eggs will hatch in 56 hours at 75° F. At first the young will grow faster and stronger if fed entirely on live food, infusoria and then newly hatched brine shrimp. After three weeks to a month, depending on their size, they may be fed fine dry food alternately with microworms.

Since zebras get barely 2 inches long and the young grow rather slowly (an inch in six months), it is best to keep them away from the larger fish, especially the cichlids.

Newest of the *Brachydanio* species is *Brachydanio frankei*, the leopard danio, with a body that is speckled with tiny dots. They spawn just like the zebra danio and are just as hardy. There is still doubt with many as to whether or not these are hybrids, but Meinken in Germany has classified them as a valid species. Leopard danios will cross with other *Brachydanio* species.

All the danios may be bred alike. It may be interesting to note that this is the same way in which goldfish spawn.

Barbs

The barbs are very desirable aquarium fish for manifold reasons: their gay, often loud coloring, their active movements, their formation when swimming, and the ease with which they may be spawned. Barbs are active eaters and not very choosy. They have occasionally been successfully reared on bread alone.

All the barbs drop adhesive-type eggs and require live food in enormous quantities for successful breeding and maturation. They are at their best when exhibited in a large tank in great numbers, where they swim in active schools and soon learn to "beg for food." A person merely walking by the tank will cause a frantic race of the entire school to the spot where food is usually introduced. The feeding hole, usually left open in most aquarium covers, should be covered by a piece of glass at all times.

Tiger Barb
(*Capoeta tetrazona*)

As *Capoeta tetrazona*, the tiger barb (once called the "Sumatranus" because it came from Sumatra), is the most popular of the barbs, we shall describe its peculiarities fully.

If a person had heard the name "zebra fish" without knowing which fish bore that name, he would most likely assume it belonged to *C. tetrazona*. *C. tetrazona* is striped something like a zebra, having four narrow bands of dark pigment running vertically completely around its body and head. It is gaily colored with yellow and red, though these colors tend to fade as the fish reaches maturity. Specimens that are over 2 inches in length and over 1 inch deep are not uncommon.

Since the *C. tetrazona* is a fast-swimming fish that drops sticky eggs when spawning, dense clumps of *Nitella* and similar plants must be provided to hold the eggs.

Sex in these barbs is easily distinguished. The female gets much broader and rounder than the male, and while she loses much color, the male increases in color and develops a red nose.

Seasoning for the female must take place in the breeding tank. Select the largest female and place her in the spawning tank. The spawning tank should be a long-type, 20-gallon size at the minimum. Feed her large quantities of tubifex and daphnia with a medicine dropper, making sure that she is able to get all the food before it gets lost in the vegetation. A small area of the tank may be left bare for this feeding purpose. The males may be conditioned in the community tank by similar processes. Live food is essential for the seasoning of the fish.

When the female seems adjusted to her conditions and she looks as though she couldn't get much larger, place two males in with her. Spawning, just as in the zebra danio, should take place in a very short time.

While the fish are spawning they should be fed daphnia by the eyedropperful. If these small crustaceans are not available, try tubifex. With luck, the fish will take the food rather than the eggs; should they elect the eggs, do not continue the feeding of live food, but try to pull out the strands of *Nitella* that contain the eggs. Place these strands in a beaker filled with some of the same water in which the eggs were laid. Have the beaker floating in the spawning tank so it will be readily available for the deposit of the "egged down" *Nitella* and be at a constant temperature. Care should be exercised not to disturb the parents in the removal of the *Nitella*.

C. tetrazona is a great jumper and jumps at the slightest provocation. After the spawning, when the young fish have reached swimming size, every possible precaution should be taken to prevent them from jumping out.

The spawning just described should not take more than a few interesting hours, after which the parent fish should be removed and, if necessary, the eggs carefully replaced in the spawning tank. The spawn will hatch in two days. The fry must be fed infusoria for the first few weeks. Follow this food with newly hatched brine shrimp, microworms, or finely sifted daphnia.

The optimum breeding temperature is 75° F. When

the fry are about three weeks old, raise the temperature to about 78° F. The lower spawning temperature helps slightly in keeping the bacterial count down.

In the other types of barbs, such as the rosy barb (*Puntius conchonius*), black ruby barb (*Puntius nigrofasciatus*), tic-tac-toe barb (*Puntius ticto*), etc., sex is easily determined by the size of the female and breeding habits are the same as in *Capoeta tetrazona*.

Medaka
(*Oryzias latipes*)

The many popular names attached to *Oryzias latipes*, such as "geisha girl," "medaka," and "rice fish," give an indication of its former popularity as an aquarium pet. Originally coming from Japan, where it is called "medaka," the fish has many traits to hold the interest of fanciers.

Such a wealth of information is available on the medaka that it would be possible to present its entire embryology. The value of such a complete study to the ordinary aquarist is doubtful, however, and with a careful selection of the important material a concise elementary study would seem to be more profitable.

The female medaka possesses a single large ovary. This organ contains hundreds of eggs, all in different stages of development. As the eggs get more fully developed, they increase in size. This accounts for the swollen abdomen so characteristic of the female egg-layer. The female may produce from one to eighty eggs a day, depending on various conditions. These eggs are squeezed out of the female's body by a special set of muscles in the tube called the "oviduct." They arrive outside the body of the female, hanging like a bunch of grapes, and are there fertilized by the male. One male may be active enough to service many females, thus it is to your advantage to have an abundance of females with a minimum number of males.

The eggs hang outside the body of the female for four or five hours, unless they happen to be brushed off by a plant or on the bottom of the tank. The medaka will eat neither the eggs nor the young.

Care should be exercised in handling medakas as they are high jumpers. More peaceful aquarium fish are hard to find, and they further make themselves desirable by eating anything and everything, though they will make better parents if seasoned on live food.

White Cloud Mountain Minnow
(Tanichthys albonubes)

This almost cold-water fish originally found near Canton, China, has long been one of the author's favorites. It is so hardy and easy to care for and it breeds so readily that it is highly recommended for beginners.

A small tank, five gallons or so, filled with *Nitella* or other spawning grass is all that is necessary besides a healthy pair of fish. The White Clouds will eat dry foods, but they should be offered some live foods to keep them in shape. They spawn continuously, and as the eggs hatch the young look like miniature cardinal tetras. Infusoria is required for the fry as soon as they become free-swimming. The parents should be removed after they have been in the aquarium for a week or so. A long-finned variety is available from time to time.

Rasboras

The genus *Rasbora* contains many lovely, gentle fishes. One of the most popular of all the rasboras is the harlequin, *Rasbora heteromorpha*. This lovely fish is very difficult to induce to spawn and, unless you like challenges, you'd better start on other species like *Rasbora trilineata*. Though that species is difficult to spawn, it is not impossible. The fish usually lay their eggs on the underside of stiff broad-leaved plants. The plants of the genus *Cryptocoryne* suit them fine. These *Cryptocoryne* plants, by the way, are excellent for your aquarium and they abound in the same streams in which most *Rasbora* are found. As a group, *Rasbora* species eat freeze-dried foods, flake foods, and just about every aquarium food small enough to be ingested. They really become most colorful when fed small live foods like brine shrimp and daphnia, so offer these whenever they are available from your local pet shop.

Sexing most rasboras is difficult, but mature fishes can easily be sexed by their size. Males are usually much more slender than the females which are filled with roe. Your pet shop will advise you about sex differences (if they are very good aquarium fish people).

Chapter 5
Scavengers

Catfish

The catfish are easily identified by the whiskerlike barbels that extend from their "noses," "lips," and "chins." Another peculiarity is that the true cats have no scales, though they sometimes possess a type of "shingle" that covers them. This "shingle" is very unlike the scales of ordinary fish and on some catfish looks much like the coats of armor worn by medieval knights; thus the name "armored catfish."

Most aquarists consider the cats as merely scavengers. The catfish are always busy poking their "snouts" into the gravel looking for any type of food. Dead leaves, food that has reached the bottom, dead snails, dead and decaying daphnia are all of interest to catfish, and they will devour them without much ado. The cats are very peaceful, seldom attacking any live fish, regardless of size—there have been only a few substantiated reports about individual cats eating small living fish. They will usually leave fish eggs alone, too, but when you spawn such fish as the zebra danio, which drops eggs onto the bottom of the tank, it would be more advisable to leave cats out of the tank.

The author has observed cats that were so bashful they would hide at the slightest provocation, yet when a school of daphnia was introduced into the tank, they would make one of their rare appearances and swim out and help themselves. This, however, is a rare example and not typical of the general behavior of catfish. After training, however, catfish even take floating food, turning upside down if necessary.

Corydoras paleatus

Though the cats are very seldom bred by the amateur, they will breed rather easily and very interestingly. Let us consider *Corydoras paleatus* as the typical catfish for the home aquarium. The *Corydoras* are small members of the family Callichthyidae and are very well suited for the small tank. *Corydoras* are among the most popular of tropical fish, not because of beauty, but for their great assistance to the keeper of an aquarium in his cleaning. *C. paleatus* also breeds to a large extent like many of the more beautiful fish kept in tanks for esthetic reasons.

Since sex in the *Corydoras* cats is very difficult to distinguish, breeding must be accompanied by natural pairing. Some authors think that a comparison of the ventral fins will offer a sexual distinction. This method is difficult to use, not only because the fins are so similar in shape, but also because the cats are nearly always in a position that makes comparison of the ventral fins impossible. The ventral fins are important in the reproductive cycle of the fish.

Should you have half a dozen mature cats in the same

tank, you might notice a male staying very close to a female, showing her more than a usual amount of attention. After a few hours of close movement on the bottom of the tank, the female will assume a position across the male that will facilitate her catching his flowing milt in her mouth. This milt is nearly invisible; the author has attempted on various occasions to introduce some sort of dye into the male that might color his sperm but has had no success.

It seems that as soon as the female has the milt in her mouth she drops a few eggs, catching them between her ventral fins. She then leaves the prostrate male and searches for a suitable location for her eggs. When a stiff leaf has been selected, she touches the spot with her mouth, there depositing some milt, and then presses a couple of eggs into the milt. She repeats this process very shortly to dispose of the remaining eggs she has clasped in between her ventral fins. The female will then return to the male.

The female does not usually drop all her eggs in one place; she more often seeks a new place for each group of eggs. Different types of cats are interested in different types of locations, some choosing the glass, some even a bubble-nest *(Hoplosternum)*.

The eggs hatch in a few days, and the young immediately disappear into the muck on the bottom of the tank, where they seem to stay for a few weeks until they are large enough to handle fairly large-sized food (grown daphnia). They mature rapidly and seem very hardy. The parents show little interest in their brood and, if well fed, usually will not disturb the eggs. Other cats will not bother the brood either.

Among the other types of cats that are popular are the bronze corydoras *(C. aeneus)*, a type that breeds by the female placing her eggs on glass; the leopard corydoras *(C. julii)*, a very active fish; *C. nattereri*, which is very similar in all respects to *C. paleatus*, though slightly darker; and the large, 4-inch *C. agassizi*.

All these corydoras catfish are peaceful, very hardy, and excellent as scavengers. They will do especially well if kept on a diet of live food (tubifex is best; cats can often dig it out of the sand by burrowing, while it is usually too deep to be pulled out by the more ordinary types of aquarium fish) and in a tank of their own. Best breeding results will be obtained if a blanket of litter is allowed to accumulate on the bottom of the tank so the fish may hide when they feel shy. This cover will also be beneficial to the young *Corydoras*. Water changes greatly stimulate spawning activity.

Glass Catfish
(Kryptopterus bicirrhis)

This fish, though not a real scavenger, earns a place in this material as a member of the catfish group.

As the name "glass" implies, this species of catfish is very nearly transparent. It may reach 3 inches in length and is rather shy and timid. It is not a bottom-feeder, but catches food on the way down. It usually does not feed from the top either.

Though rather harmless, it does go after young fish.

Breeding is apparently very difficult, and sex in the glass cat is hard to determine.

Other Scavengers

Certain fish are peculiarly adapted to do the work of a scavenger. The habits of the *Corydoras*, namely their preference for feeding off the bottom, make them ideal for this purpose. But other fish have the same property that also should make them desirable for cleaning purposes. The common guppy picks continually on any palatable matter that may be on the bottom of the tank and is often used for scavenging purposes. The name "scavenger," when used in connection with a certain class of fish, is much like the term "weed" when talking about a garden. Is a stray orchid a weed in a patch of dandelions? Yes, if you are primarily interested in raising dandelions! But there is bound to be trouble if the general name "scavenger" is used too freely.

The many fish that have tremendous appetites all might well be called "scavengers," but there must be a distinction: A scavenger is a fish that eats food that is left uneaten by the other fish in the tank. (Such animals as snails, clams, mussels, and shrimp may be included in this category.)

Scavengers eat not only food that the others have left behind, but there are those that get into places where the other ones cannot squeeze and pick up whatever is left there. This group includes the kuhli loaches, which include *Acanthophthalmus kuhli*, *A. semicinctus*, *A. shelfordi*, and *A. myersi* among others. These loaches have about the same body shape, elongated and snakelike, which lets them crowd into some very tight corners and get bits of food which would otherwise contribute toward fouling the tank.

Another type of "scavenger" has come to be known extensively as the Chinese algae-eater, *Gyrinocheilus aymonieri*. Whoever gave them the "Chinese" part of their name must have had an active imagination, because they come from Thailand, quite a stretch away from China. These fish have a very greedy appetite for algae and spend a great deal of their time foraging for it. They go over the glass sides of the tank, the rocks, plants, and gravel, and keep plucking at all the algal growths that come their way.

G. aymonieri is not alone in being a fish that will eat

great amounts of algae. There are *Otocinclus* and *Hypostomus* species, all from tropical South America, that graze happily on algal growths and bits of uneaten food. As far as looks go, they are just about the unloveliest fish in existence. With many of them this is the secret of their charm. They rarely spawn in captivity.

At one time it was believed to be necessary for every well-set-up aquarium to have a few snails, but this is not so. Snails have their "pros" and "cons," which we list here:

1. A snail consumes oxygen just like fish. For every snail you must figure one less fish of similar dimensions.

2. Snails greedily consume great amounts of algae, it is true. They often raise havoc with your valued plants as well.

3. A snail will dutifully clean up uneaten food but will also leave behind it a number of messy droppings.

4. Snails are very prolific, and disposing of the young often becomes a problem.

So there you have it. They have their good points, but in order to benefit by their good points, you have to put up with their faults.

It is well known that daphnia feed readily on most types of infusoria and green algae, and it is standard practice to introduce daphnia into a tank that is cloudy or green. In doing this, one caution, however: *Remove the fish.* Not only could the fish overeat and thus reduce the number of scavengers, but the tank might not be able to support so much life at one time. The water could become too saturated with carbon dioxide and thus poison all the inhabitants, or the fish might turn on one another and kill themselves, which often happens in densely populated aquaria.

Sometimes freshwater clams or mussels are placed in the tank to help keep the water clear. These animals serve their purpose well as they obtain food by sucking water through a set of filters and thus remove most types of suspensions, whether digestible or not. Although these animals have unusual capacities for clearing water, they do represent a hazard. Should one die it might go unnoticed for a few days, since they are not very visibly active, and their decaying would do more damage than they could ever do good. Also, several large fish may peck at them, causing them untold grief; or, as the author has witnessed, large fish (*Astronotus ocellatus*) may try to ingest them—bettas also make their lives miserable.

Snails are undoubtedly the favorite as far as shelled scavengers go. They reproduce without any help, often producing a type of very nutritious egg that is enjoyed by many fish. Some snails produce live young (Japanese livebearer). It might be worthwhile to discuss individually each of the popular types of snails and their advantages, since they are so valuable when put to the proper task.

Japanese Livebearing Snail

Most freshwater snails are hermaphroditic; that is to say, each individual snail has both male and female reproductive organs, and they can also fertilize their own eggs. This sexual independence does not stop two snails from acting as male and female together, as well. The few exceptions to the rule are the dioecious (either male or female) types that belong to the genus *Viviparus*. The Japanese snail is that type of snail in which reproduction requires the participation of a male and female of the species. This does not mean that if you have kept a female Japanese snail alone for several months she cannot have a brood. Quite to the contrary. The Japanese snail is purported to have only one fertilization a lifetime. This fertilization must take care of the entire mass of unfertilized eggs contained in the body of the female. The eggs are hatched in a space under the shell of the female, where they remain until they emerge as fully recognizable snails.

Red Ramshorn Snail
(Planorbis corneus)

The red ramshorn *(Planorbis corneus)* snail is one of the larger types of snails available for the home aquarium. When placed in a tank with daphnia they reproduce magnificently. These snails must be fed a type of food that tends to produce profuse cultures of infusoria; lettuce, celery greens, spinach, and oatmeal mush are excellent. Daphnia must be used to clear the tank of too much infusoria, since an overabundance of these small creatures is detrimental to the health of the snails.

Given the proper care and aeration, and at a temperature of about 78° F., the red ramshorn will reproduce rapidly. Eggs are laid in groups of from eight to 30 and hatch out in about three weeks. Care should be exercised in choosing the type of fish to be introduced into the tank with the red ramshorn. Cichlids will eat them when they are small, and many fish will readily take their undeveloped eggs. Many aquarists place the reds in their aquaria in order to provide some extra living food for their fish.

Mystery Snail
(Pomacea bridgesi, formerly Ampullaria cuprina)

The mystery snail or apple snail gets its name from its peculiar breeding habits. The fact that it needs a dry area upon which to spawn, coupled with the fact that the developing embryos need dry spaces to develop, makes breeding very difficult in the ordinary aquarium.

They only lay their eggs out of the water.

The mystery snails are not dioecious and are extremely valuable in tanks where infusoria is required in quantity. In the process of digesting the greens that should be provided for the infusoria as well as the snails, the mystery snail excretes organic matter that serves as excellent food to the infusoria protozoa. These snails should not be placed in a spawning tank until the young have hatched, as they eat fish eggs.

Unless they are provided with a substantial diet of greens, the mysteries may attack growing plants, so it is wise always to keep a piece of lettuce in the tank.

Pond Snails
(Lymnaea, Physa)

The two familiar forms of pond snails differ in the type of twist they possess. The *Lymnaea* curls to the left, the *Physa* to the right.

The pond snails are not dioecious and reproduce by cementing sticky masses of eggs on the plants and glass parts of the aquarium. These eggs are too hard to be eaten by most fish, though cichlids and bettas seem to enjoy them. As they usually reproduce in geometric progression, they are the most prolific snails in the average home tank. A mass of eggs will have hatched in three weeks, and in another three months, these, in turn, will have eggs of their own.

Other types of snails will usually serve the same general purpose but are not so plentiful as the aforementioned.

Care should be exercised to remove all dead snails. They might cloud the water should they be allowed to decompose in the tank. If snails become too plentiful, they may be crushed between the fingers so the fish may clean the meat from the shells. The empty shells may supply a few necessary minerals to the plants.

Chapter 6
The Annual Fishes

Mother Nature, as all who study her ways can attest, has some strange ways of keeping the world populated with her creatures. In many places in the tropical areas of Africa and South America there are spots where bodies of water fill to overflowing during the rainy season, but when the dry season comes along these places dry out completely. How can fish live in these holes? And if they can, what happens when there is no more water? Let us examine the very strange life cycle of this beautiful group of annual killifishes.

The rainy season comes on with a series of downpours on the parched land, and in the ponds and ditches that were dried out all during the dry season, water gradually appears and becomes deeper. Tiny fish appear as if by magic, and the water soon teems with them. They grow at an unbelievable rate and in a few months become sexually mature and mate, burying their eggs in the bottom silt. The males find territories for themselves and battle fiercely for them when another male appears, showing their most brilliant colors.

rbled Hatchetfish
rnegiella strigata
oto by Andre Roth

Black-winged Hatchetfish
Carnegiella marthae
Photo by Klaus Paysan

d-spotted Copeina
peina guttata
oto by Klaus Paysan

Bloodfin Tetra
Aphyocharax anisitsi
Photo by Dr. Herbert R. Axelrod

ver Tetra
enobrycon spilurus
oto by Klaus Paysan

Harrison's Pencilfish
Nannostomus harrisoni
Photo by Andre Roth

k-tailed Chalceus
alceus macrolepidotus
oto by Andre Roth

Headstander
Abramites hypselonotus
Photo by Dr. Herbert R. Axelrod

But this happy state of affairs does not last very long. The rains soon end, and the hot sun makes itself felt on the water. The result, of course, is much less water, and the fish become more and more crowded. Predators appear on the scene, as they always do when there is an easy meal at hand: kingfishers, cranes, egrets, snakes, turtles, and many others. As time goes on only the deeper spots, or what were the deeper spots, still hold water, and soon these dry out as well. The fish? They die by the millions when there is not enough water to support them. What were lovely, lush ponds become foul, malodorous puddles.

Mercifully, decay is rapid in the tropics and these areas soon become dried-out holes that bear little resemblance to what they once were. No water, but the fish life is there, just the same, in the form of eggs left by the breeding fish during the rainy season. They buried their eggs in the bottom silt, you will recall. These eggs, protected from the direct rays of the sun by this covering of silt, undergo a partial drying at this time.

Then the inevitable change of seasons takes place once more and the rain again begins falling. Life awakens within these eggs, which hatch in short order and start their strange, short life cycle all over again.

In Africa, these "annual" fishes are represented by the *Nothobranchius* species in the east and some of the *Aphyosemion* species in the west. *Aphyosemion* has two entirely different ways of spawning. Most species simply hang their eggs on plant leaves, where they hatch in two weeks, but the ones we treat here are the bottom-spawning species, such as *Aphyosemion sjoestedti*, *A. occidentale*, and *A. arnoldi*. These two genera include some of the loveliest of all aquarium fishes and are very high in cost, taking into consideration the short life span, which rarely exceeds eight months. In South America there are the *Cynolebias* and *Pterolebias* species that have exactly similar life spans.

To the fish breeder, propagating these species presents the problem of giving them similar conditions in the aquarium. Most of these species when mature and well conditioned are ready to spawn any time a male can swim up to a female. So eager are the males to spawn that many breeders make it a point to use two or three females to every male. A 2-gallon aquarium is ample in most cases. The bottom is covered with peat moss which has been well boiled in advance. Here they find a substitute for the soft mud of their habitat and lose little time digging in close beside each other and depositing eggs. Water temperature should be about 78° F., and the tank should be kept covered to keep the fish from jumping out. Live daphnia and tubifex worms are the desirable foods for conditioning, with an occasional feeding of whiteworms. Once the female has become depleted of eggs, which is shown by her lessened girth, she and the male should be taken out and kept separate until they recuperate in a week or so. This leaves a tank with a good supply of eggs buried in the peat moss. The water is then emptied carefully until there is only the wet peat moss left, and at this time the drying process is duplicated by allowing the peat moss to become partially dry and then covering the tank. The moss may also be removed to a plastic bag.

At this time a little patience is called for: the eggs must remain as they are for six weeks. Then a few inches of water is poured back into the tank. In a short time, sometimes a very short time, the fry will be seen swimming about. Sometimes the eggs are not yet fully developed, in which case they will not hatch. Leaving them dried out for another week may do the trick, and the process may have to be repeated a few times; sometimes a few hatch before the others. Various species differ in hatching times.

Eight-banded Leporinus
Leporinus octofasciatus
Photo by Andre Roth

Striped Headstander
Anostomus anostomus
Photo by H.-J. Richter

Long-finned African Tetra
Brycinus longipinnis
Photo by Klaus Paysan

Congo Tetra
Phenacogrammus interruptus
Photo by Andre Roth

Plain Metynnis
Metynnis hypsauchen
Photo by Andre Roth

Red-breasted Pacu
Colossoma brachypomum
Photo by Andre Roth

Red-bellied Piranha
Serrasalmus cf. *nattereri*
Photo by Andre Roth

Wimple Piranha
Catoprion mento
Photo by H.-J. Richter

n Barb
odes everetti
o by Dr. Herbert R. Axelrod

Spanner Barb
Barbodes lateristriga
Photo by Klaus Paysan

oil Barb
odes schwanenfeldi
to by Klaus Paysan

Tiger Barb
Capoeta tetrazona
Photo by Andre Roth

cker Barb
oeta oligolepis
to by Andre Roth

Black Ruby Barb
Puntius nigrofasciatus
Photo by Andre Roth

y Barb
tius conchonius
to by Dr. S. Frank

Striped Barb
Puntius lineatus
Photo by Dr. Karl Knaack   133

A spawning pair (female below) of fire killies, *Nothobranchius melano-spilus*, one of the many African annual killifishes. Photo by Dr. K. Knaack.

Granted the eggs have hatched, you will note that the yolk sacs have been absorbed and the fry swim freely. They are large enough at this time to eat newly hatched brine shrimp, and feedings should be frequent, as they consume unbelievable amounts. Growth is very rapid, as may be expected when their original home conditions are considered.

All this seems to be a lot of trouble to go to for a fish that will live for only about a year or so, but this group of killifishes is among the most beautiful of all aquarium fishes. You may not have them for a long time, but they are certainly a thing of beauty while they last!

Chapter 7
Plants

Let any person who believes that the only important part of an aquarium is the fish keep his fish in a bare tank, and he will soon realize the value of plants. A critical review of what plants do for the home aquarium—as well as what they do not do—has been made by Dr. James W. Atz.

Although plants have been grown in home aquaria for more than a hundred years, their functions in such small bodies of water are still largely misunderstood. Not only aquarists but teachers and scientists as well have entertained incorrect ideas about the part that plants play in the so-called "balanced aquarium" ever since vegetation was first put into the tanks with fish. Strangely enough, this century of error has not handicapped the keepers of home aquaria to any great extent. Being empirically minded, aquarists have accepted and employed practices and techniques that "worked" without concerning themselves too much as to just *why* they worked. This practical attitude has produced beautiful tanks and healthy fish but has sometimes placed fish

Zebra Danio
Brachydanio rerio
Photo by Klaus Paysan

Long-finned Zebra Danio
Brachydanio rerio
Photo by Klaus Paysan

Pearl Danio
Brachydanio albolineatus
Photo by Andre Roth

Leopard Danio
Brachydanio frankei
Photo by Andre Roth

Giant Danio
Danio aequipinnatus
Photo by Dr. Herbert R. Axelrod

Harlequin Rasbora
Rasbora heteromorpha "hengeli'
Photo by H.-J. Richter

Big-spot Rasbora
Rasbora kalochroma
Photo by Andre Roth

Scissortail Rasbora
Rasbora trilineata
Photo by H.-J. Richter

bow Shark
eo erythrurus
to by Klaus Paysan

Red-tailed Black Shark
Labeo bicolor
Photo by Andre Roth

:k Shark
ulius chrysophekadion
to by A. Kochetov

Bala Shark
Balantiocheilos melanopterus
Photo by Andre Roth

g-finned White Cloud
ichthys albonubes
to by H.-J. Richter

Bitterling
Rhodeus sericeus
Photo by Dr. Herbert R. Axelrod

mon Comet Goldfish
ssius auratus
to by Dr. Herbert R. Axelrod

Celestial Goldfish
Carassius auratus
Photo by Dr. Herbert R. Axelrod

fanciers in the comfortable but somewhat strange position of doing the right thing for the wrong reason.

There are perhaps half a dozen different reasons why the aquarist should try to keep plants in his aquarium, but the oxygenation of tank water is *not* one of them. In fact, the idea that the fish and plants of an aquarium balance each other in their production and consumption of carbon dioxide and oxygen is a false one of such long standing and general acceptance that it perhaps deserves to be called a myth.

The usual concept of the balanced aquarium is quite simple and a little too pat, it turns out. Fish and aquatic plants utilize gases, oxygen and carbon dioxide, that are *dissolved* in water. Animals, including fish, of course, respire, taking in oxygen and giving off carbon dioxide. Plants also respire, but in the presence of light that is strong enough and of the proper wave lengths they also carry on the process of photosynthesis as a result of which carbon dioxide and water are taken in and oxygen released. In the actively photosynthesizing plant, this process well overbalances that of respiration so that the *net* result is the consumption of carbon dioxide and production of oxygen.

The respiring animal "burns" carbohydrates and other energy-producing materials and obtains energy. On the other hand, the photosynthesizing plant stores up energy in manufactured food with the aid of green chlorophyll. Here is a chemical simplification of the essential process involved:

$$6H_2O + 6CO_2 \underset{\text{photosynthesis}}{\overset{\text{respiration}}{\rightleftarrows}} C_6H_{12}O_6 + 6O_2$$

water   carbon   glucose   oxygen
         dioxide

It is obvious that these processes counterbalance one another, and it might be thought that this is evidence in favor of the idea that plants balance fish in an aquarium. This reasoning involves one false assumption, however; namely that an aquarium is a closed system, cut off completely from the outside world. To be more specific, the oxygen and carbon dioxide in the air above the water have not been taken into consideration.

It was Dr. Charles M. Breder, Jr., who first pointed out that the oxygen dissolved in the water of an aquarium comes not from the plants but from the atmosphere. He found that whenever tank water was oversaturated or undersaturated with oxygen to the slightest degree, it very quickly returned to equilibrium with the oxygen in the air above—whether or not plants were present or whether the measurements were taken in bright sunlight or in the dark. Obviously plants could not have been affecting the oxygen content of the water to any significant extent. The oxygen comes in from the air as fast as the smallest deficiency exists in the water. Similarly, surplus oxygen immediately passes off into the atmosphere whenever any excess is present. Except under extraordinary conditions, there is neither any lack nor excess of oxygen in an aquarium.

How is it, then, that fish sometimes seem to "smother" so obviously—in an overcrowded aquarium, for example? The answer is that carbon dioxide causes their distress and eventually kills them. According to experiments made by physiologists, fish can be killed by carbon dioxide even though there is plenty of oxygen present. Carbon dioxide moves in and out of water much more slowly than oxygen. When aquatic plants were actively engaged in photosynthesis, Breder found that the amount of carbon dioxide in tank water remained far below the equilibrium point. In other words, plants can use up carbon dioxide more rapidly than the carbon dioxide can enter the water from the air. Similarly, dissolved carbon dioxide can accumulate in an

Prickly Pleco
Pseudacanthicus spinosus
Photo by Dr. Herbert R. Axelrod

Spotted Pleco
Hypostomus cf. *punctatus*
Photo by Andre Roth

Bristlenose Pleco
Ancistrus species
Photo by Andre Roth

Clown Pleco
Panaque sp.
Photo by Dr. Herbert R. Axelrod

Twig Catfish
Farlowella species
Photo by H.-J. Richter

Whiptailed Catfish
Rineloricaria cf. *hasemani*
Photo by Andre Roth

Plane-head Sucking Catfish
Hypoptopoma inexpectatum
Photo by Dr. Herbert R. Axelrod

Peppered Sucking Catfish
Otocinclus flexilis
Photo by Dr. Warren E. Burgess

Iridescent Plated Catfish
Brochis splendens
Photo by Andre Roth

Iridescent Plated Catfish (juvenile)
Brochis splendens
Photo by Dr. Warren E. Burgess

Bronzed Corydoras
Corydoras aeneus
Photo by Andre Roth

Peppered Corydoras
Corydoras paleatus
Photo by Dr. Warren E. Burgess

Three-lined Corydoras
Corydoras cf. *trilineatus*
Photo by Andre Roth

Gold-naped Corydoras
Corydoras adolfoi
Photo by Dr. Herbert R. Axelrod

Stripe-tailed Corydoras
Corydoras robineae
Photo by Dr. Herbert R. Axelrod

Port Hoplo
Hoplosternum thoracatum
Photo by Andre Roth   141

aquarium more rapidly than it is able to pass off into the atmosphere. Unless the carbon dioxide content is then reduced in some way, the fish are unable to adjust themselves to the excessive accumulation of this gas and may die—even though there is plenty of oxygen all around them. It should be realized that the amount of carbon dioxide dissolved in water is to all intents and purposes independent of the amount of dissolved oxygen, and vice versa.

When fish come gaping to the top of an aquarium, the cause is an excess of carbon dioxide, not a deficiency of oxygen—except under extraordinary conditions when an oxygen deficiency may exist. For instance, a tank that has gone completely "bad" may contain so many bacteria that the oxygen content of its water is kept dangerously low. Even in such an aquarium, however, the accumulation of carbon dioxide must also play a part in causing the distress of fish, since bacteria produce this gas just as do higher plants and animals.

It has been shown *in experimental tanks* that the greater the carbon dioxide content of water, the higher must be the concentration of oxygen to "offset" its harmful effects. Anything that tends both to lower the oxygen and increase the carbon dioxide will have a doubly detrimental effect, so to speak. High temperature is such a factor, since it decreases the amount of oxygen (and carbon dioxide) that water can hold in solution but increases the rate at which carbon dioxide is produced by speeding up the metabolism of the fish. It is true that less carbon dioxide can be held in solution, but this gas, we must remember, often builds up concentrations above its saturation point, a thing that oxygen does not do. Rising temperatures therefore cause a relative increase in the carbon dioxide content of aquarium water if not an absolute one. Nevertheless, Breder's measurements show that carbon dioxide, not oxygen, is the limiting gas, so far as respiration is concerned, under all ordinary conditions in aquaria.

Carbon dioxide and not oxygen should therefore be the aquarist's concern. When a tank is aerated artificially by air pumps, very little, if any, oxygen is being introduced—since the water is practically saturated with that gas at all times—but the release of carbon dioxide is being facilitated, carbon dioxide that can build up to dangerously high concentrations, since it can be produced more rapidly than it can escape into the atmosphere. In effect, the myriads of tiny bubbles rising from an aerator increase the surface through which the gas can leave the water. As has been emphasized by a number of experienced fish fanciers, the surface of water exposed to the atmosphere is the all-important factor in a standing aquarium. In calculating the number of fish that a certain tank will comfortably support, the most critical element is the area of the water's surface, not the volume. Another result of aeration may be the circulation of water within the tank, preventing stratification and bringing carbon dioxide-laden water to the surface.

It is often said that keeping plants in an aquarium will enable it to maintain more fish. If plants were actively photosynthesizing at all times, they would keep down the carbon dioxide concentration appreciably, as Breder showed, thus permitting more fish to live in a given tank. But plants continually respire, just as animals do, and it is only in bright light that their respiration is more than offset by photosynthesis with the net result that carbon dioxide is consumed and oxygen produced. At night or on dark days they are not engaged in photosynthesis and produce carbon dioxide and consume oxygen exactly as do fish. At such times the presence of plants theoretically lessens the number of fish a tank

Angelicus Catfish
Pimelodus pictus
Photo by Andre Roth

White-striped Spiny Catfish
Acanthodoras spinosissimus
Photo by Klaus Paysan

Iridescent Shark Catfish
Pangasius sutchi
Photo by Dr. Herbert R. Axelrod

Two-spot Catfish
Mystus micracanthus
Photo by Andre Roth

Glass Catfish
Kryptopterus bicirrhus
Photo by Andre Roth

Banjo Catfish
Bunocephalus coracoideus
Photo by Andre Roth

Polka-dot Upside-down Catfish
Synodontis angelicus
Photo by Dr. Herbert R. Axelrod

Lancer Upside-down Catfish
Synodontis alberti
Photo by Andre Roth

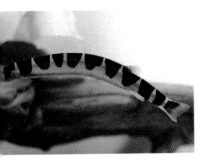

ommon Coolie Loach
canthophthalmus kuhli
hoto by Dr. Herbert R. Axelrod

Broad-banded Coolie Loach
Acanthophthalmus myersi
Photo by Dr. Herbert R. Axelrod

alf-banded Coolie Loach
canthophthalmus semicinctus
hoto by Dr. Herbert R. Axelrod

Spot-banded Coolie Loach
Acanthophthalmus shelfordi
Photo by Dr. Herbert R. Axelrod

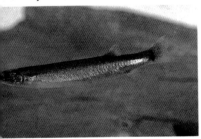

Plain Coolie Loach
Acanthophthalmus javanicus
Photo by Dr. Herbert R. Axelrod

Worm Coolie Loach
Acanthophthalmus anguillaris
Photo by Dr. Herbert R. Axelrod

Horse-faced Loach
Acanthopsis choirorhynchus
Photo by Andre Roth

Chinese Algae-eater
Gyrinocheilus aymonieri
Photo by Andre Roth

145

will support. The amounts of gas exchanged by plants during respiration are much less than those by animals, however, so it is doubtful whether the consumption of oxygen and production of carbon dioxide by plants are ever of sufficient magnitude to cause aquarium fish any trouble. For this reason the aquarist need hardly ever worry about having his tank too heavily planted. In all probability, a tank would have to be almost completely choked with plants before seeing the effect.

Anyone who wants proof that plants are not essential to any so-called "balanced aquarium" need only remove all of them from such a tank; the fish will show no respiratory distress whatsoever. This simple experiment should convince aquarists that plants do not oxygenate the water in an aquarium.

Since plants act as oxygenators only to an insignificant extent in an aquarium, it might be thought that they are useless or even deleterious. That such a view is completely erroneous will be apparent from the following remarks, outlining the principal functions of plants in aquaria. For convenience, these have been treated under six different headings:

1. *To decorate the tank.* This is put first even though it may seem the least utilitarian. If aquaria could not be made attractive or an asset to the appearance of a room, how many fish fanciers would there be? To be sure, there are many who are interested in fish *per se*, but by and large it is the beauty of a well-decorated tank that attracts people to the hobby. We believe that the vegetation of an aquarium is by far the greatest contributor to its beauty.

2. *To minimize the likelihood of excessive multiplication of algae.* In general, tanks that are well-planted suffer less frequently from green water or any other overabundance of algae. This phenomenon has also been noticed in outdoor ponds and pools and has been demonstrated

experimentally out-of-doors. Several theories have been advanced to explain why it occurs. One is that the large plants shade the water sufficiently to prevent the growth of the small types, but it seems unlikely that this could happen in a glass-sided tank. Another idea is that the large plants produce some substance inhibiting the growth of the small ones, but no one has yet detected such a material.

A third theory has been suggested by Dr. C. M. Breder, Jr., and other workers. Since plant physiologists have shown that plants are dependent upon a number of substances for growth, a well-established stand of higher plants may use up one or more of the available growth-promoting materials as fast as they appear in an aquarium, or keep them at so low a level that no large amount of algae can be formed. Johnstone's application of Liebig's Law of the Minimum to planktonic growth is perhaps pertinent here: "A plant requires a certain number of foodstuffs if it is to continue and grow, and each of these food substances must be present in a certain proportion. If one of them is absent, the plant will die; if one is present in a minimal proportion, the growth will also be minimal. This will be the case no matter how abundant the other foodstuffs may be. Thus the growth of a plant is dependent upon the amount of that foodstuff which is presented to it in minimal quantity." Drs. F. W. Kavanagh and H. W. Rickett of the New York Botanical Garden have pointed out, however, that the amounts of nitrogenous and mineral substances used by plants in an ordinary aquarium are minute and unlikely to become a limiting factor. In fact, ordinary tap water is often a pretty good nutrient solution for plants, the very small amount of materials dissolved in it being sufficient for them. The reason a good growth of higher plants tends to prevent excessive mul-

Yellow-finned Loach
Botia lecontei
Photo by Andre Roth

Clown Loach
Botia macracantha
Photo by Klaus Paysan

Banded Loach
Botia hymenophysa
Photo by Andre Roth

Dwarf Loach
Botia sidthimunki
Photo by Andre Roth

Asian Weatherfish
Misgurnus anguillicaudatus
Photo by Andre Roth

Golden European Weatherfish
Misgurnus fossilis
Photo by Dr. Herbert R. Axelrod

Broken-banded Loach
Nemacheilus botia
Photo by Dr. Herbert R. Axelrod

Myers's Hillstream Loach
Pseudogastromyzon myersi
Photo by Dr. Herbert R. Axelrod

Lyretailed Panchax
Aphyosemion australe
Photo by Klaus Paysan

Two-striped Panchax
Aphyosemion bivittatum "loennbergi"
Photo by Andre Roth

Cinnamon Panchax
Aphyosemion cinnamomeum
Photo by Dr. Karl Knaack

Blue Gularis
Aphyosemion sjoestedti
Photo by Klaus Paysan

Golden Pheasant
Aphyosemion occidentalis
Photo by Andre Roth

Palmqvest's Notho
Nothobranchius palmqvesti
Photo by Andre Roth

Rachow's Fire Killie
Nothobranchius rachovi
Photo by H.-J. Richter

Korthaus's Notho
Nothobranchius korthausae
Photo by H.-J. Richter 149

tiplication of algae is thus a mystery, and if the Law of the Minimum applies, it does not concern the fertilizing substances in fish wastes since these are present far in excess of the plants' needs.

Many aquarists have believed that plants help maintain a more nearly uniform water chemistry in an aquarium by utilizing appreciable quantities of the nitrogenous wastes of fish. Because the amounts of these fertilizers necessary for aquatics' growth are insignificant compared to what the fish are producing, this effect does not operate to any extent. In this connection, it should be remembered that fish have been known to live in unplanted tanks for years without any change of water. They have also lived for long periods in standing aquaria kept in total darkness, where not even algae can grow.

3. *To provide food for the fish, both directly and indirectly, by promoting the growth of various micro-organisms and other small animals.* Fish that eat leafy plants are not popular with the great majority of aquarists, so the use of higher plants directly as fish food is relatively unimportant. Only algae are regularly eaten by the common species of tropical fish kept in aquaria. Indirectly, however, leafy plants and stoneworts may be quite important. The behavior of many fish gives ample demonstration of this, for they spend much time picking or grazing on the leaves and stems of submerged aquatics. In nature a great variety of very small creatures lives on aquatic plants. Undoubtedly fewer exist on the plants in aquaria, but, so far as we know, they help provide a more adequate and natural diet for captive fish. *Nitella*, one of the stoneworts or Charales, is especially valuable in this regard.

4. *To shelter less dominant fish from attacks of their more aggressive neighbors.* A careful study of the behavior of practically any group of fish in captivity reveals that cer-

tain individuals dominate others whenever there is competition for food, swimming space, or potential mates. Sometimes this domination appears to border on persecution, and the only way a less aggressive fish may be able to escape harassment from its more domineering tankmate is by hiding. Nothing can provide more or better hiding places in an aquarium than a generous growth of plants. It has also been demonstrated that dividing a tank into partially separated compartments reduces the amount of aggressive behavior among territory-holding fish, apparently by enabling them to establish their domains securely with less fighting. It would seem quite probable that plants act in a similar way, providing fish with niches, nooks, or crannies that they can call their own, so to speak, or as refuges when hard pressed by some other fish.

5. *To provide sites for the attachment of eggs and refuges for the protection of young fish.* These are well-recognized functions of aquatic plants. A large number of different fish place or scatter their eggs on plants. Among the better known genera that include species with such reproductive habits are: *Hyphessobrycon, Hemigrammus, Nannostomus, Barbodes, Puntius, Capoeta, Carassius, Rasbora, Corydoras, Rivulus, Epiplatys, Melanotaenia, Pachypanchax, Aplocheilus, Pterophyllum,* and *Chanda.* For baby fish, hiding places are life-or-death matters. Without a suitable sanctuary from hungry larger fish, few young would survive. A heavy growth of floating plants seems to be the best protection for tiny fish, and it also provides them with good feeding grounds for microscopic and near-microscopic prey.

6. *To give the fish a natural habitat more conducive to their well-being—in the broadest sense of the term.* This somewhat intangible function of plants is placed last because it forms a sort of catch-all for any items not included in the first five—most of which it overlaps in several respects. It is quite reasonable to suppose that,

Red-chinned Panchax
Epiplatys dageti
Photo by Andre Roth

Golden-spotted Panchax
Epiplatys fasciolatus
Photo by Dr. Karl Knaack

Striped Green Panchax
Aplocheilus lineatus
Photo by Andre Roth

Blue Panchax
Aplocheilus panchax
Photo by Klaus Paysan

Argentine Pearlfish
Cynolebias bellotti
Photo by Klaus Paysan

White's Pearlfish
Cynolebias whitei
Photo by H.-J. Richter

Bloodmark Long-finned Killie
Pterolebias longipinnis
Photo by Dr. Karl Knaack

Magdalena Spot-finned Killie
Rachovia brevis
Photo by H.-J. Richter

Cuban Rivulus
Rivulus cylindraceus
Photo by Klaus Paysan

Golden-eared Killie
Fundulus chrysotus
Photo by Andre Roth

Yucatan Pupfish
Garmanella pulchra
Photo by H.-J. Richter

American Flagfish
Jordanella floridae
Photo by Andre Roth

Bluefin Killifish
Lucania goodei
Photo by Dr. Herbert R. Axelrod

Graceful Lady Killie
Procatopus gracilis
Photo by Dr. Karl Knaack

Persian Minnow
Aphanius mento
Photo by Dr. Karl Knaack

Javan Ricefish
Oryzias javanicus
Photo by Klaus Paysan

153

in general, captive fish will behave more normally, be more healthy, and will live longer and more natural lives the more closely their man-made environment approximates or betters their native environment. Plants form an integral part of the natural habitat of most tropical fish; for this reason, if no other, the aquarist should give them careful consideration.

Undoubtedly some of the functions of plants in aquaria have been omitted from the above. For example, Dr. Myron Gordon has found that *Nitella* can be used to condition raw tap water. It is nevertheless evident that fish benefit greatly from the presence of plants in their aquaria.

The benefits that accrue from keeping plants and fish together do not extend only to the fish, however; the plants, too, profit from the association. It is common experience that aquatic plants grow better when kept with fish than when kept alone, provided, of course, that the fish are not of the plant-molesting type. Aquatic plants need fertilizer just as terrestrial ones do, and fish wastes are evidently excellent fertilizer, although fish produce far in excess of what the plants require. Of much greater importance is the carbon dioxide given off by the fish. There is good evidence that this gas is usually a limiting factor in the growth of at least the higher aquatic plants. Without it photosynthesis cannot take place, and these plants apparently quickly exhaust the supply dissolved in water. Breder's measurements of carbon dioxide concentrations in aquaria lend support to this view, since he found that the carbon dioxide remained far below its equilibrium point with the atmosphere for long periods when the plants in an aquarium were actively photosynthesizing. A more adequate supply of carbon dioxide is undoubtedly the reason plants kept with fish grow better than those kept in old tanks rich in fish wastes but without any fish.

For both utilitarian and esthetic reasons, aquatic plants should be an essential part of the home aquarium, and successful aquarists will continue to use them generously.

In selecting aquatic plants, careful consideration should be given each individual species and its physical requirements. Following are discussions of the most important of these plants.

Anacharis, Elodea
(Elodea canadensis)

An important plant in practically any type of aquarium is the popular anacharis, more commonly called elodea. This plant may be purchased at any store that carries fish of any kind. As noted in the discussion of the balanced aquarium, the amount of oxygen that a plant gives off during photosynthesis is of little importance to the amount of oxygen dissolved in the water; oxygen that is needed would more readily be picked up from the air that is in contact with the water surface. Many dealers, as well as authors of texts on tropical fish, might nevertheless be tempted to claim that anacharis is the best plant for oxygenating purposes. As explained above, this is not so. Plants should be selected for other purposes. If you are looking for a plant that will reproduce quickly and beautifully in a tank that gets a few hours of direct sunlight a day, as well as a plant that will offer considerable protection to fish and young during spawning time, anacharis is the answer. The only drawback to including anacharis in every type of tank is that it needs a certain minimum amount of direct sunlight or equivalent artificial light per day to maintain its fineness. This is true of most of the cheaper and more popular plants. Should you attempt to raise

Red-lined Australian Rainbowfish
Melanotaenia splendida
Photo by Andre Roth

New Guinea Red Rainbowfish
Glossolepis incisus
Photo by H.-J. Richter

Plain-fin Popondetta Rainbowfish
Popondetta connieae
Photo by H.-J. Richter

Madagascar Rainbowfish
Bedotia geayi
Photo by Ruda Zukal

Badis
Badis badis
Photo by Klaus Paysan

Leaf Fish
Monocirrhus polyacanthus
Photo by H.-J. Richter

Schomburgk's Leaf Fish
Polycentrus schomburgki
Photo by Dr. Herbert R. Axelrod

Five-spotted Archer Fish
Toxotes jaculator
Photo by Andre Roth

Siamese Tiger Fish
Datnioides microlepis
Photo by Andre Roth

Indian Glassfish
Chanda ranga
Photo by Dr. Herbert R. Axelrod

Scat
Scatophagus argus
Photo by Andre Roth

Banded Snakehead
Channa striatus
Photo by Andre Roth

Hooded Bumblebee Goby
Brachygobius nunus
Photo by H.-J. Richter

Mono
Monodactylus argenteus
Photo by Andre Roth

Freshwater Butterfly Fish
Pantodon buchholzi
Photo by H.-J. Richter

Pirarucu, Giant Arowana
Arapaima gigas
Photo by Andre Roth

157

the anacharis in a dark tank, it would become stringy and scrawny, developing more and more space between its leaves.

When anacharis is purchased from a dealer, it usually comes in bunches bound together at the bottom with a strip of lead or a rubber band. Remove the lead or rubber band and tear off about an inch of the bottom of the plant. Then stick the stems into about an inch of sand. The arrangement of the plants is important mostly for esthetic reasons. It is usually wiser to have the taller growing plants at the rear and sides of the aquarium so the smaller ones may be easily seen. Should taller plants be placed all through the tank, the fish will not be shown off to their best advantage since they will always be partially hidden by the vegetation.

Milfoil
(Myriophyllum spicatum)

The long, fine leaves of this plant afford maximum efficiency in catching the eggs of the egglaying fish. It needs plenty of strong light to maintain its closely knit leaves. When such light is afforded the plant, it will grow astoundingly fast, sometimes as much as 3 or 4 inches a week. This plant is very sensitive to the salt-permanganate solution and should be removed from any tank undergoing such treatment.

Plant *Myriophyllum* the same way as anacharis, tearing off an inch or so before putting it in the sand. Should growth be too rapid, the plant may be uprooted and left to float around in the water. In time, however, it will send down fine roots into the sand. All plants seem to be able to distinguish between the top of the aquarium and the bottom. This property is known as "geotropism." If plants bend toward the source of light ("photo-tropism")—and they all should—make sure that the light is placed directly above them. Should one lamp suffice for the entire tank, all the plants will grow toward that light.

Fanwort
(Cabomba caroliniana)

This plant looks like a cross between the anacharis and the *Myriophyllum:* it has properties common to each and acts like both of them. More than the rest, it requires a great amount of light to maintain its dense appearance. Should there be insufficient light, it will become very stringy.

The author used *Cabomba* in a demonstration tank at New York University. This tank contained a few hundred guppies and, other than a little green algae, *Cabomba* was its sole plant. It got exactly eight hours of light a day from three 25-watt bulbs, six days a week. The *Cabomba* did so well that specimens 3 or 4 feet long were taken from it. One of the plants flowered, giving off eight blossoms. The blossoms were miniature lilies, a really beautiful sight.

Cabomba should be treated the same as anacharis.

Tape Grass, Val
(Vallisneria americana)

Vallisneria americana, though not the most familiar type to be used in the home aquarium, is of tremendous importance for all sorts of wild life; muskrats, fish, ducks, and geese all relish this plant and eat it readily.

Vallisneria reproduces by sending out runners that sink into the sand a few inches from the parent plant and produce new plants. This plant may flower.

Three-spined Stickleback
Gasterosteus aculeatus
Photo by Klaus Paysan

Peter's Elephantnose
Gnathonemus petersii
Photo by H.-J. Richter

African Knifefish
Xenomystus nigri
Photo by Andre Roth

White-spotted Spiny Eel
Mastacembelus armatus
Photo by Andre Roth

Variable Ghost Knifefish
Sternopygus macrurus
Photo by Andre Roth

Green Knifefish
Eigenmannia virescens
Photo by Andre Roth

Silver Needlefish
Xenentodon cancila
Photo by Andre Roth

Round-spotted Puffer
Tetraodon fluviatilis
Photo by Klaus Paysan

Sagittaria
(Sagittaria graminea)

Sagittaria looks much like the *Vallisneria* except that it is much thicker and stronger and will usually grow longer, sometimes reaching a length of 2 feet.

When planting *Sagittaria*, as well as other similar types of "crowned" plants, be sure that the crown (the place where the roots are fastened into the plant proper) is above the level of the sand. This will ensure maximum growth.

Sagittaria produces beautiful flowers and reproduces by sending out runners. These runners may be severed if there is need to separate the plants.

Hygrophila
(Hygrophila polysperma)

This member of the group of aquarium plants comes from Asia and is unequaled for rapid growth. Given sufficient light, it will soon fill up the aquarium. The author has had it grow right out of its tank and into the air some 3 or 4 inches.

Hygrophila will grow well under almost any type of conditions and can survive extremes of temperatures and pH. New plants grow from the old by a series of roots dropping into the sand from the old plant. These roots may sprout from the parent plant as high as a foot above the sand level, though any joint is a possible crown.

Hygrophila should be planted low in the water, as it grows very quickly. Cuttings should be made every few weeks to keep the tank clear. The cuttings may be transplanted into another tank or merely stored in a jar of water.

This plant is not a true aquatic and may grow out into the air if the stem is strong enough. Since it will grow toward the light, be careful that it does not get dehydrated from getting too close to the reflector.

Nitella

Nitella is a type of stonewort or Charales, one of the groups of plants forming a connecting link between the algae and flowering plants. It looks much like emaciated *Cabomba*. It has a fine, long main stem from which very fine filaments protrude in all directions. It does not root and is excellent for use when spawning egglayers. Many fish will eat this plant, as it is very palatable.

Many schools use *Nitella* for protoplasmic demonstrations. It may be kept in a jar of water and will get along very well. Its growth is sometimes very rapid, and the more light the *Nitella* gets, the more dense it will be.

Amazon Sword Plants
(*Echinodorus* species)

The most majestic of aquatic plants is truly the Amazon sword. It is a crown-type plant that has 30 to 40 leaves coming off the main stem, much as in stalks of celery. The plant looks so beautiful when it gets the proper light that it defies description.

Since it is a rather delicate plant, it must not be subjected to the treatment that plant-molesting fish like most cichlids would give it. It grows to a height of 18 inches and may cover an area of 2 feet. It reproduces by runners, but also blossoms. Runners should be weighted into the sand. The price of these plants is usually what makes them uncommon in the average home aquarium.

Ludwigia

Though not a true water plant, *Ludwigia* has, nevertheless, found its way into those aquaria where light and richly fertilized sand is available.

Ludwigia, like anacharis, tends to become very stringy and dies if sufficient light is not available. The beautiful red species which has been grown so successfully in Florida rarely maintains its luster in the environs of the Northeast.

The fact that *Ludwigia* does best in a rich soil culture bears out the fact that it is primarily a bog plant. Reproduction can be accomplished vegetatively; that is, the parent is divided into smaller plants. Cuttings planted in damp sand and humus will root quickly. The cuttings can then be placed in the aquarium.

Cryptocoryne
(Cryptocoryne species)

The antithesis of *Ludwigia* is *Cryptocoryne*. *Cryptocoryne* needs a minimum of light and looks much like a terrestrial plant, with its long stem and broad green leaves, yellowish green on the under side. Planting is best done in a rich sand (containing some humus or earth). Many aquarists plant *Cryptocoryne* in 6-inch bulb pots and place these right in the sand. This will usually help keep earth or humus from fouling a nicely set up tank.

The plant reproduces by sending out shoots. Under optimum conditions it sometimes flowers. As there are many species of *Cryptocoryne*, even plant taxonomists have trouble in differentiating them.

Floating Plants

Some floating plants have a place in the home aquarium. Many bubble-nest builders will use them in nest building, and other types of fish will nibble on their roots now and then.

About the most popular type of floating plant is duckweed. It looks like merely a set of leaves about three-eighths of an inch long, all attached at the center. Only a few species exist, *Lemna minor* and *Spirodela polyrhiza* being the most popular, but they are all quite similar.

Reproduction is vegetative. The roots may drop about an inch into the water; fish like to nibble on them. If given too much light, the duckweeds will cover the top of an aquarium in a week. This will prohibit desirable top light from entering the tank through the surface and may also interfere with the elimination of carbon dioxide from the water.

Riccia is another type of floating plant that is useful for specific purposes, but it grows so rapidly that it soon chokes out the sunlight that may enter from the top. *Riccia* serves well for spawning purposes but should be used with caution. Many enemies of fish like to lurk in the dark masses of this plant and await their prey.

Other types of floating plants, such as *Salvinia*, bladderworts, and water hyacinth, have the same practical value as the aforementioned plants but are more delicate and expensive. Their uses are limited to bubble-nest builders and those types of fish that drop light eggs. The long roots of the water hyacinth may be a help to adhesive egglayers, but the expense and trouble of maintaining the hyacinth are prohibitive.

Chapter 8
How to Keep Fish Healthy

Aquarium Conditions

Tropical fish, like most living organisms, are subject to various types of disease. Dr. Ross F. Nigrelli of the New York Aquarium has made a complete study of those factors that affect fish in captivity. Dr. Nigrelli lists the following factors that he believes account for the loss of fish in captivity:

1. CROWDING. A given aquarium will support only a certain number of fish before they will turn against each other in an effort to reduce their density. More carbon dioxide will also be present in the water and thus further add to the destruction. Diseases that are infectious will be more easily spread in the smaller tanks.

2. TEMPERATURE. Temperature fluctuations must be kept to a minimum. Though many fish have wide ranges of tolerance, successful adaptations to temperature changes require a long period of time. Higher temperatures may activate certain types of parasites, while

lower temperatures might cause them to encyst (encase themselves and become inactive).

3. LIGHT. The fish generally kept in home aquaria are tolerant of a wide variety of light conditions. The quality—natural daylight, incandescent, or fluorescent—and quantity—providing they are not kept in total darkness or semidarkness for more than about two-thirds of the time—seem to make little difference to tropicals' well-being. The direction of light is important, however; most aquarists agree that artificial side lighting is detrimental. In other words, all artificial lighting should come from above the water's surface. Indeed, it is claimed that the best natural illumination also comes from above. It is widely believed that the principal reason fish in captivity spawn most frequently in the spring is because of the increasing length of daylight most apparent at that season. Certain types of flatworms (Trematoda) are phototropic (attracted to light) when in the larval stage. These trematodes, especially the gyrodactylids, cause very nasty diseases of the skin and gills.

4. pH OF THE WATER. The most suitable pH (acidity or alkalinity) of the water is variable for individual types of fish. Marine fish require a pH of about 8.0, slightly alkaline, while most tropicals require a pH of about 7.0, neutral. Most species of fish when kept in a tank of their own will tend to keep the pH of the water at the most desirable level.

5. SPECIFIC GRAVITY OF THE WATER. Specific gravity (s.g.) may be defined as weight per unit volume as compared with an equal volume of water. The specific gravity of water is 1. Should water get heavier from an increase in dissolved substances it would increase some of the chemical changes that take place within the bodies of the fish. For example, their breathing would get more rapid. An increase in s.g. has a harmful effect upon many parasites in some instances.

6. FLOW AND AERATION OF WATER. Several gases are toxic to fish when they reach a certain concentration. Various fish require different amounts of aeration to rid the water of gases such as carbon dioxide, hydrogen sulphide, and nitrogen.

7. METABOLIC WASTE PRODUCTS. Water contains many types of matter dissolved in it. Some of this material comes from the waste excreted by the fish. Certain types of this material are beneficial to some fish, but too strong a concentration is undoubtedly not good.

8. DIET. Many fish get poor diets and may suffer from various deficiencies. Liver and kidney troubles are frequent manifestations of vitamin deficiencies.

9. HANDLING. Many fish get scratched or lose a few scales when being handled. These openings are often sites of attack by harmful organisms.

10. PARASITES. Certain types of organisms attack the fish and live on them. Some parasites will attack only a specific fish, but there are many types of fish parasites that show no specificity. These types are the most dangerous.

Certain different types of ailments may be treated by the same methods, but there is definitely no "cure-all" for fish. Many types of medicines sold as cure-alls should be ignored. About the only medication that can be offered many ill fish is a bath in a gallon of water containing about 2 1/2 tablespoons of plain household salt. The temperature of the water should then be raised so any encysted parasites may become active. It is wise to treat the whole tank with this salt treatment. Most diseases of fish are very infectious, and salt is the best type of nontoxic medicine to be recommended.

The widespread *Ichthyophthirius*, a type of protozoan parasite causing "ich," is very successfully treated this way. The white spots, which usually indicate the presence of ich, are the encysted parasite. A rise in temperature in this case is needed to enable the parasites to be free-swimming and thus become poisoned by the salt.

The author has been told by one of the greatest authorities on fish diseases that the only recommended remedy for fish ills is the salt treatment. Other treatments are usually toxic and may be more dangerous than the disease itself.

The antibiotics have successfully entered fish-cultural practices. Aureomycin has been found an excellent treatment for fungus and certain bacterial infections. A concentration of about 250 milligrams per 10 gallons of water is recommended. The whole dose of the drug is simply put into the water all at once. Other newly developed antibiotics also give promise of helping the aquarist both cure and prevent disease.

Professor Roberts Rugh suggested the following precautions when dealing with fish:

It is almost safe to say that there is no reliable remedy for sick fish, no matter what the cause. Prevention is all-important. However, there are several simple rules to keep in mind:

1. Never add new fish to an old aquarium until they have been sterilized and quarantined for a few days. All new fish should be given a salt treatment, regardless of their source.

2. Provide separate aquaria for sick fish and isolate them as soon as there is any indication of trouble.

3. When shipping large numbers of fish, it is said that mortality will be reduced if a small amount of aspirin is added to the water (reasons unknown).

4. When sick fish are found in a regular aquarium, this aquarium should be put through a thorough process of cleaning and sterilization. Fish diseases are generally very contagious (for the fish!).

5. Overcrowding and overfeeding are probably the second and third most frequent causes of illness, the

first being parasitization.

6. The chlorine in drinking (tap) water is a good bactericide for human beings but harmful to fish. Chlorine will naturally evaporate from standing water if there is sufficient exposed surface, but warming or agitating the water will hasten the process.

Because sick fish, as previously explained, are usually weaker than healthy ones, they should be separated from the rest of the fish, even though they all may be getting the same treatment. To eliminate the trouble of temperature controls in a separate tank, a glass beaker filled with some of the water from the tank may be floated on the surface of the aquarium. A single small fish will do very well in such a small body of water, at least for a few days.

Feeding

One of the greatest assets to a healthy tank is the food that the fish receive. How, as well as what, you feed your fish is a very important consideration. Most fish can safely be fed once a day, all they can eat in about five minutes. Uneaten food should not be left to decay in the aquarium. Many more fish die from overfeeding, especially at the hands of beginners, than from starvation. Several important factors should be recognized when feeding fish:

1. SIZE OF FOOD PARTICLES. Make sure the particles are small enough for the fish to ingest.

2. VARIETY OF FOOD. Alternate different types of food.

3. QUANTITY OF FOOD. Larger fish, of course, need more food than smaller ones. Feed the fish small

portions for about five minutes. This will ensure a minimum waste of food. Some very active fish require several such feedings a day. More food should be given fish during the summer than winter. Also feed more food to fish in tanks that have more light than is normal.

It is up to the individual fancier, however, to judge the optimal feeding techniques and the varieties of food to be used.

Live Food

1. PLANTS. Such plants as algae, duckweed, and lettuce are required in the diet of many fish (scats, mollies, guppies, etc.). Many of the larger types of plants, such as *Vallisneria, Cabomba,* etc., also are good for fish to nibble on.

2. BRINE SHRIMP. These little salt-loving animals are very handy. They are obtained in egg form and hatched in a solution of 6 tablespoons of salt to a gallon of water. The eggs should hatch out in two days at 75° F. The brine shrimp (*Artemia*) may be fed on plankton (salt-water infusion), algae, or lettuce and raised to quite a size. The larvae are excellent food for newborn fish.

For the hatching of brine shrimp eggs fill a few deep glass dishes with the salt solution to a depth of not less than 1 inch. Add eggs in the proportion of one teaspoon to the gallon, or just roughly sprinkle some eggs over the surface of the water. Do not move the water after the eggs have been placed on it, as the eggs will usually stick to the sides of the dish.

After the culture has remained for two days, place a light at some part of the dish. The brine shrimp show positive phototropism, all congregating near the light, and are easily scooped up with a fine net.

It is impossible to pick up live brine shrimp without getting some eggs also. Snails usually take care of the uneaten eggs.

3. INFUSORIA. These include such organisms as amoebae, paramecia, blepharisma, rotifers, etc. They are made readily available in pill form that may be cultivated into a strong infusion by the addition of a little lettuce. The infusoria should be fed to newborn fry with an eyedropper. It is inadvisable to drop the pill into the spawning tank, as certain pills will form a scum on the surface.

4. DAPHNIA. These small relatives of shrimp, crabs, and lobsters are excellent food for every type of fish large enough to ingest them. Sifted daphnia are excellent for fry. It is sometimes advisable to enter a few large daphnia into the spawning tank so they may throw off young that will be small enough for the fry. Daphnia may be raised in beakers or battery jars with a minimum capacity of 2 pints. After about six adult daphnia have been selected and placed in the jars, some malted milk, dried, shredded lettuce, infusoria, or hay should be placed in the jar for food. Daphnia will reproduce in large numbers. The water may turn cloudy after the food is placed in it—perhaps because of the infusoria—but this should not be a detriment as long as it does not turn moldy. The culture should be changed every month.

5. ENCHYTRAEIDS. These whiteworms are excellent food for all types of fish. They may be chopped up into fine particles for the young fish. Cultures of whiteworms may be started with an inoculation of a few worms into some humus. This humus should be kept in a clay pot or wooden vessel. The temperature should be in the fifties, and the humidity should be very high. It may be a good idea to keep the culture in a dark, damp cellar. Food in the form of malted milk, dried milk, and bread of any kind is good. Cereal boiled in milk until it is pasty may also be inserted into the humus for food.

The culture should stand about a month before being used.

6. TUBIFEX. These red worms are usually available all year round. They are very popular and nutritious for fish. Feedings of tubifex may present two problems. First, tubifex are sludge worms and are usually sold with much of the debris still intact in the culture. This decaying matter is liable to cloud up the culture if the worms are not thoroughly cleaned under cold running water. The second factor is that tubifex may carry with them several types of parasites that are quite dangerous to tropical fish. This is another reason the red worms must be thoroughly cleaned.

These worms may be stored in the refrigerator for weeks in glass jars containing no less than 2 pints of water. The water in the jars should be changed daily. First, pour off as much water from the jar as possible. Then shoot a stream of water, as cold as possible, into the culture so the worms will all be separated. Allow the water to settle—the worms will sink to the bottom. Do this until the worms get very red and the water that comes off is clean. Then feed the fish a few worms, making sure that they are able to ingest the worms before they fall to the bottom of the tank. Should the worms fall to the bottom, they will burrow into the sand and be very difficult for the fish to pull out. Tubifex may be fed to the fish two or three times a week. Special feeding rings are available for this purpose.

In 1953 I wrote a booklet entitled *Tropical Fish as Pets*. Several of my associates challenged the wisdom of this title since fish are not really "pets" in the sense that a horse, dog, or cat is actually "pettable." Though I couldn't convince them that you can handle fishes in one way or another, it didn't make me change the title of the booklet. Since that time I have been very sensitive about training fishes; but, until now, I haven't had much luck.

Now the story changes. A few years ago a Chinese from Taiwan sent me samples of dried tubifex. Within three weeks I had samples on my desk of five different types of dried tubifex worms. The fishes ignored most of them.

Laughingly, Bernie Duke, who ran Gulf Fish Farms in Palmetto, Florida, said, "Herb, you need catnip for your fish food." He laughed. I laughed. I started thinking.

Scientifically, we know that certain substances increase the appetites of fish and attract them to investigate certain "odors" that might be food. I worked with a few of them and finally found my "fish nip." Once fishes discover it in the aquarium, they tear it apart with such vigor that you would think that they hadn't eaten for a month. After almost a year of testing, I discovered that I could raise angelfish, bettas, *Corydoras*, all the livebearers, most of the tetras, and even African water frogs solely on a diet of these freeze-dried tubifex worms.* The food was great! I called them "Miracle Worms."

Further refinements in the processing made possible the following characteristics:

a. If allowed to soak in a glass of clear water, the worms will float for days and will not cloud or discolor the water. The food is also odorless.

b. As the worms pick up moisture, they expand and look exactly like live tubifex worms.

c. When pressed against the inside of an aquarium they adhere, and the fish can be fed so that every bit they eat can be observed. This prevents overfeeding since you can easily remove any uneaten bits of worms. Overfeeding is the single greatest "disaster" that can

*The author was granted a patent on freeze-drying but he never enforced it.

foul the tank (and enthusiasm) of any beginner.

d. It is so nutritious that it can bring almost every known aquarium fish into breeding condition. This food and brine shrimp are perfect diets for most small fish.

e. The fish enjoy eating it so much, as evidenced by their voracious attacks on it, that they become tame and will eagerly pick at it from between your fingers. I have proven this with nocturnal catfish, mollies, gouramis, angelfish, cardinal tetras, and most cichlids.

Here is the proper method to train your fish. For the first three days merely affix a small piece of freeze-dried tubifex worms to the center of your aquarium glass (or just drop it into the aquarium if you don't want to get your hands wet). Let your fish develop a taste for it. It may take them five or ten minutes actually to attack it since the food emits powerful "odors" and they may be "suspicious." Once they have acclimated themselves to the worms, don't feed them for one day. The next day they will almost eat the freeze-dried tubifex from between your fingers.

7. MOSQUITO LARVAE. Immature mosquitos are fine food for the tropicals. These wrigglers are actually both pupae and larvae of the mosquito. They may be purchased or gathered from swampy pools along with daphnia. The only objection to these larvae is that should they metamorphose before they are eaten, you are liable to have a houseful of mosquitos.

8. EARTHWORMS. These familiar organisms are ideal for large types of fish such as the cichlids. They may be chopped up and fed to the smaller tropicals. Bloodworms and sandworms also fall into the same category.

9. DROSOPHILA. These little fruitflies may be obtained from any high school or college that offers a course in biology or from a biological supply house or a

dealer in live foods. A certain mutant type called "vestigial" has very small wings and cannot fly. If a male and female *Drosophila* are placed in a small cream container or similar jar with a piece of banana or other type of nutrient, they will reproduce very profusely.

10. MICROWORMS. Imported from Europe, these thread-like worms, technically called *Anguillula silusiae*, are about an eighth of an inch long and make excellent food for all types of newly hatched fish. Young live-bearers also relish this food. The original cost of starting the culture is about the only expense necessary to have a year-round supply of live food for all the young that would be spawned in any home aquarium. They may be purchased at any large tropical fish store. The best type of container for their quickly growing culture is a refrigerator jar. Most purchased cultures come in such a container. They can be kept at room temperature, 68° F.

Since most of the microworms are females and reproduce by giving off living young, the food supply diminishes rapidly and new food is required; owing to its contents, the food supply should be changed every two weeks, in any case. The usual mixture that has been found successful is a watery mixture of three parts Pablum to one part yeast. This paste should be placed about one-half inch deep in the refrigerator jars. The worms will not be able to eat all the culture medium before it turns sour. Care must be exercised that the medium does not dehydrate. Some people tape the edges of the refrigerator jar to prevent the loss of water through evaporation. This is a good idea, also, because the worms seem to fare very well with a limited air supply.

Separation of the worms from the culture medium is no problem since the worms do not actually live in the medium but rather prefer to stay on the sides of the glass near the surface of the culture. They may be fed to the fish directly after being scraped off the sides with a finger or knife.

Starting a new culture is usually done by adding a "fingerful" of worms to a freshly prepared culture dish. This dish, containing the same food as the old, should be started a few days before you intend to throw out the old medium—a culture should not be kept more than two weeks—so you will always have an abundance of microworms for the young fish.

Prepared Foods and Formulas

There are many types of prepared food which, if interspersed with other types, are very beneficial to captive fish. Listed below are probably the most nutritious ones. Caution should be exercised, however, to avoid being too repetitious with these foods.

1. Beef heart
2. Cereals—the smaller grained ones
3. Eggs—chopped up yolk of hard-boiled eggs
4. Potato—boiled thoroughly and broken up into fine pieces
5. Fish—all sorts of raw fish may be chopped into small pieces and fed sparingly to all types of fish. Frozen fillet of flounder is easy to keep. Merely cut off a small piece every day and feed with a little dry food. Cichlids do very well on this diet.
6. Shrimps—fresh, shelled, and chopped into fine pieces or dropped into the tank on pieces of string so they may be pulled out after ten or fifteen minutes. Care should be used to remove them soon enough, for shrimp will cloud the water if left in the tank for too long a period.
7. All sorts of dry prepared foods for sale in pet shops and other stores. They are all usually satisfactory, but they should not be used exclusively.

Gordon's Formula

This requires a pound of liver, 20 tablespoons of Pablum or Ceravim, and 1 tablespoon of salt. Cut the liver into one-half-inch pieces and remove all the sinewy material. Add an equivalent weight of water. Grind the liver into a mash (a blender is excellent for this purpose), and then drain through a fine sieve. Then add Pablum or Ceravim slowly to the liver to form a thick paste. Mix this meal in well, seeing that there are no lumps. The salt may be added during this process. Now place the mixture in small glass jars. Place the jars in a pot of water and boil. Put the covers on the jars, but do not screw them down or the jars may burst from the expanding gases. When the water has boiled, turn off the heat and allow the jars to cool with the water for half an hour. Screw the caps on, if possible, as soon as the heat is turned off. When the jars have been thoroughly cooled, they may be placed in the refrigerator and safely stored for a month or so. All fish seem to have a hearty appetite for this mixture, so feed it sparingly, allowing the fish to eat only small amounts at a time.

Chapter 9
Appliances—Use and Repair

The most important consideration to be given an appliance is its usefulness in the aquarium. As there are an infinite number of appliances that can be purchased to add to the complexity—or simplicity—of aquarium management, we shall explain the operation of only those few that are a necessity to every aquarium.

A necessary requirement for every appliance is that it be made of a noncorrosive material. Stainless steel, glass, and certain plastics are the safest materials to put in an aquarium. If an appliance is not available in a safe material, do without it.

Thermometers

Thermometers measure the temperature of the water. Most thermometers for use in the aquarium are filled with mercury, colored alcohol, or colored water. The best is the mercury thermometer. As accuracy is obviously the criterion of a good thermometer, it would be profitable to analyze here what makes a thermometer accurate.

A thermometer works on the principle of an expanding liquid. A calibrated glass tube is used to measure this expansion. Mercury is the most accurate liquid for this purpose, as it expands the most evenly with every rise in temperature. It is obvious that the longer the thermometer, the more accurately it can be read.

Aquarium thermometers are sold in different models. Some are filled with air and float. Other are weighted with lead shot and stand on the bottom of the tank. Still another model is fastened to the side of the aquarium with a suction cup. The easiest to read without removal from the water is the one fastened to the side of the tank, though the standing type can also be set to allow for easy reading.

Since the temperature of a large tank of water is not uniform throughout—it may be 10 degrees warmer at the top of the water than at the bottom—it may be wise to have both a floating thermometer and a standing thermometer. Aeration helps to maintain an even temperature throughout the aquarium.

Do not use boiling water, or even very hot water, to clean the algae off a thermometer, or the thermometer will undoubtedly break. Aquarium thermometers are usually set between 50° and 100° F.; the temperature of boiling water is 212° F. To get the algae off, merely run some steel wool over it a few times and rinse it in some water that has a temperature in the tolerable range of the thermometer.

Most aquarium thermometers are accurate to within about 2 degrees. When comparing the temperature of two or more tanks, use the same thermometer and measure the temperature at the same depth of water.

Heat-sensitive resin strips are usually not very accurate in the long run.

Thermostats

Since the majority of tropical fish come from waters where the temperature is rather constantly above 75° F., you must see that the temperature of the water in your aquarium never drops below that point. A thermostat, composed of a bimetallic strip that bends backward and forward with each rise and fall of the temperature, will make this easy. This bending action can be utilized to make and break an electrical circuit. An electrical heater in the circuit will go on when the circuit is completed. As soon as the water in which the thermostat is located reaches a predetermined temperature, the bimetallic strip bends away from its contact and breaks the circuit, thus shutting off the heater. Almost all thermostats can be regulated by a set screw that moves closer or farther away from the bimetallic strip as it is turned. By regulating the distance from the screw to the strip, the temperature at which you want the thermostat to operate can be regulated. Most thermostats fail to operate because of corrosion on the point of contact between the thermostat and the set screw. It is advisable to check on this factor every few months. Sometimes it is good to run a nail file over the contacts to make sure that conducting surfaces are in contact. Of course, the thermostat has to be readjusted after such a treatment.

Many thermostats are located in the same unit as the heater. Thermostatic units which are located separately from the heater, besides being most advantageous, are usually most economical, since more than one heater can be operated from a single thermostatic unit. When operating such a system, it is advisable to use a thermostat in the smallest tank as far from the heater as possible, as smaller bodies of water are liable to more drastic temperature changes. When operating a great number of heaters from a single thermostatic unit, the wattage rating of the thermostat should be checked. Thermostats are all rated at the maximum safe load they can carry, and if overloaded they will burn out. When overloaded, the spark that jumps across from the bimetallic strip to the set screw will be so hot that it will actually weld the two units together. This can be most disastrous since the thermostat will not be able to turn off the heater and the fish will be cooked to death. To calculate whether the load on the thermostat is safe, add up the total wattage of the heaters and be sure that it does not add up greater than the wattage rating of the thermostat.

Many thermostats are built with condensers (capacitors) to eliminate static or interference in radio and television sets. These capacitors are easily added to any unit that does not already have one. They may be easily installed by placing them across the circuit at any point. If you are skeptical about your ability to make this minor adjustment, let your electronics man do it.

The quality of a thermostat can generally be determined by the material of which the points of contact are composed. Silver contacts are usually the only low-priced acceptable contacts.

Heaters

Closely allied to thermostats, as seen from the discussion above, are the heaters. These are essentially small electric coils enclosed in a conduction jacket. This jacket is usually made of Pyrex glass. The Pyrex glass test tubes make the best all around jackets.

It is of the utmost importance that no water be allowed to seep into the heater. If it does, it evaporates when the heater goes on; the water vapor then builds up great pressure in the closed container and is very liable to explode. The pressure is sometimes great enough to blow out the sides of an aquarium.

Of the different kinds of heaters, the submersible type is the most advantageous in principle, although it is most susceptible to explosion. (Should it fail to operate, take it back to the store, as the waterproofing is not guaranteed if the heater has been tampered with.) It heats the water at the bottom of the tank, thus allowing convection currents to heat the tank more evenly than if the surface of the water is heated. Make sure that the heater does not get buried in the sand. Stratification takes place when the top of the water is heated and the bottom is at a much lower temperature. This is a dangerous situation that jeopardizes the health of the fish in the aquarium. Many people advise the use of two heaters, one the regular immersion type, the other the submersible type. This tends to stabilize and equalize the temperature in the tank. Both heaters should operate from the same thermostat.

To calculate the wattage heater necessary for a given tank, allow 5 watts for every gallon of water to be heated. Thus, in a 10-gallon tank a 50-watt heater should be used. Should a lower wattage heater be used, there would be danger that the heater would not give off enough heat to raise the temperature to that required by the thermostat. This would mean that the heater would burn continuously, thus greatly reducing its life span. Using too powerful a heater is just as bad; it will go off and on every few seconds and probably burn out the thermostat.

When hanging an immersion-type, nonsubmersible heater in an aquarium, be sure that the heater is only as far in the water as will safely ensure against the admittance of water into the jacket. On the other hand the danger of having too much of the heater exposed to the air is apparent when you consider the conductivity of water as compared with that of air. Naturally the part exposed to air will get very hot since air is a very poor conductor of heat and will not cool the glass to any great degree; on the other hand the water will cool off the bottom part of the jacket, thus creating a drastic difference in temperature between the top of the jacket and the bottom. Most glass jackets would crack under the strain. If the heater has a built-in thermostat, the thermostatic unit will probably be located near the top of the heater. Again the consequences are apparent should the heater not be deep enough in the water.

Heaters are measured in watts. The higher the wattage, the more heat it can give off in a given period of time. The wattage you require is determined mathematically, taking into account such things as the lowest temperature in the room in which the aquarium is located, how large the tank is, and how well it is insulated. If the room temperature drops at night, you might consider protecting the sides, bottom, and back with thick styrofoam board. This will keep in the heat.

A 20-gallon aquarium kept at 78° requires a 100-watt heater if the room temperature doesn't drop below 73° F. If it drops to 68° then the wattage of the heater doubles to 200 watts.

Air Pumps

The advantages of aeration of water are twofold. First, it is helpful in ridding the water of the harmful carbon dioxide which, when allowed to accumulate, has such a detrimental effect on most fish. Second, it serves the very useful purpose of aiding in the circulation of the water, thus ensuring a more even distribution of heat.

The mechanism for the supply of air is the commercial air pump, of which several different types are available to the aquarist. In the piston type of pump, air is compressed and forced through the air lines, usually plastic tubing, to run the air stones or filters. The piston-type pump has two cycles, the compression stroke and the intake stroke. When the piston is pushed down into the cylinder, the air is compressed, thus the compression stroke. When the piston is raised up, it sucks in air by creating a vacuum in the cylinder. The cylinder is fitted with a valve that is closed during the compression stroke and open to admit air during the intake stroke.

Another type of pump is the vibrating-membrane type. A rubber membrane that vibrates quite rapidly takes the place of the cylinder-piston arrangement just described. Most of the vibrating-membrane type pumps have lower capacities than do the piston types. The rubber membranes need replacing after a period of six months to a year, and there is a definite air loss when slight cracks develop in the rubber membrane because of the incessant vibration. Most manufacturers have facilities for the replacement of these parts and it is the wisest policy to return the pumps to the manufacturer for adjustment and repair. The cost is usually trivial, so don't try to replace the membrane yourself!

The air pressure built up by most vibrating-membrane pumps runs between 3 and 6 pounds per square inch. Naturally, the greater the pressure the greater the number of outlets the pump can maintain.

In general, insofar as price alone is concerned, the cheaper pumps are vibrating-membrane types. The principal objection to this type of pump is the noise that it makes. It has the advantages of being cheaper to buy, cheaper to operate, and it is usually sufficient for two to three small tanks.

The proper arrangement of air stones, filters, and escape valve is most important in utilizing the full capacity of the pump.

It is sometimes very desirable to calculate the cost of

operation of a certain pump or other electrical appliance for a given period of time. This is easily accomplished merely by finding out the rate of electricity in your neighborhood.

The formula is as follows:

$$\text{Cost} = \frac{\text{wattage} \times \text{number of hours} \times \text{rate per kw hour}}{1000}$$

Not all appliances give the wattage. All, however, must give enough information so that wattage can be easily figured out.

$$\text{Wattage} = \text{Amperage} \times \text{Voltage}$$

$$\text{Amperage} \times \text{Ohms} = \text{Voltage}$$

Some things to look for in a good pump are: low wattage (less than 40 watts), a year's guarantee, easy to repair, easy to lubricate, static free (equipped with a condenser), beltless, replaceable rings for pistons (felt or leather being best), noiseless, and great output (in cubic inches of air).

Filters

Aside from aeration, filtration is the best aid to a "balanced" aquarium. Not only does it eliminate solid waste particles floating in the water but, with the use of activated charcoal, it helps to remove the harmful gases dissolved in the water. Filtration is also very useful in aiding the circulation of water.

The mechanics of filtration are easily understood. A

filter system is set up so that water is forced to pass through a straining device—usually filter floss or sand, or both—to remove solid debris, and then on through some activated charcoal to remove the dissolved gases.

The advantages of outside and inside filters are open to debate. About the only great advantage the inside filter has over the outside filter is that should the filter fall from the tank or develop a leak, the water will not continue to run out, as in the outside filter, until the siphon loses contact with the water. The inside filter, however, occupies more space than the outside filter, and will crowd the aquarium a little and be rather unsightly.

Cleaning of the sand and floss is easy. Merely run hot water over the sand for a few minutes to get all the dirt and debris out of it. The floss should be changed. To recharge the activated charcoal, you need only to cook it on the stove for 15 or 20 minutes. Filter stems and return stems should be cleaned periodically with a brush made just for this purpose.

Undergravel filtration, a principle that was responsible for a major boom in the aquarium hobby, was invented by Norman Hovlid. The Hovlid principle is in placing a flat plastic slotted tray under the gravel. The tray has about a one-fourth-inch space between it and the bottom of the aquarium. Water is drawn through the gravel by means of the filter and returned to the top of the aquarium.

The great advantage of this type of filtration is that there are no messy filters to be cleaned and floss to change.

Power Filters

The filter of choice for the larger aquarium (20 gallons+) is the power filter. This is a filter that pushes water directly through a filter medium by means of an impeller that is mounted on a round magnet and driven by another round magnet on the driveshaft end of an electric motor. Separating the motor and the impeller is a plastic wall that keeps the motor away from the water. There are many brands on the market. The one you should buy is the one your local dealer can service; service and spare parts are the deciding factors in which brand to get. Certain of these power filters have rather special filtering media, one of which is diatomaceous earth. These so-called "diatom filters" have proven to be very effective in keeping aquarium water very clean.

Water Changers

The single most valuable tool for the aquarist is the water changer. Invented by Merrill Cohen, Baltimore, Md., the water changer may have made the pump, heater, and filter almost obsolete. Here's how it works. You hook up the water changer to a dedicated water outlet. The outlet should enable hot water and cold water to mix in a single spout. By setting the proper temperature and drip, you can slowly add warm tap water to the aquarium. The proper flow is, naturally, determined by the size of your aquarium. Ideally, a 20-gallon aquarium should have 2 gallons of water change every day. You can estimate how to do this by measuring the amount of water coming through the water changer. A gallon jug should be used. Calculate the time it takes for the jug to be filled and that will be the standard for how long the water changer should be allowed to run. A 10% water change every day or two is ideal for almost all fishes. The water changer also removes the old water as the new water is added. Usually this fresh water, because it is slowly being mixed with old, established water, does not require chlorine neutralization.

Siphoning Tubes

As much of the debris—dead snails, feces, and un-eaten food—is usually too heavy to float or be suspended in the water, the filter will not be able to gather it up. The auxiliary tank cleaner to be used to remove this heavy debris is the siphon.

Originally, most siphons were constructed primarily for the removal of water, but recently new types of siphons have been placed on the market to siphon the dirt out of the tank. Special valves have been devised that allow for the picking up of the lighter debris without disturbing the heavier sand.

Those siphons, which are known as vacuum or dip tubes, work on the siphon principle but are not continuous. When you place your finger over the top of a straw and then put the straw deep into some water, you notice that the water rushes into the straw as soon as you release the finger from the top. This principle was utilized in constructing a widemouth "straw" to pick up bottom debris. Obviously the dip tube must be emptied after each insertion.

Fish Nets

This is one accessory that apparently seems rather insignificant to the average aquarist. Many people fail to realize the importance of using a proper-sized net to catch fish. Small nets make the actual capture of the fish more difficult, besides increasing the danger to the fish itself. It is much easier to damage a fish in a small net than in a large one. It is also much easier for a fish to jump out of a small net than from the larger, deeper size.

The correct size of net should be at least two inches longer than the fish. Widths run accordingly. If one net is all the budget allows, buy the largest practical. Even small guppies should be handled in 3-inch nets.

Most nets for tropical fish are made of Brussels net. Brussels net is a strong, porous material that makes excellent netting. The gauze netting, being more closely knit than Brussels, is usually used in the cheaper nets.

Nylon nets now have become popular. The only objection to them is that they do not allow the water to pass through very easily and thus they hinder the aquarist in the capture of fast-moving fish. Nylon nets are excellent for the capture of brine shrimp or small daphnia. Fry and daphnia nets are specially made of a very fine material.

As the frames of good nets are usually made of strong stainless wire, they always seem to outlast the netting. It is rather easy to cut out a piece of white cotton or purchase regular netting and construct a new net. However, nets are so inexpensive that it hardly pays to make one's own.

pH Test Kits

It is sometimes of the utmost importance to check the pH of the water. This is sometimes measured so accurately that a simple exposure to air will make a marked difference. That kind of calculation, however, is not necessary at all for the aquarist. You need only be interested in fluctuations of a unit or so. Neutral pH is 7.0. Acidity runs from 0 to 7.0; alkalinity runs from 7.0 to 14.0. The maximum tolerance for most tropical fish for any period of time is from about 6.0 to 8.0.

Certain indicators, such as bromthymol blue, litmus, and phenolphthalein, change color with a change in pH. These indicators can be so calibrated that by comparing the amount of change of any given dye—this comparison is usually accomplished by a color chart—you can tell the acidity or alkalinity of the water.

Chemicals are available separately or a complete pH test kit may be purchased. For more accurate measurements, electrical pH test meters are available.

Buffer solutions may be purchased to aid in the alteration and stabilization of the pH. Care should be exercised that the buffer does not harm the fish.

Your pet shop will certainly stock a variety of water test kits that are useful to aquarists. Many hobbyists consider that kits to measure water hardness and ammonia or nitrite level are essential for maintaining a successful aquarium.

Planting Tongs and Snips

Special tongs are available to assist in the planting of new vegetation after the tank is already set. These tongs are useful in deep tanks and in tanks where dangerous fish, such as the piranha, are kept. They should be so constructed that they will not damage the plants. They should also be rustproof.

Planting snips are used to trim plants. They are merely long-handled scissors. Again, they should be rustproof, as should every aquarium accessory.

Other Gadgets

Your pet shop will be able to help you with many other gadgets. Special aquarium glass cleaners and scrapers are available to remove algae from the front glass (leave it alone on the sides and back). Ornaments, plastic plants, automatic feeders, colored gravel, and colored lamps are just some of the many gadgets that make aquarium life a bit more interesting. Breeding traps, tank dividers, air valves, digital thermometers, and various chemical test kits are also available. If you

The automatic water changer is perhaps the most revolutionary gadget developed for the aquarium in the last 50 years. It aids filtering and makes tedious water changes unnecessary, as well as promoting breeding by many aquarium species.

are a scientifically oriented individual and are interested in the chemistry of your aquarium...or fish genetics...or just about any other aquarium subject, ask your pet shop about a book on the subject. There really are books on aquarium genetics, water chemistry, fish diseases, etc.

Chapter 10
Aquarium Genetics
by Dr. Myron Gordon

Genetics, the study of heredity, is playing an increasingly important role in agriculture and medicine. Although aquarists may be aware of the benefits that have resulted from the application of genetic principles to the breeding of farm animals, they probably have not considered that the same principles could be applied to their domesticated fish. Moreover, they may not know that many scientific investigations have already been made on inheritance in fish and that these studies have made fundamental contributions to the science of genetics. Fish fanciers themselves have benefited, too. For example, the popular black wag platy and swordtail and the bleeding-heart platy all resulted from the deliberate use of well-established genetic techniques.

Mendelian Laws of Inheritance in Aquarium Fish

The best way to understand the working of Mendelian laws of inheritance is to conduct a simple experiment yourself. Before keeping tropical fish became nationally popular, mice, rats, guinea pigs, and certain insects were universally used in these studies of heredity. Plants of many species were used, too; indeed,

Mendel himself discovered the laws of inheritance by study of the common pea.

The tropical fish keeper will be interested to know that some of his fish are excellent material for genetic work. Three species have been used with great success by geneticists (scientists who study inheritance phenomena), the medaka (*Oryzias latipes*), the guppy (*Poecilia reticulata*), and the platy (*Xiphophorus maculatus*).

The author's own work has been concerned with the platy. Since the platy is one of the most common of all tropical aquarium fish and the characteristics studied are quite distinct and easily recognizable, this species will be used to illustrate how the laws of Mendel operate. The reader is urged to set up similar matings, for it is amazing how much interest can be aroused from a personal investigation of these remarkable laws of nature.

A few precautions are of paramount importance for accurate work with viviparous fish. The female fish that are to be used for studies of inheritance must never have been mated before, because a female fish that has once mated carries the sperm of the male in her body for as long as six months. Both the males and females must come from pure breeding lines. For example, if you wish to cross a gold platy with a gray platy, the gold platy should come from a strain that produces gold platy offspring only. Similarly, the gray platy parent should come from a family of 100 per cent gray platy offspring.

Inheritance of Gray in the Platy

The simplest law of inheritance may be illustrated by mating a gray-colored platy with a common gold platy. Owing to the fact that the plain gray-colored platy is difficult to obtain from dealers because of its so-called uninteresting color pattern, the blue platy may be used; but pay no attention to the iridescent qualities or to the black blotch in front of the tail that may be present. These characteristics are also inherited, but success in the interpretation of the results of breedng experiments depends upon concentration of attention on *one* characteristic at a time. The restriction of study to *one* characteristic at a time was the key to success by Mendel over preceding plant and animal breeders. As experience is gained, two or more characteristics may be studied simultaneously.

The diagram illustrates the mating of a gray platy father with a gold platy mother. These are the *parental* fish and are referred to as *P*. Many gold sisters of the gold platy mother may be crossed with gray brothers of the father in order to get a large number of offspring. Since the accuracy of interpretation of results of breeding depends upon the number of each type that appears, it is fundamental to get large broods. Where one mating will not provide sufficient young, many similar matings should be set up.

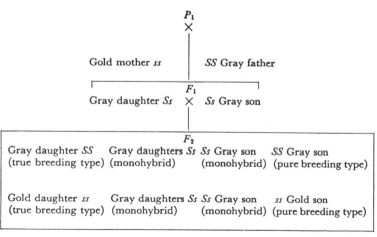

When a gray platy father is mated with a gold platy mother, it will be found that *all* the offspring will be gray platies. This means that the gray is *dominant* to gold. This, in turn, may be expressed as follows: gray (gold), where gold in the parentheses is represented but is temporarily suppressed by the presence of gray. Another way of expressing this same case is to let the capital letter S represent gray and the small letter s represent gold. The gray parent then is SS and the gold parent is ss, and their offspring become Ss. The offspring appear gray because S is *dominant* over s. The offspring, Ss, are indistinguishable visually from their father, SS.

The parental fish, it will be remembered, are referred to as P_1 and are symbolized as SS or ss. The fish resulting from this cross represent the first generation, or the first *filial* generation, and are referred to as F_1 and symbolized as Ss.

The first generation is represented by gray fish. It will be found that some of these fish will develop into males and others into females; the proportion of males to females will be approximately one to one.

If the first generation (F_1) gray females (Ss) are mated to their gray brothers (Ss), and if counts are kept as to the color of their offspring, it will be found that there will be approximately *three* gray fish to every *gold* one. These second-generation fish are referred to as F_2. If the F_2 fish are reared to sexual differentiation, it will be found that in the gray group 50 per cent of them are males and 50 per cent females. Similarly, in the gold group of the F_2 fish, the sex ratio, males to females, will be one is to one.

How did the ratio of *three to one* (three gray to one gold) appear in the number of the second generation, and what does it mean?

Before answering these questions, let us repeat the same experiment from the beginning but merely reverse the colors of the (P_1) parents. In other words, instead of using a gray father and a gold mother, let us mate a pure gold father with a pure gray mother. This is called the *"reciprocal"* cross. In this case, the gold father may be represented by the symbols *ss* (small *ss*) and the gray mother by *SS* (large *SS*).

From the diagram it will be seen that in this case *all* the offspring (F_1) are gray (*Ss*). When these grow up, it will be found that there are approximately as many males as females. When these F_1 *Ss* offspring are mated together and the offspring of the second generation are sorted, it will be discovered again that there are *three* gray fish to every gold *one*. Again, also, the sex ratios are one to one in each group. In other words, exactly the *same* results are obtained in the reciprocal cross as in the original one. This is of great significance.

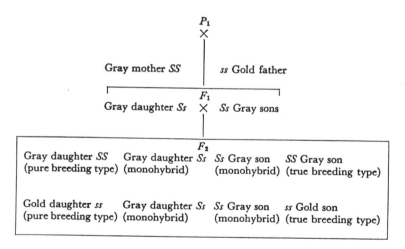

P_1
×

Gray mother *SS* | *ss* Gold father

F_1
Gray daughter *Ss* × *Ss* Gray sons

F_2

Gray daughter *SS* (pure breeding type)   Gray daughter *Ss* (monohybrid)   *Ss* Gray son (monohybrid)   *SS* Gray son (true breeding type)

Gold daughter *ss* (pure breeding type)   Gray daughter *Ss* (monohybrid)   *Ss* Gray son (monohybrid)   *ss* Gold son (true breeding type)

To answer the question as to the meaning of the *three to one* ratio and the significance of the similar results obtained in the original mating and its reciprocal, we must resort to the use of a few symbols and arrange them in a diagrammatic way to represent parent and offspring.

From the observations that direct and reciprocal crosses yield *similar* results, we may conclude that the offspring inherit equally from their paternal and maternal parents.

The symbols SS of the first cross indicate the hereditary constitution of the gray father and ss the hereditary constitution of the mother. The hereditary elements, the sperms of the males, each carry hereditary factor S in the single phase, and each egg of the mother carries the hereditary factor s in the single phase. At the time of mating, the s eggs become impregnated with S sperms—the fertilized egg Ss results, which hatches into a gray Ss fish. Similarly, in the reciprocal cross, the gray mother produces S eggs, and these are impregnated with s sperms; the result is an Ss offspring entirely similar to those produced in the original cross.

Now when brother and sister gray fish of the first generation are crossed, we may diagram the mating as follows:

$$Ss \left(\begin{matrix} \text{son} \\ \text{father} \end{matrix} \right) \times \left(\begin{matrix} \text{daughter} \\ \text{mother} \end{matrix} \right) Ss$$

The sperms of the father are of two kinds: S or s.

The eggs of the mother are of two kinds: S or s.

The sperm S may impregnate egg S, producing an SS individual which is *gray*.

The sperm S may impregnate egg s, producing an Ss individual which is also *gray*.

The sperm s may impregnate egg S, producing an Ss individual which is *gray*, again.

Finally, sperm s may impregnate egg s, producing an ss individual which is *gold* and occurs only once out of every four individuals.

The results may be summarized as follows:

P_1 father is gray, SS x mother is gold, ss. Fathers produce sperms of S constitution only. Mothers produce eggs of s constitution only.

F_1 sons are Ss, daughters are Ss. Sons produce

sperms, S or s, daughters produce eggs, S or s.

F_2 table of all possible combinations is as follows:

	F_1 Sperm, S	F_1 Sperm, s
F_1 Egg, S	F_2 SS, gray fish	F_2 Ss, gray fish
F_1 Egg, s	F_2 sS, gray fish	F_2 ss, Gold Platy

Summarizing, there are *three* gray platies, but one of them is SS and two of them are Ss.

There is *one* gold platy that is ss.

The SS type of gray can be distinguished from the Ss type, not by sight, but by a breeding test only. When an F_2 gray platy is mated to a gold platy and only gray fish are produced, we may conclude that the F_2 gray platy tested was pure, and its genetic formula may be written as SS and its offspring as Ss. When another F_2 gray platy is mated to a gold platy and two types of offspring result, namely, gray and gold, and these occur in equal numbers, then we must conclude that the F_2 gray parent was not pure and its genetic formula must have been Ss and its offspring were either Ss (gray) or SS (gold). By making this test, one can find out which are the *true breeding types*. After this preliminary testing, the pure breeding forms may be crossed to each other, and in this way *a true breeding line may be established*. The gold platy, being a recessive-type ss, is always pure. If gold platies are mated to gold platies, they cannot normally throw any other color. If they do, it is probably an exceptional sport or mutation.

In a genetic sense, the nontrue breeding type Ss is called a "hybrid," monohybrid, or "mongrel." The latter term has been dropped and "monohybrid" is used. The word "hybrid" as used here should not be confused with the word "hybrid" used in connection with results of crosses between different species, and indeed between different genera.

Inheritance of Black (Nigra) in the Platy

A different type of inheritance may be illustrated by mating the *black platy* with a *not-black* type of platy. The not-black type may either be a gold or gray platy. For simplicity, let us take the gray platy.

When a black platy father, P_1, is mated to a gray mother, P_1, the first generation offspring, F_1, will be all black like their black father. If these black sons are mated to their black sisters, it will be discovered that there will be *three* black fish in the F_2 (the second-generation) brood to *every non-black* or gray fish.

Concerning the *three-to-one* ratio obtained in the second generation from the mating of *black x nonblack*, it seems that this is the same as is found in the *gray x nongray* cross previously discussed. But the difference lies in the sex ratios shown. In the *gray x nongray* cross, there were males and females among the nongray fish of the second generation. In the *black x nonblack* cross, there are *only females* in the *nonblack fish group*. To compensate for the unisexuality of the nonblack fish, there are two males to every female in the black group of the second generation. This brings the sex ratio back to one to one.

Now if the reciprocal mating with the black and nonblack varieties of platies is made, namely, a *black mother* and a *nonblack father*, total dominance of the black pattern will *not* be exhibited in the brood of the first generation. If a black mother is mated with a gray father, one-half of the first generation will be black while the other half is nonblack. If the young are reared to sex recognition, it will be found that all the F_1 black fish are males and all the *nonblack fish are females*. In other words, the black pattern of the P_1 female parent has *"crisscrossed"* to her F_1 sons while the gray pattern of the P_1 father has crisscrossed to his daughters. This type of inheritance is known as *"sex-linked inheritance"* because a particular character is associated with a particular sex.

By mating an F_1 black son with its nonblack sister, also of the F_1 brood, an interesting brood appears. Again there are 50 per cent black offspring and 50 per cent nonblack offspring in F_2. In each group, however, both males and females appear in the black group and in the nonblack, or gray, group. This is, of course, different from the F_1 because in the F_1 males were black and females were nonblack.

In order to explain the results of inheritance of the black pattern in face of the different evidence for the inheritance of the gray pattern, we must resort to a modified form of diagram.

The *eggs* of the black female fish *are unlike* with respect to hereditary carriers of the black pattern. In other words, 50 per cent of the eggs elaborated by the black female carry the hereditary factor for black pattern and half of them do not. Those that do not carry the black-pattern factor are female-determining eggs while the other with the black-pattern factor are male-determining.

Suppose the two qualities of the black females are designated as Z and W, then the egg containing black-pattern factor may be written as Z_N (N for nigra or black pattern) and W_n may be used to designate the nonblack pattern and female-determining (small n for lack of nigra or black pattern).

Assume, also, that the sperms of the male platy are Z only, and since the male used in this cross is nonblack (black female x nonblack male), his formula will be $Z_n Z_n$ (small n's for lack of black).

Let us indicate what happens when a $Z_n Z_n$ male mates with a $Z_N W_n$ female.

	P_1 sperms, Z_n	
P_1 egg, Z_N	F_1 male, $Z_N Z_n$	= black males
P_1 egg, W_n	F_1 female, $W_n Z_n$	= nonblack females

A female black platy, *Xiphophorus maculatus*. Courtesy New York Zoological Society.

When an $F_1 Z_N Z_n$ black son is mated with a $Z_n W_n$ non-black daughter, the following recombinations are anticipated:

	F_1 sperm, Z_N	F_1 sperm, Z_n	
F_1 egg, Z_n	F_2 male, $Z_N Z_n$	F_2 male, $Z_n Z_n$	= black and nonblack males
F_1 egg, W_n	F_2 female, $W_n Z_N$	F_2 female, $W_n Z_n$	= black and nonblack females

From the knowledge of the mode of inheritance of the black pattern in the platy, it is possible to predict the sex of the young fish with great accuracy when certain types of crosses using this character are made. For instance, if a black female is mated with a not-black male (gold platy), it is to be expected that those fish which show the black pattern in the brood will later differentiate into males, while those that do not develop the black pattern will be females. Similar characters are present in fowl, and poultry husbandrymen use this knowledge of hereditary laws to cull out surplus males from their chicks.

Problem Suggested for the Reader

Above a solution has been attempted to be given to the problem of inheritance of gray (a simple Mendelian character) and black (a sex-linked character) and it has been indicated how many fish of each type appear in the first and second generation for each character. In addition, the probable sex ratio of each group was indicated.

Suppose, now, that both black and gray characters were present in one parent and none in the other. With the information already at hand, one should be able to trace, in advance of making the actual cross, the inheritance of both characters at the same time and indicate the frequency with which both characters appear in the offspring, the frequency with which either black or gray appears singly, and the frequency with which no character appears, the gold platy. Furthermore, the sex ratio for each group may be calculated in advance. Try to figure the results of the following two matings to the first and second generations:

1. Gold platy mother (not gray, not black) x gray-black father.

2. Black-gray mother x gold platy father (not gray, not black).

When you have finished your figuring, check your answer with the answer below.

Answer to Problem

When a gold platy mother (not gray, not black) is mated to a gray-black father platy, the results in the first generation (F_1) are: sons and daughters are black and gray.

In the second generation, the following proportions are expected (F_2):

SONS
6 black, gray
2 black only

DAUGHTERS
3 black, gray
1 black only
3 gray only
1 gold (not gray, not black)

When a black-gray platy mother is mated to a gold platy father (not black, not gray), the results in the first generation (F_1) are: sons are black and gray; daughters are gray only.

In the second generation, the following proportions are expected (F_2):

SONS
3 black, gray
1 black only
3 gray only
1 gold

DAUGHTERS
3 black, gray
1 black only
3 gray only
1 gold

Further Examples of How Fish Inherit

The results of mating the gold platy to the gray platy have already been illustrated. In this section examples will be given of what happens when other platies are crossed with the gold platy. Those to be so discussed are: the one-spot platy, the twin-spot platy, the crescent platy, and the moon platy.

If we study the inheritance of each pattern separately as indicated below, we see in each case the complete dominance of the pattern introduced. When the first-generation intervarietal hybrids are mated together, we get, in the second generation, three platies with a pattern to every gold platy (with no pattern).

MATING	FIRST GENERATION	SECOND GENERATION
1. One-spot x gold platy	all one-spot	3 one-spot, 1 gold
2. Twin-spot x gold platy	all twin-spot	3 twin-spot, 1 gold
3. Crescent x gold platy	all crescent	3 moon, 1 gold
4. Moon x gold platy	all moon	3 crescent, 1 gold

When two platies are mated, each having a singular pattern, the new platy combines the patterns of both its parents. For instance:

1. One-spot x twin-spot produces a *one-spot twin-spot* platy (it has three spots).

2. One-spot x crescent produces a *one-spot crescent* platy.

3. One-spot x moon produces a *one-spot moon* platy (*you have to look closely*).

4. Twin-spot x crescent produces a *twin-spot crescent* platy.

5. Twin-spot x moon produces a *twin-spot moon* platy.

6. Crescent x moon produces the celestial *crescent moon* platy.

Now let us see what happens when two platies are mated, each of which has two patterns. The results are surprising. Let us follow through the results when the domino-patterned one-spot twin-spot platy is crossed with the celestial crescent moon platy.

One-spot Twin-spot x Crescent Moon Platy

According to simple Mendelian principles we should expect to get 16 different types because there are four heritable patterns involved:

PLATY PATTERNS EXPECTED	PATTERNS OBTAINED
1. One-spot twin-spot crescent moon	none
2. One-spot twin-spot crescent	none
3. One-spot twin-spot moon	none
4. One-spot twin-spot	none
5. One-spot crescent moon	none
6. One-spot crescent	obtained, 25%
7. One-spot moon	obtained, 25%
8. One-spot	none
9. Twin-spot crescent moon	none
10. Twin-spot crescent	obtained, 25%
11. Twin-spot moon	obtained, 25%
12. Twin-spot	none
13. Crescent moon	none
14. Crescent	none
15. Moon	none
16. (Gold platy)	none

We expected 16 platy types, but we got only four of them; furthermore, of those that we did get, none has the exact combination that their parents had!

This is all very strange, and if you ask why it is that you do not get any other patterns except these four given immediately above, the answer is that the hereditary patterns one-spot, twin-spot, crescent, and moon belong to a common hereditary series technically called *"multiple allelomorphic series"*! The matter can be explained no further here.

One more point might be mentioned. The kind of inheritance that is treated here *(multiple allelomorphism)* was unknown to Mendel, that great discoverer of the fundamental principles of heredity. Someone has said that nothing new in heredity has been found since Mendel. This is not true. The science of genetics has gone far since Mendel. Even before Mendel, breeders did pioneer work. This Mendel freely admits in his reports. No one knows better than present-day workers the great contributions that Mendel had made. They honor Mendel and call him the "Father of Genetics." Mendel's theories are still fundamental. They have guided his disciples to make further progress and extend the original principles.

These varieties are common aquarium types. Cross them yourself and experience the thrill of testing a biological principle in your aquaria.

Discovery of the Gold Platy

Any gold miner will tell you that when you are lucky enough to discover gold you do not usually find that noble metal in a pure state. Often the run-of-the-mine ore is pretty poor stuff, for gold in nature has many baser physical and chemical associates. Refiners through various technical processes isolate the pure metal or combine gold with known quantities of other metals.

So with the gold platy. There are no *pure* gold platies in nature—or in the *rios* and *arroyos* of southern Mexico. Yet in every platy in Mexico there is the making of a gold platy. It can further be said (and the chances of its being right are good) that if you have platies in your aquarium, no matter what their superficial colors may be, and you may have the red or ruber, the blue or gray platy, your platies are in part gold platies. Most platies are gold platies, basically; the gold color of the masquerading platy is hidden by other pigment effects. Get rid of the reds and grays and black spots and you will have gold as a residue.

If, however, you have a white platy or an albino platy, you do not have a gold platy, but you have something far rarer. You may refer to your true white platy, quite appropriately, as the platinum platy.

When it was said, among other things, that the *ruber* platy is a gold platy plus a disguise, it was meant that the ruber platy is a gold platy plus a red platy plus a black-spotted platy plus a gray platy. In other words, the ruber platy is a composite of four distinct color varieties, each of which may be, and has been, isolated or, to use a technological term in gold mining, "refined." The metallurgist's technique of purification is by means of chemical and physical analyses. The fish fancier's technique is selection, appropriate mating, and inbreeding.

If there are no *pure* gold platies in Mexico's streams, where did the first *pure* gold platy come from? From what strain of platy was it isolated? After it was obtained, how was it multiplied to produce the pure race of true-breeding gold platies?

Let us review, hastily, a few suggestions on some of these points in four early American aquarium encyclopedias. They say that the first true gold platy appeared ready-made as a sport about 1920 in an aquarium of a German fish fancier. Upon this point there is inspiring accord, for witness these quotations:

Stoye—"The Gold Platy is a sport...a variation that occurs unexpected in nature."

Mann—"The Gold Platy is a sport...a freak of nature."

Uhlig—"The Gold Platy is a color mutation....It just happened in the aquarium of a fancier who...appreciated it and 'fixed' it."

Peters—"A sport in nature is a sudden departure from the typical form of color....The Gold Platy was such a sport....Just what method was used in the propagation is not known."

As you see, they say that the gold platy is a sport but its genealogy is unknown.

The First Gold Platy

The first question: Where did the first gold platy appear?

Herr Otto Struve, a German fish fancier, produced it first in a pure form and named it about 1920. In his paper published in 1920 he promised to tell us how he developed the gold platy, but, alas, nothing more was ever said. Herr Sachs tried to come to his rescue, two years later, and made many suggestions relying upon some experimental work on permanent color changes in other animals, but his ideas cannot be regarded as very plausible in the light of modern work in biology. While Herr Struve does not say how he got his gold platies, he drops a hint that turns out to be most significant. He says that a man had described a *golden* platy, lightly spotted with black, in the *Wochenschrift* in 1916 and again in 1918. This clue is too good to be passed up. The description of these is found to have been written by Herr Friedr. Kammerzell; here is a brief abstract of the salient points of his very illuminating notes:

"A brown platy female with black spotted sides [*braun mit schwarzer Seitenzeichnung*]" gave birth to some unusually marked and colored animals. The ground color of the new adult fish was *yellowish red and they were marked with black spots*. When young, the new platies were pale yellow and fairly transparent; the black spots, which were to develop in a decided manner later, were barely visible. Since, to his knowledge, the female had been with no platy male, Kammerzell thought these unusual golden young were the product of hybridization with some other species. Later he gives up the idea.

The brown, black-spotted female platy that Kammerzell described as the mother of the yellow brood was undoubtedly what we now know as the old-fashioned ruber platy, in which the males are brilliant red but the females are dull red.

Kammerzell related sadly his experiences with the golden, black-spotted platies. He lost his original brood of golden platies owing to the difficulties of getting fuel during the winter while the war was going on. He was elated when another female, in 1918, produced a brood of *"twenty young among which I found five which showed that striking gold color."* Again these golden platies were black-spotted. This ratio of *one* golden ruber to *three* normal rubers is the hereditary clue that will eventually solve the problem of the gold platy's origin. But no help in its solution comes from Herr Kammerzell directly. Herr Kammerzell whets our appetite for an explanation of these unusual platy goings-on by saying that he plans "to show how a normally colored parent may produce young which in part exhibit totally dissimilar color." But, sad to relate, he, like Struve, fails to appear with the story.

Two important facts are gleaned from the reports of Kammerzell and Struve: the first *gold-like platy* appeared in the Kammerzell Brothers' aquaria not later than 1916. The first *true gold platy* was reported by Herr Struve in 1920. The Kammerzell gold platies were black-spotted; Struve's platies were *not* spotted. Are these phases of the gold platy (one spotted, the other nonspotted) related? If it can be shown that they are then this and one other link in the hereditary chain, when properly arranged, should solve the problem of the origin of the pure gold platies. One link will join the old-fashioned ruber platy to the golden rubers of Kammerzell. The second link will join the golden rubers to the pure gold platies of Struve.

The First Link: The Ruber to Golden Ruber

There seems to be no question about the fact that Kammerzell's golden ruber platies were derived from the old-fashioned ruber, for even Kammerzell's 1918 papter is entitled: *"Ueber Gelbfärbung (Xanthorismus) bei Platypoecilus maculatus rote Varietät."* He says his *"rote Varietät"* is black-spotted.

How was it possible for Kammerzell to have obtained five golden rubers in a brood of 20? Some may suggest that these five golden rubers were sports. But sports rarely, if ever, occur in 25 per cent of the brood. They are probably the first visible result of a sport to the gold far back in their ruber platy family tree. It is as if we were witnessing a *première* performance of a play of the five golden platies. We know that the golden platies must have existed before in rehearsal, but they were hidden from our view and we did not see them until the opening night.

Because there were five golden rubers to 15 normal gray rubers in the show under Kammerzell's tent, the hereditary spotlight (the three-to-one ratio) focuses attention on one of the *grandparents* of these five golden rubers. These five golden rubers are merely the actors making their initial bow. The author of the play goes back two generations. The golden actors owe everything to their grandfather ruber who was given gold-developing qualities by a stroke of nature. Some call it "sporting" or "mutating" to the gold. Touched to gold by nature, this grandfather ruber platy was, nevertheless, unable to display its inheritance, for two gold elements are necessary before a platy can be gold-colored.

This grandfather ruber platy passed on its potential gold-developing power to its offspring. Throughout the lifetime of these young, too, the display of gold was withheld from public view, for while one-half of the young rubers inherited one gold-developing element from their father, none of them had the two gold elements necessary for the complete development of a gold costume.

The *première* performance of the gold act, in the formal dress of gold, takes place when the second generation appears. One-fourth of the young have managed to collect two golden hereditary elements and have stepped forward into the public gaze for the first time in glittering costumes of gold. Those satisfied with superficialities would bestow glory on the first five golden ruber actors, but those who know give the credit to their creator, their grandfather ruber. Plain though he appeared, it was he who led his tribe along the golden path.

The origin of the golden rubers may be told in a more matter-of-fact way. A sport to the gold occurred in a ruber platy, one of the grandparents of Kammerzell's golden ruber platies. This mutation to the gold in the ruber platy affected one of the pair of hereditary color factors which governs the development of small black pigment cells that make the fish look gray. The effect of this mutation to the gold in the grandfather ruber platy was not revealed because the other and normal color factor of the gray-gold pair remained constant. The consequences of this mutation in the grandfather ruber affected the ruber's breeding performance but not its appearance. When mated to a normal ruber, the gold sport grandfather ruber spread the new hereditary color factor gold (lack of gray pigment cells) to many (just half) of its offspring, but at this point his sons and daughters of the first generation were no different from the usual ruber in appearance.

When, by pure chance, two gold-carrying rubers of the first generation, each of which carries one gold factor, mate there is opportunity for two gold factors (one from each parent) to combine, and a gold offspring is born in the second generation. As a matter of chance, if two such gold-carrying rubers mate, there will be among their offspring *one* gold platy to every *three* normal ones. This briefly sets up a hypothetical case which gives us results similar to those reported by Kammerzell.

The Second Link: Golden Ruber to Gold Platy

How can we get a pure gold platy of the Struve type from the golden rubers of Kammerzell? Wait for another sport? This is not necessary. Mate the golden, spotted ruber of the Kammerzell type to a gray platy. The gray platy has *no* large black spots and *no* red body color. If a golden ruber female is mated to a gray male as stated, normal-looking ruber males with spots and gray-looking females without spots appear. It looks as if the gold standard-bearers desert their colors. This is more apparent than real, for note what happens.

When the normal-looking gray daughters mate with their normal-looking ruber brothers, quite an array of variously colored platies appears. Each type of platy appears in a definite numerical ratio; among every three graylike platies there is one goldlike platy; and for every golden ruber there is one pure gold platy.

The color types of platies line up in this manner:
FEMALES
3 ruber (gray and spotted)
1 golden ruber (spotted)
3 gray
1 pure gold

MALES
3 ruber (gray and spotted)
1 golden ruber (spotted)

3 gray
1 pure gold

By selecting the pure-gold females and males and mating them, it is easy to get a pure breeding line of gold platies. This part of the story is not a description of a theoretical setup; experiments similar to these have been performed time after time. No claim is made that Struve deliberately obtained his gold platies in the manner described. It is entirely possible that, by sheer chance, unbeknown to Struve, a series of matings such as outlined above led to the establishment of the pure-gold line.

Struve insists that his gold platies did not descend from ruber platies because *his gold platies throw only gold-colored young.* This is not good reasoning. His gold platies breed true because the gold platy is a recessive in inheritance. It hides nothing; it cannot produce anything else when mated to its own type.

Here, then, are the questions asked and their answers:

Q. Where did the first pure gold platy appear?

A. It appeared in the aquarium of Herr Otto Struve not later than 1920.

Q. What were the ancestors of the pure gold platy?

A. The old-fashioned ruber produced the Kammerzell golden ruber. The golden ruber, when mated to a gray platy, produced the pure gold platies in the second generation.

Q. How was the pure gold platy strain established?

A. It was established by inbreeding the gold platies.

Black Lace for the Gold Platy

This story begins in a small stream hidden in the hot, mite-infested jungles of Mexico's southern state of Oaxaca and stops, for the present, in the tanks behind the counters of any pet shop in New York.

According to reports from a tropical-fish exhibit held by the Aquarium Society of New York at the American Museum of Natural History in the early 1940's and from statements of sales from tropical fish dealers all over the United States and Canada, the golden wagtail platy, an old favorite in a dazzling new costume, had climbed close to first place in the popular demand as a toy fish for the home aquarium by 1943. Yet only three years before, one of the grandparents of these colorful, home-bred and reared aquarium fish was the wild, gray, undistinguished platy that abounds by the thousands in the arroyos and lagoons of the southern states of Mexico.

Within a few fish generations, by a system of careful selection and scientific breeding, the olive-drab body color of the wild platy has been transformed to bright gold, and each fin of the wild specimens, which was colorless, has been darkened to produce the effect of an old-fashioned black-ribbed lace fan. The sharp contrast of dull black on bright gold in the golden wagtail platyfish is particularly appealing, for rarely is this striking color scheme seen in fish.

The wagtail platies are fine living examples of what cordial Pan-American cooperation may produce, for they are the direct result of mating a wild Mexican platy with the domesticated gold platy that was perfected in the United States.

With the consent of the Mexican government and the generosity of the John Simon Guggenheim Memorial Foundation of New York, an expedition was organized with the cooperation of the New York Aquarium in 1939 for the purpose of studying the freshwater fish of the Atlantic coastal rivers of Mexico.

Large collections, particularly of the platy, were made for special studies that have been going on for many

214

years in connection with the problems of species origins and cancerous growths. Altogether, we collected more than 8,000 specimens, and when they were classified, we found some 135 different color types among them. This proves, we believe, that the southern platy, *Xiphophorus maculatus*, is North America's most variable wild vertebrate with respect to color patterns. Yet in none of these patterns was there anything that remotely resembled the wagtails of today. Among them was a variety that was distinguished from others by a black line on the upper and lower margin of the tail. The rest of the tail was transparent, as were all the other fins. We called this color type "the comet." A number of these together with a larger assortment of other types of platies were shipped 4,000 miles north to our Aquarium laboratories.

The comet platy at the Aquarium was subjected to a routine breeding test to see whether its pattern was inherited or whether it was just a chance variation that occasionally appears and then disappears without leaving any living representative to carry on the type. The test was simple. A wild platy with the comet markings was mated with another platy without them. We found that their offspring all had the comet pattern. When these offspring were mated together, they produced three fish with the comet pattern to every plain type. This indicated to us clearly that the comet was inherited.

Then a comet platy of our original wild stock was mated to the plain gold platy, a strain that has been domesticated for a long time, the first of which appeared about 1920. When their young were born, one could easily see that the gray body color of the wild platy was dominant, for all the young were gray. Later, as the gray hybrids developed, their tails became darker and darker. And when they were about half an inch long, the other fins darkened, too. These were the first black wagtails, so named because of their wagging black tails.

Among our domesticated animals, the color scheme of the Siamese cat is comparable to that of the gray wagtail platy because its feet, tail, and snout are so much darker than its body; so are, to a lesser degree, the dilute fawn breed of the Great Dane dog and the Hampshire Down sheep. But above all others, the Himalayan rabbit and the giant panda, with their strong contrast of jet black extremities on a snow-white body, appealed to us as being the most attractive. So we used them as models in designing a somewhat similar costume for the platy.

Since we already had the gray wagtails, a plan to produce a black-finned and black-snouted gold platy was easily worked out. All we had to do was to mate the gray wagtails to each other, or mate them back to the pure gold platy. We did both. In the first instance, we obtained the anticipated golden wagtails once in about every seven young, or, to be exact, nine in every 64. In the second case, we obtained the predicted and desired type once in every eight offspring. Later, when these black-finned gold platies were isolated and mated to each other, some bred true to type. Others produced a number of comets; these were throwbacks, indicating the wagtail's ancestral origin, the wild comet-marked platy.

The golden wagtails have turned out to be so popular that fish breeders have used them to improve other varieties. Thus, now you can buy red platies with black fins; even the related swordtail has been dressed up in black tails, gloves, and socks. But the golden wagtail remains the key type and the most popular. Besides its sharply contrasting color scheme, there is another feature, the peculiar markings of its head, which enhances its attractiveness. The upper and lower margins of its jaws are outlined in black, and the black trim runs along the lower lines of its gill covers. It looks like a golden harlequin wearing a black mask. The golden wagtail is an amusing fish to watch in the aquarium. It has the rare trick of exciting one's sense of humor.

Back to Their Ancestors

If a number of fancy breeds of an animal or of a plant be turned loose to mate at random, such a mixed population will tend to revert, in time, to its common ancestral type. Charles Darwin noticed this phenomenon in the free-living pigeons in the parks of London and described it in *The Variation of Animals and Plants Under Domestication.*

Any person strolling in a park and observing the variously colored pigeons that come fluttering down to pick up crumbs along the paths may perceive this phenomenon of nature, for these wild flocks are under the control of no man. They appear to be a conglomerate stock made up of escaped birds from many lofts. A few pigeons are off-color, mottled black and white, or red and white; some are predominantly red, others deep blue, but the majority is like its ancestral type, the wild blue rock pigeon, *Columba livia.*

In the days before Gregor Johann Mendel, plant and animal breeders were puzzled by the appearance of "throwbacks" to the ancestral type. Now these are explained in terms of ordinary Mendelian inheritance. The reappearance of ancestral traits is usually brought about by the reunion of hereditary characters that had become separated during the period of their domestication.

Reversions in Plants and Animals

The plant breeder may obtain the original type of the sweet pea that is still found wild in Sicily by crossing the bush and cupid varieties. By crossing two different white-flowering sweet pea stocks the horticulturist may recreate plants having the wild purple flowers. The corn breeder, by mating two different stocks of dwarfs, can produce a plant normal in height. A rabbit fancier, by crossing the yellow rabbit with the Himalayan breed, may reestablish the wild agouti color.

According to Shisan C. Chen, the wild goldfish (*Carassius auratus*) was first domesticated in China during the Sung Dynasty (A.D. 960-1278). Today goldfish revert to their ancestral olive-green color so persistently that commercial breeders of the fancier color types find small pickings in any given brood. However, the case for reversion in the goldfish is not complete, for many in a brood that are olive-green when young, if kept alive sufficiently long, eventually display the fancy colors of their breed.

Reversion at the Aquarium

A clear-cut example of complete color reversion in a tropical fish appeared at the New York Aquarium when a bright golden swordtail was mated with an almost white, pink-eyed albino. The mating of these two light-colored domesticated swordtail breeds produced the dark, olive-green, wild type, similar to those still found in the jungle streams of southern Mexico.

The wild swordtails were imported into Europe for the first time in 1909, yet during a relatively short period of domestication a remarkably large number of color varieties were developed. The golden and the albino are but two out of dozens of strains.

The ancestral olive-green color is really a mosaic pattern of two kinds of tiny pigment-carrying cells, the blacks and the yellows. There are thousands of them in the skin of a swordtail. For example, the area occupied by a single scale may have 20 black cells and almost as many yellow ones.

The Golden Swordtail

The golden swordtail owes its distinctive color pattern to the fact that it has lost all but a few black cells, but retains, in full force, all the yellow ones. It is like the quick-change artist in an old-time vaudeville show who sheds one coat to reveal a more brilliant one beneath.

This change from the wild to the golden, from a full complement of many tiny black pigment cells to a rare few, may be expressed this way: The hereditary factor *St* representing the *stippling* effect of the small black cells in the normal wild swordtail mutated from *St* to *st*, from the dominant phase to the recessive, from the olive-green phase to the golden. This must have taken place prior to 1921 for in that year Krasper, an aquarist, first described the golden sport. Later, another aquarist, Hildebrand, pointed out that in one mating the wild swordtail was dominant over the golden. In 1934, the author showed in a series of genetic tests that the golden character in the swordtail was definitely recessive and was typically Mendelian. This has since been confirmed by Kosswig.

The golden sport indicates a breakdown in the swordtail's ability to produce black pigment cells at a normal rate. What this failure is we do not know for certain. We do know that the machinery for black pigment formation does not break down completely because the golden swordtail has black eyes and a few black cells along its back, but these are so few that they do not diminish its vivid yellow color. It may be that the golden swordtail fails to produce sufficient raw material in the color cells for normal pigmentation to develop. It may also be that the chemical constitution of the cell is different, so that the melanin reactions are not carried to completion.

Pink-eyed Albinos

The albino, with its white body and pink eyes, appeared suddenly about 1934. A few of them were discovered in aquaria containing ordinary black-eyed olive-green swordtails. Curiously, these mutants appeared almost simultaneously in American and in European aquaria. Once the albinos were detected and isolated, they were easily perpetuated by inbreeding. Like albinism in other animals, this character is usually recessive. Critical studies proving this were made by Kosswig and they have been confirmed by the author's experiments.

The albino mutation brought about the almost complete elimination of the black pigment cells normally present in the skin, in the retina of the eyes, and in many other areas of the body. The albino's eyes appear pink in the swordtail not because of any special red pigment, but because, as in pink-eyed albino amphibians, birds, and mammals, the clear lens of the eye transmits the color of the blood as seen through the many transparent blood vessels in the retina. The albino mutation involved a second hereditary factor influencing black pigment. In this instance, a dominant factor I representing the wild type mutated to the recessive i phase. The factor i stops practically all the machinery responsible for the production of black pigment. With the i factor in control, there may be an abundance of raw material for black-pigment production provided by the hereditary factor St, but none can be converted.

Wild Equals Golden Plus Albino

When a golden swordtail is mated with an albino, the wild, fully pigmented swordtail is re-created because each variety brings to its offspring the essential dominant factor which the other lacks.

From their golden parent, the wild olive-green swordtail offspring inherit the machinery (I), and from the albino swordtail they obtain plenty of raw materials (St) for the normal large-scale production of black pigment cells.

This may be expressed in a diagram:

Golden X Albino = Wild, Olive-Green
stst II X StSt ii = Stst Ii

The wild-colored offspring of the golden and albino parents, after being mated brother to sister, are producing, out of every 16 born, nine young that are typically wild, three that are golden, and four that are albinos. One of every four albinos must be a double recessive, but as yet they cannot be distinguished from the ordinary albinos. They may eventually turn out to be a more attractive variety; perhaps a superblond swordtail will emerge.

Use for the Albinos

Whether or not the albinos will be attractive is not particularly important. But they are extremely useful in current genetic studies of melanomas that develop in fish hybrids when the albino swordtail and the spotted or black-banded platy are mated. Breider and Kosswig have shown that when a black-banded hybrid is back-crossed to an albino swordtail and their black offspring are back-crossed again to the albino, some of the young of the last mating develop tumors without black pigment. With the cooperation of Fred Flathman of Woodhaven, Long Island, we have succeeded in obtaining fish hybrids with black tumors in the first generation and colorless tumors in the offspring of the second generation. Melanomas that are white instead of black are biological anomalies.

The ordinary albino swordtails transmit micromelanophores (the technical name of the small black pigment cells) to their hybrids, just as they transmit these same cells to their own wild, olive-green-colored young of their own species. With the development of the strain of double-recessive albinos, it will be possible to eliminate the micromelanophores that are regarded as nonessential for tumor production; thus, pathologically, the study of the colorless melanomas can be simplified. More emphasis will be placed upon the large black pigment cells, the macromelanophores, brought to the hybrid by the spotted platy. Under the influence of the albino factor, i, it appears that macromelanophores, just as the micromelanophores, cannot elaborate melanin pigment, yet the large colorless pigment cells may still be able to evoke colorless melanomas in the fish hybrids.

Practically nothing is known about the inheritance of melanomas in man, the mouse, or the horse; still less is known about human colorless melanomas. Melanoma studies with fish should be of value in interpreting the development of these neoplastic diseases in the more specialized vertebrates, including man.

In the tissue-culture laboratory of the Department of Biology of the Washington Square College, biologists were successful in growing, for the first time, tiny fragments of fish melanomas in a medium composed of fish serum and chick-embryo extract. They compared the cell types that emerged from the fish-melanoma fragment with the cells that emerged from fragments of mouse and human melanoma previously studied. They found that the cell types, the melanoblasts, the melanin-bearing macrophages, and the fibrocytes, in fish, in mice, and in men were identical in structure.

Conclusions

The mating of the golden swordtail with the albino was conducted as a routine study of inheritance in fish, a subject of which comparatively little is known. Reversion to the ancestral color pattern was demonstrated. The double-recessive albinos obtained as a by-product of this study will be of great value in explaining the curious pathological anomaly, colorless melanomas.

For more information on both the general background of inheritance in fish and the problems associated with developing and maintaining certain patterns in aquarium fish, see the book *Genetics for the Aquarist* by Dr. J. Schroder (T.F.H. PS-656).

Chapter 11
The Balanced Aquarium Myth
by James W. Atz

The idea that the animals and plants of an aquarium balance each other in their production and consumption of carbon dioxide and oxygen was a little over one hundred years old when it was proven wrong. Although it was disproved by 1930, the myth of the balanced aquarium still holds sway—in the tropical fish fancy, in the schoolroom, and in the laboratory. Such is the power of the too felicitous phrase, the too trim theory.

Joseph Priestley was the first to demonstrate the reciprocal action of plants and animals on the atmosphere when he showed that a limited amount of air in which rats were smothered would again support more of them after green plants had remained in it for a time. In 1777 he also reported that fish affect the water in which they live in the same way that terrestrial animals affect the air surrounding them, although he apparently had not availed himself of Robert Boyle's experiments, performed a century earlier. In 1670 Boyle showed that a fish breathes air dissolved in water, since it dies when its container is placed in a chamber from which most of the air is exhausted by a vacuum pump or when its glass, "quite filled with water," is "so closely stoppered" that it "cannot enjoy the benefit of air."

Priestly paved the way for the fundamental work of Ingenhousz, de Saussure, and Senebier on plant physiology and of Lavoisier on the chemistry of animal respiration. Thus, by the first decade of the nineteenth century it was well established that plants, like animals, respire, taking in oxygen and giving off carbon dioxide, but that in the presence of strong enough light this function is far overbalanced by the assimilative one, later called "photosynthesis," in which carbon dioxide and water are consumed and oxygen released.

It is believed today that almost all the oxygen in our atmosphere results from the photosynthesis of plants, so the savants of Priestley's time were not incorrect in emphasizing the far-reaching importance of this plant-animal relationship. But they gave to it a teleological twist, using it to illustrate the marvelous goodness of the world in which man lives. Sir John Pringle, President of the Royal Society in 1773, declared:

From these discoveries we are assured that no vegetable grows in vain, but that from the oak of the forest to the grass of the field, every individual plant is serviceable to mankind; if not always distinguished by some private virtue, yet making a part of the whole which cleanses and purifies our atmosphere. In this the fragrant rose and deadly nightshade cooperate: nor is the herbage, nor the woods that flourish in the most remote and unpeopled regions unprofitable to us, nor we to them; considering how constantly the winds convey to them our vitiated air, for our relief, and for their nourishment.

This florid vein continued on into the cynical twentieth century, when J. E. Taylor wrote, in 1901, that

every teacher in physical geography now imparts to his class that the oxygen generated in the virgin forests of the Amazon valley may be brought by the wind to bring health to the fetid streets and alleys of crowded European cities, and that in return the carbonic acid breathed forth from our overpopulated towns may be carried on the "wings of the wind," to be eventually absorbed by the incalculable stomata which crowd the under surfaces of the leaves in the same forest-clad region!

These were the compost mixers for our myth; they prepared each successive generation with successively more fertile minds for its seeding and growth. Who, preoccupied with the world-wide implications of the balance between plants and animals, could suspect that so insignificant a part of the earth as a home aquarium would not conform?

The first aquarium: where and when was it devised? The word itself was not used to indicate a container of water with aquatic animals living in it until 1852; but before that, who was the first to keep fish captive in some small, water-containing receptacle? As far back as 2500 B.C., the Sumerians kept living fish for food. The ancient Romans had pet moray eels and mullet, while the Chinese domesticated the carp more than two thousand years ago and the goldfish in their Sung Dynasty (960-1278), but all these fish were maintained in pools or ponds. There is evidence, however, that in some places in China goldfish were kept indoors in porcelain vessels during the winter months. Perhaps these were the first aquaria, although we cannot be sure.

If we consider the aquarium properly to be only a

glass or glass-sided water container, we can fix its origins a little more definitely. The earliest record of putting fish into glass containers comes down to us from the Romans of the first century. They did not do this to keep the fish alive, however, but to watch their change of color as they died.

The maintenance of fish in small glasses was still noteworthy enough in 1746 to warrant the publication of Fellow William Arderon's letter on the "keeping of small fish in glass jars" in the *Philosophical Transactions* of the Royal Society of London; yet this was certainly not the first attempt to do so. According to Boyle, Guillaume Rondelet, a Renaissance student of aquatic life who died in 1566, once claimed that his wife had kept a fish alive in a glass of water for three years. Samuel Pepys, indefatigable recorder of minutiae, made the following entry in his diary on May 28, 1665: "Thence home and to see my Lady Pen, where my wife and I were shown a fine rarity: of fishes kept in a glass of water, that will live so for ever; and finely marked they are, being foreign."

But the keeping of fish as pets did not become a popular pastime until after the goldfish was widely introduced into England during the first half of the eighteenth century. At first they were maintained in ponds on the lands of the well-to-do. Sir John Hawkins, noted editor of Izaak Walton and Charles Cotton, wrote in 1760: "There has also been lately brought hither from *China,* those beautiful creatures Gold and Silver Fish....These fish are usually kept in ponds, basins and small reservoirs of water, to which they are a delightful ornament; and I have known a few of them kept for years in a large glass vessel like a punch-bowl...." In the second and third editions of *The Compleat Angler* which he edited, dated 1766 and 1775 respectively, the above footnote was repeated, but in the fourth edition, printed in 1784, Hawkins saw fit to alter it, stating that "it is now a very common practice to keep them in a large glass vessel like a punch-bowl...." The Reverend Gilbert White corroborates Hawkins in Letter LIV of *The Natural History of Selborne*, based on an entry from his Journal dated October 27, 1782: "When I happen to visit a family where gold and silver fishes are kept in a glass bowl, I am always pleased with the occurrence, because it offers me an opportunity of observing the activities and propensities of those beings with whom we can be little acquainted in their natural state."

If we accept this evidence at face value, we can declare that between 1775 and 1784 the goldfish bowl became a popular household appliance in England.

The elements of our myth were now at hand; it only remained for someone to apply the principle of plant-animal balance to an aquarium by growing aquatic plants in it.

Looking at the matter in historical perspective, one is not impressed by the ingenuity of the idea or surprised that a number of people claimed to have stumbled upon it independently and more or less at the same time. The wonder is, perhaps, why no one hit upon it before. For it was not until after 1840 that aquarists began to employ aquatic plants in their tanks. Moreover, it was a French invertebrate zoologist, Charles des Moulins, who first claimed to have discovered that the presence of green plants in small containers of water kept that medium suitable indefinitely for small animals (planarians in this instance) and who attributed this effect to the physiology of the plants. Charles des Moulins was President of the Linnaean Society of Bordeaux, and he reported his experiments in the *Actes* of that organization in 1830.

Credit for the earliest clear enunciation of the benefits resulting from the interactions between aquatic plants and fish should, however, go to the author of the chemistry textbook, William Thomas Brande. As early as 1821, his *Manual of Chemistry* stated: "Fishes breathe air which is dissolved in water; they therefore soon deprive it of its oxygen, the place of which is supplied by carbonic acid; this is in many instances decomposed by aquatic vegetables, which restore oxygen and absorb the carbon; hence the advantage of cultivating growing vegetables in artificial fish-ponds." That this information should appear in a book on chemistry makes one wonder if it were not common knowledge among fish culturists of the time, but a search of the literature has failed to reveal even an allusion to it.

Perhaps this disjunction of knowledge explains why the five or six amateur and professional biologists who at this time came upon the idea of using plants to "purify" their aquaria each claimed to be the originator of it and why they quarreled (albeit genteelly) as to who was the first among them to do so.

One of them, Robert Warington, later said that it was Brande's statement that had incited him to set up his experimental tank with goldfish and tape grass (*Vallisneria*). Warington was a chemist himself, and his was the first unequivocal exposition of the conception of mutual interdependence of the plants and animals in a small container of water. Both des Moulins and George Johnston, who had worked with sea water, marine animals, and seaweed previous to 1842, had been somewhat vague in their writings. Not so Warington. His paper, read before the Chemical Society of London early in 1850, is perfectly clear and could be used today as a summation of what practically all teachers, most aquarists, and many professional biologists believe:

Thus we have that admirable balance sustained between the

animal and vegetable kingdoms, and that in a liquid element. The fish, in its respiration, consumes the oxygen held in solution by the water as atmospheric air; furnishes carbonic acid; feeds on the insects and young snails; and excretes material well adapted as a rich food to the plant and well fitted for its luxuriant growth.

The plant, by its respiration, consumes the carbonic acid produced by the fish, appropriating the carbon to the construction of its tissues and fibre, and liberates the oxygen in its gaseous state to sustain the healthy functions of the animal life, at the same time it feeds on the rejected matter which has fulfilled its purposes in the nourishment of the fish...

The key word was "balance," and it appears in the writings of N. B. Ward, Philip Henry Gosse, Edwin Lankester, and Mrs. Anne Thynne, co-claimants for the honor of first applying the oxygen-carbon dioxide interactions of plants and animals to small aquaria. Probably the first to set up a tank containing both fish and plants with the idea of balancing one against the other was Nathaniel Bagshaw Ward, an English botanist who originated the Wardian Case, that glass-sided box with ferns and other plants growing inside it so often seen in latter nineteenth-century parlors. Whether it was this miniature greenhouse (admittedly not airtight) that gave Ward the idea for setting up his aquarium in 1842 was never made clear. At any rate, Ward did not publish an account of his work until 1852. Ward was apparently indirectly responsible for the first public aquarium. His tank inspired a Mr. Bowerbank to set up one of his own, and this in turn gave David W. Mitchell, Secretary of the Zoological Society of London, the idea of an exhibit made up of a series of such tanks. This took form in Regent's Park as the Fish House, which was opened to the public in the spring of 1853 and consisted of a number of standing aquaria, some with fresh, some with salt water, housed in a conservatory-like building.

Judging from the remarks of the times, the exhibition was a tremendous success. Moreover, it stimulated the hobby of keeping fish as pets at home so much that the maintenance of small aquaria became more or less of a craze. Dealers in tanks and aquatic plants and animals established themselves in London and Edinburgh. Prices for a readymade home aquarium ranged from two shillings to ten pounds. The experience of one J. Paul was perhaps typical: "I saw the aquarium first at the Regent's Park Gardens," he wrote, "then in a shop-window in the City Road, and then—everywhere; and I at once determined to be the happy possessor of a tank. Alas," he continued, somewhat ruefully, "I knew not the penalty attendant on this worship of Neptune."

Punch poked fun at the fancy in its issue of December 13, 1856:

Oh, come with me,
And you shall see
My beautiful Aquarium;
Or if that word
You call absurd,
We'll say instead Vivarium.

'Tis a glass case,
In fluid space,
Where, over pebbles weedy,
Small fishes play:
Now do not say
You think they must be seedy...

My Dicky sings,
And claps his wings,
I know that what he wishes

Is to escape
His cage, and scrape
Acquaintance with the fishes.

Now tell me, do,
Suppose that you
Your mode of life could vary;
Which would you like?
To be my Pike?
Or to be my Canary?

By 1858, at least nine books on the keeping of aquaria had been published in London, and an encyclopedia of 1854 included an article on the subject. In all these and in various newspaper and magazine articles, too, the idea of balance between the aquarium's plants and animals was stressed. Our myth was now firmly fixed in the common knowledge; a host of amateur aquarists practiced its precepts daily, and they and their friends saw living proof of it each time they looked into a tank.

There was living disproof of it to be seen also, but this was either overlooked or reasoned away. For many years previous, fish had been successfully maintained in bowls and tanks without any plant life in their water. How did that fit into the scheme? In 1856, Shirley Hibberd expressed the view taken by aquarists on this matter:

The Philosophy of the Aquarium must be clearly understood....It is a self-supporting, self-renovating collection, in which the various influences of animal and vegetable life balance each other and maintain within the vessel a correspondence of action which preserves the whole. A mere globe of fish is not an aquarium in the sense here indicated; because to preserve the fish for any length of time, the water must be frequently changed....

And yet hundreds of aquarists before and since have kept fish in tanks without plants and without changing the water for months on end. Hibberd himself kept a tank of goldfish with no plants and without changing the water for seven years. He explained this by attributing the oxygenation of the water to microscopic and algal growths. He wrote that, although it may take some time for a tank

to become richly clothed with suitable oxygen makers, some supply of oxygen is secured from the very first, for I have seen ciliated spores and beginnings of genuine vegetable deposits within a few hours of the first furnishing of a tank. Hence it was that...I did not hesitate to introduce the fishes as soon as the tank was furnished, without waiting for the full development of the microscopic forest, for I knew that before the fishes exhausted the oxygen in the fresh river water, there would be the beginning of a new supply for them, and there was never any distress through that procedure.

Since fish can live in a newly set up tank without any apparent plants at all—either introduced or grown *in situ*—there must be enough unseen ones present to oxygenate the water, else the fish would die! The reasoning was fallacious but somehow the facts had to be made to fit the belief.

Conclusive proof of the falsity of Hibberd's assertions was given when it was shown that fish could live as long as four months under axenic conditions, that is, in vessels and water not only free of all higher plants and algae but absolutely free of all demonstrable bacteria and other microorganisms.

In addition, it has always been well known that at night or on dull days plants consume oxygen and give off carbon dioxide just as animals do. How did fish survive such periods in an aquarium? Was it by breathing oxygen that had been stored up in the water while the plants were producing it? No aquarist ever said so, but this was implied in some of their works. A little thought on the properties of oxygen dissolved in water would have shown this to be impossible. Some concepts are simply too good to discard, even if they are untrue; the balanced aquarium is one of them.

Proof that the balanced aquarium existed only in the minds of its devotees and an uncritical public was published in *Copeia* in 1931 by Charles M. Breder, Jr., at that time Research Associate at the old New York Aquarium in Battery Park. His proof that "the production of oxygen by the photosynthesis of plants in open balanced aquaria contributes little, if any, to that consumed by the animal life therein" was obtained most directly—simply by *measuring* the amount of oxygen present under different conditions. No one had ever bothered to do this before, and Breder found that as far as oxygen was concerned, an "over or under saturation returns with extreme rapidity to equilibria" with the air above the water. In other words, the water is practically never under or oversaturated with dissolved oxygen. As soon as the slightest deficiency in oxygen exists in a tank, oxygen from the atmosphere passes into solution to make it up. Similarly, if an excess is produced by plants under the influence of bright light, this quickly passes off into the air.

In fact, one might say: Just try to keep oxygen out! Research workers in fish physiology sometimes want to determine exactly how much oxygen a fish consumes, and to do this, they must measure the oxygen in a *sealed* container of water before and after a fish has lived in it. The problem is to get a seal that will keep out the atmospheric oxygen during the course of the experiment.

Even 1½ inches of heavy mineral oil floated on the top of an aquarium's water will not entirely keep out atmospheric oxygen from above, when the fish begin to use up the gas already dissolved in the water below. Scientists have had to design some complicated apparatus to circumvent this difficulty.

Despite this omnipresence of oxygen, every aquarist has at one time or another seen his fish gather at the surface of their tank, "gaping." What makes them come to the top, breathing rapidly, seeming to be in some sort of respiratory distress? Not a lack of oxygen, but an excess of carbon dioxide. Compared with oxygen, this gas passes from the water into the air and from the atmosphere into solution much more sluggishly. Consequently, when an excess amount of it appears in an aquarium, it takes an appreciable length of time for it to pass off. On the other hand, Dr. Breder found that in tanks where plants were actively engaged in photosynthesis—building up carbohydrates out of water and carbon dioxide and giving off oxygen—the carbon dioxide remained far below its equilibrium level with the atmosphere for extended periods.

Plants, then, can and do make an aquarium more habitable for aquatic animals by using up the carbon dioxide that the latter produce—carbon dioxide which, as Dr. Breder put it, is "the limiting factor as regards the respiratory gases." If plants were at work all the time, a tank containing them could support more animals than one without. But at night or on dark days, when they cannot carry on photosynthesis, plants breathe like animals, adding their share of suffocating carbon dioxide to the water. They breathe, of course, in bright light, too, but then their respiration is far outweighed by their photosynthetic activity, and they consume far more carbon dioxide than they produce. Without bright light, however, the presence of plants in a tank theoretically lessens the number of fish that the tank will support. Contrary to general belief, putting plants into an aquarium does not make it possible to keep more fish in it without suffocation taking place.

It has long been known that carbon dioxide in excess can kill fish or man. Both amateur and professional ichthyologists, however, have usually neglected the effects of this gas, assuming that oxygen alone was concerned with the respiration of fish. Whether or not a fish will be asphyxiated depends on the concentrations of both oxygen and carbon dioxide dissolved in the water. The more carbon dioxide present, the greater must be the concentration of oxygen to prevent asphyxiation. The principal reason for this seems to be that small amounts of carbon dioxide increase the efficiency with which the blood of a number of fish can deliver life-sustaining oxygen to the tissues but at the same time sharply decrease the ability of the blood to take on oxygen at the gills. Physiologists call this an "exaggerated Bohr effect."

The extent to which this effect operates in fish varies greatly from species to species. Trout, several characins, and a number of marine fish have been demonstrated to be quite sensitive to carbon dioxide. Carp, goldfish, and various armored catfish show less sensitivity, and the common bullhead shows hardly any at all. As would be expected, those species known by aquarists and fish culturists to be most easily asphyxiated are the ones whose blood is most affected by carbon dioxide.

It is possible for a fish to be unable to utilize oxygen that is present in ordinarily ample quantities all about it simply because there is too much carbon dioxide present. This must be the physiological explanation why carbon dioxide, and not oxygen, is the critical respiratory gas in an aquarium. As Dr. Breder discovered, there is always sufficient oxygen present, but carbon dioxide may build up to relatively high concentrations, since it is a slow-moving gas and can be produced by the respiration of the tank's inhabitants at a faster rate than it can escape through the water surface. The fish will then be starved for oxygen even though there is plenty of it around, because they cannot utilize it in the presence of excessive amounts of carbon dioxide.

The reason the aquarist gets along so well, even while working under the wrong premise, is that he is doing the right thing—for the wrong reason. For example, when he aerates his tank's water or circulates it, he is not introducing more oxygen, as he usually believes, but facilitating the escape of carbon dioxide.

"A vessel of water containing plants and animals must be looked upon as a little world," wrote Edwin Lankester in 1856. We can now just as categorically state that it must *not* be so considered. Although the physiology of plants and animals in an aquarium is identical with the physiology of those in the world at large, the part they play in the ecology, or bionomics, of their tank is quite different from that taken by the sum total of all life in the earth's grand economy. In this sense, an aquarium is not at all a microcosm but merely a part of a macrocosm—part of a larger world from which it cannot be either physically or ideally separated. No balance could be expected to exist in such an open system. Looked at logically, the idea of a balanced aquarium, as far as respiratory gases are concerned, seems baseless. But then, most myths never made a pretense of being logical.

Does the balanced aquarium exist in any sense whatsoever? Most certainly, so far as the chemistry of the water is concerned. In a well-established freshwater standing aquarium the water remains crystal clear and in a relatively static chemical state. This stability, or balance, can be most clearly brought out by comparing

No matter how many plants you put in your tank, they will never "balance" the oxygen and carbon dioxide levels in the water.

marine and freshwater aquaria. Sea water in which animals are living continuously deteriorates in its ability to support life. That is the principal reason marine aquaria are so much more difficult to maintain than freshwater ones.

Chapter 12
How the Cardinal Tetra Got Its Name

As one goes through life, one often glances backward into time and wonders what would have happened should things have worked out differently. One of my favorite subjects for reminiscence is the story of the cardinal tetra, *Paracheirodon axelrodi*. For me it is a fascinating story; for you, the casual reader, it might shed some light into the workings of a scientist, how fishes get their names, and the interesting associations that develop between colleagues.

Unquestionably, the cardinal tetra is the most colorful of all freshwater aquarium fishes. It is imported from Brazil and Colombia in huge quantities, perhaps up to 40,000,000 per year, and quite likely that makes it the most imported of all aquarium fishes.

The story of the cardinal tetra started when I came back from Korea in 1952. While teaching at N.Y.U., I opened a fish shop in New York and soon became interested in importing fishes directly from Southeast Asia and South America. In those days the only economical manner of fish transportation was to charter the refrigerated, insulated rooms in trans-oceanic ships which normally carried bananas and other perishable foods. These rooms were then fitted with heating, air conditioning and racks to hold wooden containers of fish. The wooden containers were lined with plastic bags. Air compressors supplied air to the wooden aquaria, and tight-fitting lids kept the water and fish in the aquarium during stormy periods. As the ship left, say Singapore or Hong Kong, with its loads of fishes, I would cable the next stop, alerting the local fish people that I was coming in and that I had fishes to sell; in many cases I traded for other fishes. This kept up until I landed in New York usually about 7 weeks after I left Singapore. The key to success in this operation was in getting enough fish together at the initial point so the boat could be loaded within a 24-hour period. I usually had 500 wooden boxes of fish, each with at least 1,000 *Rasbora heteromorpha,* and lots of boxes with kuhli loaches, chocolate gouramis, *Belontia signata,* barbs, etc.

When I got to New York I would usually trade with Fred Cochu of Paramount Aquarium...one *Rasbora heteromorpha* for one neon tetra in order to have a greater variety to offer for sale. It was then that I decided to try to break the monopoly that Fred had on discus and neons.

In 1952 there were two names that were making history in the tropical fish business: Fred Cochu and Auguste Rabaut. At that time Cochu and Rabaut traveled the world to collect all the rare aquarium fishes, bringing back boatloads of *Rasbora* from Singapore and discusfish and neons from South America. Cochu owned the world-famous Paramount Aquarium in Ardsley, New York, while Rabaut was a collector who bought fish for Cochu, eventually going into business for himself with his son-in-law. This mistake in judgment resulted in his departure from tropical fish collecting.

It was in 1955 that I made my first trip to Brazil to try to find the discusfish, which was imported only by Cochu at that time. After tracing the range of the various species of discusfishes in the literature, I discovered that they all came from the Amazon River and its tributaries. A map and a call to the airlines indicated that Belem do Para, Brazil, was the place to stop to begin my search. So, laden with nets, tin cans for holding and shipping the fish and $400, I landed in Belem. It didn't take me long to find out that the nearest discusfish was a thousand miles away and that even if I could get there I would not be allowed to take the fish out of Brazil, since I didn't have a permit. At that time the Goeldi Museum was in charge of all fish exports from Brazil, and I was told that Fred Cochu had the exclusive license to export Brazilian fishes. This exclusive license was given to Cochu because of his extraordinary courage and skill in discovering many new fishes deep in the jungle, his training of local natives on how to collect and ship them to a central point, and for his fearless journeys into wild, uncharted jungle where many white men simply disappeared.

I sold my tin cans to the Museu Goeldi and took a river boat up-river to Manaus. I could hardly imagine how discusfishes could live in such muddy, filthy water anyway, so at Manaus I joined another boat which made its way into the black but clear and clean Rio Negro water. The boat journey lasted about three days out of Manaus, and we stopped along the way to take on wood (for the wood-burning steam engine of the boat) and to transfer passengers and cargo. I well remember how we all slept in hammocks, with every inch of space occupied at night by the hammocks slung in every direction, one atop the other, making the slightest movement a cause of irritation to several neighbors. The loud snoring drowned out the usually incessant drone of the steam engine.

We landed at a very small town with the Indian name of Tapurucuara, and I was quite happy to get off the boat and look for a hotel. There were none! Where could I sleep? Where could I find a place to sling my hammock? "Try the church," I was advised. So off to the church I went; as my luck would have it, the priest spoke German (so do I) and he was a fish hobbyist of sorts!!

"Yes," he said, "there are discusfish near here. But we also have neon tetras!"

"Where are they?" I asked.

"Everywhere around here. Wherever there is shade; wherever they can escape from other fishes that might eat them. Come, I'll show you. There are some only a few yards from the church."

We walked out onto the shore of a Rio Negro tributary which the local people called an *igarapé*. This *igarapé*, or creek, held water that hardly moved and was only a foot or two deep. Lifting his cassock, the German priest didn't bother to remove his sandals as he walked gently into the water. Of course I followed him, sneakers and all, and got my pants wet, too.

"Stand quietly. Don't move, and look carefully into the water and you will see neon tetras."

I stared hard but couldn't see a thing. It took some time until I could focus my gaze at something moving. Finally I determined that the moving thing was a small school of about 20 fishes; it wasn't until they crossed my sneakers that their magnificent red and blue bodies offset against the white sneakers made the neon tetras recognizable.

"Can I catch some, Father?" I asked.

"Why not buy them from the boys? The boys have small hand nets and they can capture them for you." With that, he called to a group of 10-year-olds who were busy doing nothing and explained to them in a strange language (*lingua geral*) what he wanted.

"How much must I pay them, Father?" I asked, thinking about my rapidly diminishing bankroll.

"They agree to catch 100 fishes for you for a price of one cent. Can I tell them to catch 1,000 neon tetras and that you will pay them a dime?"

"Of course," I magnanimously agreed, quite relieved that the whole project was well within my budget. "Come, Father, let's look for other fishes."

"First, let's have some coffee. Come to the church and I'll ask one of the girls to prepare us some *cafe zinho*."

I watched in awe as a small girl pounded some coffee beans into a pulp, put them into an old stocking, added some hot water and, using two sticks, rolled the stocking tightly, forcing the water out into a large old tin can which was to serve as our coffee pot. I took my coffee black, but the priest added at least 8 tablespoons of sugar to the coffee, then some evaporated milk. We sat down in comfortable but crude chairs and talked about fishes, the weather and his job. The priest was a fat old man who was quite devoted to the Catholic Church, but he seemed to be more interested in bringing financial aid to the miserably poor Indians in his area than in saving their souls! His primary function as he saw it was to keep the poor natives alive and healthy, rather than trying to have them adjust to some of the unrealistic (for the Indians) church rites.

In a few moments the boys came to the door and announced they had collected some fishes. I eagerly inspected my purchase, and even though there were only about 100 neon tetras out of the 1,000 fishes (the rest were small tetras with shiny lines on their sides), they were the largest neons I had ever seen.

I was able to get most of them back alive. After leaving what I thought at that time was Porto Velho, I headed home. I was writing a book with the famed Dr. Leonard P. Schultz, then Curator of Fishes at the Smithsonian Institution, and when I got back I sent him some of the neon tetras which had died in the tank of Sol Kessler. Sol had bought the fish from me. Dr. Schultz excitedly called me a few days later to announce that these were not neon tetras at all. They were a new species!

Coincidentally with this development, the German priest also was friendly with the people at Paramount Aquarium, and he passed the word along innocently that I was collecting giant neons. Paramount started collecting these same fishes and they sent some to William Innes, who sent them to Dr. George Myers. Innes was at that time my "competitor." He owned the *Aquarium* magazine, which was the foremost magazine at that time, and he published his famous book on tropical fishes. Further, the neon tetra had been named in his honor by Dr. George Myers as *Hyphessobrycon innesi*.

Myers published the description of the new "giant neon" in a four-page issue of the *Stanford Ichthyological Bulletin* without illustrating the fish, also in the same month as the *TFH* magazine description by Dr. Schultz. The fact that it would take *TFH* a minimum of 30 days to produce and distribute its magazine and that it might take but a few hours to print the four-page issue of the *Stanford Bulletin* tends to indicate a little bit of strategy to beat Schultz to the punch with a name. But Myers was too late when he wrote that the new fish "is a very close relative of *H. innesi* Myers and to place it in a different genus would do violence to the obvious relationships." This proved prophetic as both *H. innesi* and *H. axelrodi* are now put in one genus, *Paracheiro-don*. Myers called the fish *Hyphessobrycon cardinalis*, while Schultz called it *Cheirodon axelrodi*.

Aquarists were confused at this turn of events and they appealed to the International Commission on Zoological Nomenclature in London for a decision as to which was the correct name. The actual vote was 19 votes in favor of the Schultz paper; 5 votes in favor of the Myers paper; one abstention.

These documents are presented in this book to show you exactly how these things work.

Subsequently, I discovered the neon tetra in one other river in Brazil, the Rio Purus, and I found the cardinal tetra once again, but this time in Colombia in the Rio Meta area.

You can imagine the big hit this fish was making and how everybody who was interested in fish breeding tried to be the first to breed the new fish, now officially known as *Paracheirodon axelrodi*, with the popular name of "cardinal tetra." *TFH* magazine offered a reward of $50 for the first person to spawn the fish and send us documentary evidence that he did. The winner was Prof. Dr. C. W. Emmens at the University of Sydney in Australia.

A few years later still another fish in the "neon" group was discovered. This fish was named *Hyphesso-brycon simulans* by Gery. It is probably a mimic of *Para-cheirodon axelrodi*, with which it is sympatric; that is, it is found in the same area. (It is probable that *innesi* was a mimic of *Paracheirodon axelrodi* also, many years ago.) Dr. Gery described this mimic in 1963 and gave it the name *simulans*.

Scientists spend most of their time studying dead fishes, and when comparing these three neons aquarists are immediately impressed with their **similarity** and not their **difference**. To have these three neon tetras, that is, fishes with electric blue stripes and deep red bellies, in three different genera seems wrong. They are much too similar in size, shape, and, most importantly, behavior. This was recently recognized when one of the more live-fish-oriented scientists, Dr. Stanley H. Weitzman, in cooperation with Dr. William L. Fink, proposed placing all three known neon tetras into the genus *Paracheirodon*.

How the Cardinal Tetra Got Its Name

On February 15, 1956, Dr. Schultz wrote to me that the neon tetra I had sent him was a new species which he named *"Cheirodon axelrodi."* His letter was published in the March-April, 1956 issue of *Tropical Fish Hobbyist*, as follows:

"Dear Mr. Axelrod:

The two little characins you sent me are a gorgeous species referable to the subfamily Cheirodontinae and to the genus *Cheirodon*. It is indeed an exquisitely colored species and should be one of the popular favorites for aquarists.

As I have told you many times, characins are notoriously difficult to identify and this one was no exception. Because of the small size, detailed observations of characters must be made under the microscope. The following characters placed these 2 specimens in the genus *Cheirodon*, (1) teeth in both jaws in a single series and similar in shape, (2) distal edges of teeth "multicuspid" or with 5 cusps, a large central one and 2 smaller ones on each side, (3) 1 or 2, probably 2, teeth on maxillary, (4) teeth in neither jaw forming a continuous cutting edge, (5) lateral line incomplete, with 5 or 6 pores, (6) adipose fin present, (7) caudal fin scaled basally, (8) origin of dorsal fin equidistant between tip of snout and base of caudal fin, (9) origin of anal fin slightly behind a vertical line through the rear of base of dorsal fin, (10) gill membranes free from isthmus and attached far forward, (11) midline of belly rounded and covered with scales, not trenchant.

This scarlet characin as defined above should be referred to the genus *Cheirodon* as broadly defined by the late Dr. Eigenmann and by work in progress by Dr. Böhlke of the Academy of Natural Sciences of Philadelphia. However, in reviewing the literature available to me I am unable to find any species in that genus or a closely related genus that fits these 2 scarlet colored specimens. Therefore, I conclude that it represents an undescribed species and since you have been so kind as to send it to me for scientific study and to the U.S. National Museum for permanent preservation, I am pleased to name it in your honor.

CHEIRODON AXELRODI, new species

The holotype bears USNM 164483 and the paratype USNM 164484. They measure 22 and 20.5mm. respectively, from snout tip to base of caudal fin, and came from near Porto Velho, Brazil [really Tapurucuara— HRA].

The following counts were made on the two specimens: Dorsal rays ii,9 and ii,9 ; anal iii,17 and iii,17; pectoral i,9 -i,9 and i,10; scales from upper edge of gill opening to base of caudal fin 31 and 32; pores in lateral line 5 and 5 possibly 6 on one side; scales in a row from dorsal origin to midventral line just in front of anal origin 10 and 10; predorsal scales 10 and 10; prepelvic scales 10 and 10; teeth on premaxillaries 5-5 and 5-5; gill rakers on holotype 7 + 11.

The proportional measurements are: Head 3.6 and 3.4; greatest depth 3.4 and 3.3; length of caudal peduncle 6.0, all in the standard length. Eye 2.6 and 2.7; snout 4.1 and 4.1; interorbital space 3.8 and 4.0; tip of snout to rear end of maxillary 2.6 and 2.8; least depth of caudal peduncle 2.9 and 3.0; length of caudal peduncle 1.9 and 1.8, all in head length.

Pectoral fins reach almost opposite pelvic insertion; pelvics do not reach quite to anal origin; dorsal origin equidistant between tip of snout and midbase of caudal fins; anal origin equidistant between rear edge of pectoral base and midbase of caudal fin; second suborbital expanded to cover area from eye to preopercle below eye; third and fourth suborbitals not quite touching the preopercular edge.

Coloration consists of a brownish back and upper sides with the lower half of the fish bright red including the caudal and anal fins; dorsal surface of the head behind orbits dark brown; a narrow wedge-shaped dark pigment streak on preorbital area, adipose fin with dark pigment.

The two type specimens upon dissection were found to be fully mature females. I am unable to find the usual glandular scales on the caudal fin base nor do the peduncular "spines" appear to be present along the dorsal or ventral edges of the caudal peduncle, characters usually found only in males.

This species differs from all other members of the genus in having the lower half of the body, along with the caudal and anal fins, bright red. There is no dark caudal spot, nor a dark shoulder spot, and the dorsal fin is plain in color.

Dr. Eigenmann (*Mem. Carnegie Mus.* Vol. 7, pp. 64-83, 1915) revised the genus *Cheirodon* and summarized the then known knowledge about the species referable to the genus. Among the species listed by Eigenmann the following have more than 32 scales: *parahybae* Eigenmann; *interruptus* (Jenyns); *monodon* Cope; *ibicuhensis* Fowler; *madeirae* Eigenmann; *microdon* Eigenmann and *stenodon* Eigenmann. *C. pisculus* Girard and *C. annae* McAtee with only 12 to 15 anal rays differ strikingly from *Cheirodon axelrodi*. *C. notomelas* Eigenmann, *C. insignis* Steindachner, *C.piaba* Lutken, *C. microdon* Eigenmann and *C. stenodon* Eigenmann all differ from *C. axelrodi* in having a black caudal spot. *C. leuciscus* Ahl with 32 to 35 scales and 7 to 9 pores in the lateral line along with a grayish green coloration differs from this new *Cheirodon*. *C. jaguaribensis* Fowler by having only 8 teeth on the premaxillaries, none on the maxillary, along with a deeper body 2.4 to 2.5 in standard length, differs from *C. axelrodi*. *C. macropterus* Fowler by having iii,19 to iii, 23 anal rays differs from *C. axelrodi* which has only iii,17. *Cheirodon kriegi* Schindler is described without teeth on the maxillary and with a strong caudal spot, whereas *C. axelrodi* has 1 or 2 maxillary teeth and no caudal spot. *Cheirodon meinkeni* Ahl, in having the following characters, 17 (iii,14) to 19 (iii, 16) anal rays, 35 scales along the side 12 or 13 in a crossrow and a caudal spot, also differs from this new species.

Fowler (*Os peixes de água do Brasil*, Arquivos Zool. Sao Paulo Vol. 6, pp. 181, 185, 1948) lists 2 other species of *Cheirodon*. Dr. Böhlke kindly examined the types of *Cheirodon troemneri* Fowler and *C. pallidifrons* Fowler and reports they do not belong to the genus *Cheirodon*.

As time goes on I shall keep this new species in mind and check on it further. There may be a species of *Cheirodon* unknown to me at this moment that is close to this new one but if so it is not listed in our usual bibliographic sources."

By this time Fred Cochu heard about the new fish and had already organized their collection in quantity. He brought in these fish by the thousands and called them "cardinal tetras." The name stuck even though Dr. Schultz suggested the common name of "scarlet characin" in his original description of the fish. Of course I was thrilled to have the fish named *Cheirodon axelrodi*...the first fish named after me.

STANFORD
ICHTHYOLOGICAL BULLETIN

Published by the

NATURAL HISTORY MUSEUM OF STANFORD UNIVERSITY

All communications concerning purchase or exchange of this publication should be addressed to the Director, Natural History Museum, Stanford University, Stanford, California. Remittances should be made payable to Stanford University.

| Volume 7 | February 21, 1956 | Number 1 |

TWO NEW BRAZILIAN FRESH-WATER FISHES

By George S. Myers and Stanley H. Weitzman

FAMILY CHARACIDAE

Hyphessobrycon cardinalis, new species

TYPES: Holotype SU 48710, standard length 22.5 mm, from the Rio Negro, Amazonas, Brazil, received from Paramount Aquarium through Dr. William T. Innes. Paratypes, standard length 19.5-21.5 mm, two lots with the same data: 8 specimens in alcohol (SU 48711) and 2 stained in alizarin and cleared in glycerine (SU 48712).

This species is very similar in color, proportions, scale counts and dorsal fin-ray counts to *H. innesi* Myers (1936, Proc. Biol. Soc. Washington, vol. 49, pp. 97-98), the neon tetra, found in the Leticia-Tabatinga region, but differs greatly in the structure of the teeth and jaws; also the anal and pectoral fin-ray counts appear significantly different. A photograph of living specimens of this fish appeared in The Aquarium, 1956, vol. 25, no. 2, p. 41, under the name of "cardinal tetra." In the following description the first numbers given refer to the holotype, the second (in parentheses) to the paratypes, and the third [in brackets] to five specimens of *H. innesi*: SU 47055, one specimen, from the "upper Amazon"; SU 48714, 2 aquarium specimens; and SU 48715, 2 cleared and stained aquarium specimens. All other data unless otherwise stated refer to the specimens of *H. cardinalis*.

DESCRIPTION: Dorsal ii,9 (ii,9)[ii,9]. Dorsal insertion from tip of snout 1.88 (1.93-2.02)[1.85-1.90] in standard length. Anal iii,16 (iii,16-17)[iii,19-20] total count, last ray divided to its base. Anal origin behind last dorsal ray. Anal margin concave; anterior lobe 1.2 in head in holotype. Pectorals i,10 (i,10)[i,11-12]. Pelvics i,7 (i,7)[i,7] reaching to origin of anal in both species. Adipose fin present. Principal caudal rays 10/9 in both species. Caudal naked. Scales in a lateral series 33 (32-33)[32]. Lateral line scales 6 (4-6) [4-5]. Predorsal scales 9 (9) [9]. Gill rakers (stained specimens) (5+11-5+12)[5+10-5+11]. Head 3.7 (3.35-3.90)[3.36-3.42] and depth 3.22 (3.42-3.50)[3.18-3.34] in standard length. Eye 2.40 (2.36-2.47)[2.30-2.75] and least depth of caudal peduncle 3.04 (2.70-2.84)[2.76-3.00] in head. Interorbital 1.56 (1.46-1.57) [1.38-1.70] and snout 1.78 (1.75-1.84)[1-45-1.70] in eye. Great orbital (third orbital bone) rather reduced in size, with a naked border between it

[1]

d the preopercle. Occipital process bordered by 2.5 scales in both
ecies, its length about equal to diameter of pupil. Premaxillary with a
ngle row of 5 broad, penticuspid teeth, the central cusp the largest.
xillary with 1 or 2 tri- or quadricuspid teeth. Dentary with 4-5 large
nticuspid teeth and 2-3 small tri- to monocuspid teeth. Total number of
ntary teeth in cleared specimens 7-8.

COLOR (in alcohol): A dark silvery band (emerald to blue in life) above
dline, extending from snout to upper part of caudal peduncle. Humeral
ot indistinct; no caudal spot. Dorsum dark with centers of scales light.
tire body below silvery band light (red in life) except for a few scat-
red melanophores along base of caudal peduncle and around mouth. Fins
ther clear, but distal parts of first four or five rays with scattered
lanophores. Lobe of anal with a rather dark area distally.

Hyphessobrycon cardinalis differs from *H. innesi* most significantly in
oth structure and arrangement. All the jaw teeth of *innesi* are tricuspid
xcept the few small ones in the lower jaw), narrow and with a high cen-
al cusp. Those of *cardinalis* are broad and with five cusps. The pre-
xillary of *innesi* has 6 to 9 teeth and a rather irregular tooth-placement
ttern with two rows represented. The number of teeth in the lower jaw of
ch species is about the same. In life the coloration of *cardinalis* dif-
rs from that of *innesi* mainly in that the intense red of the sides ex-
nds anteriorly beyond the pelvics and on to the head.

The name *cardinalis* refers to the brilliant red color of the sides.

Because of the absence of what has been known technically as an anterior
w of premaxillary teeth, this species would have to be placed, if we fol-
w Eigenmann's system of classification, in the "subfamily" Cheirodontinae.
wever, recent study, especially by Dr. James Böhlke of the Academy of
tural Sciences of Philadelphia, has demonstrated that this feature (and
hers) of Eigenmann's classification is highly artificial, some "cheiro-
ntines" being closest to certain "tetragonopterines", and vice versa.
phessobrycon cardinalis* is a very close relative of *H. innesi* Myers and
place it in a different genus would do violence to the obvious relation-
ips. Until the completion of a thorough revision of the generic limits
thin the "cheirodontines" and "tetragonopterines", any new generic assign-
nt of this species would be both speculative and unwarranted.

FAMILY DORADIDAE

Hassar praelongus, new species
Figure 1

HOLOTYPE: SU 48679, collected at the São Gabriel Rapids of the Rio
gro, Amazonas, Brazil, by Dr. Carl Ternetz, February 1 to 3, 1925.

Of the eight previously known species of the genus, this species agrees
ly with *H. lipophthalmus* in having (a) the scutes anterior to the pelvic
se strong, deep, and easily seen, and (b) the basal part of the dorsal
n blackish. In the following description, the words in parentheses refer
H. lipophthalmus.

Dorsal I,6. Anal 13. Lateral scutes 36, strong, the anterior ones
epest and with four or five subsidiary spines above the main median spine
d five below, the uppermost of the lower spines nearly as large as the
dian spine (anterior scutes less deep than those above anal origin). A
rrow but evident mid-nuchal groove running back from the fontanelle al-
st to the end of the occipital process (no such groove present). Eye,
th its long adipose eyelid, three fourths as deep as long (almost or

quite twice as long as deep). Length of snout from adipose eyelid to tip over half head length (approximately half head length). Head 3.06 in standard length (3.2 to 3.3). Adipose fin low and longer than high, with no anterior keel (same, but shorter).

MEASUREMENTS OF HOLOTYPE IN MM (and of two examples of *H. lipophthalmus* in parentheses): Standard length to end of last scute 116 (112, 135). Depth 22 (21, 27). Head length to end of bony opercle 36 (33, 41). Snout length from end adipose eyelid 19 (17, 20). Eye length, including adipose lid 12 (13, 16). Vertical diameter of eye 9 (7, 8). Bony interorbital width 5 (5.5, 6). Predorsal length 46 (44, 52). End dorsal base to adipose fin origin 32 (36, 43). Greatest breadth caudal peduncle including scute spines 10 (9, 13). Least depth caudal peduncle 6 (5, 7). Length dorsal spine 28 (32, 39). Length pectoral spine 27 (28, 32). Length pelvic fin 17 (20, 25). Greatest body width, in humeral region before pectoral base, 20 (19, 24).

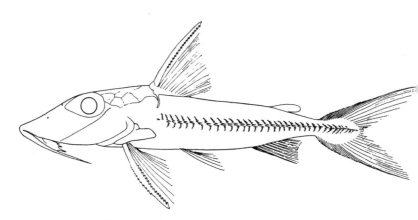

Fig. 1. *Hassar praelongus*. Holotype.

COLOR: Pale yellow-brown above, the scutes, belly and opercle whitish. Dorsum darkest adjacent to scutes, a darkish streak running out on caudal fin above and along scutes and another below, the rest of the fin whitish. Pectoral fin membrane dark. Proximal half of dorsal spine and base of dorsal fin black, this color rising towards the spine. Rest of dorsal fin clear. (In *H. lipophthalmus*: Body and fins generally dark smoky brown all over, the belly a little paler. Scutes not notably lighter in color. No streaks on caudal fin. Pectoral fin membranes dark brown. Dorsal with blackish coloration like *H. praelongus*.)

NOTES: This species differs strongly from *H. lipophthalmus* in color; the presence of a nuchal groove; the less elongate eye and adipose lid; a longer snout; a shorter dorsal spine; shorter pelvics; the better developed nature and deeper form of the anteriormost scutes; the greater number of subsidiary spines on the scutes; the lesser cranial bulge directly before the eyes; the slightly longer adipose fin; and several lesser characters. It is not close to any other known *Hassar*. The type is unique.

The type has been compared with Stanford material of *Hassar lipophthalmus* (Kner)(48713; São Gabriel, Rio Negro); *H. orestis* (Stdr.)(2234; Itaituba); and *H. wilderi* (Kindle)(2243; originally Cornell 1704; a syntype,

ereby designated lectoholotype of *wilderi;* Trocera, Rio Tocantins). Other
known species are *affinis* (Stdr.), *notospilus* (Eig.)(all the above forms being referred to in Eigenmann's review (1925, Trans. Amer. Philos. Soc.,
n.s., vol. 21)), and three species more recently described by Fowler,
I. ucayalensis (1939) and *woodi* and *iheringi* (1941).

Our comparative material of *H. lipophthalmus* from the Rio Negro differs
somewhat from Kner's description and figure (1855, Sitzb. math.-naturw. Cl.
K. Akad. Wiss. Wien, Bd. 17, p. 58, pl. 5, fig. 3), especially in the
smaller size of the anterior scutes, but we believe it to be correctly
identified.

OPINIONS AND DECLARATIONS RENDERED BY THE INTERNATIONAL COMMISSION ON ZOOLOGICAL NOMENCLATURE

Edited by

FRANCIS HEMMING, c.m.g., c.b.e.
Secretary to the Commission

VOLUME 17. Part 7. Pp. 87—104

OPINION 485
Determination of the relative priority to be assigned to the names *Cheirodon axelrodi* Schultz (L.P.) and *Hyphessobrycon cardinalis* Myers (G.S.) & Weitzman (S.H.) (Class Pisces), both being names published in February 1956

LONDON:
Printed by Order of the International Trust for Zoological Nomenclature
and
Sold on behalf of the International Commission on Zoological Nomenclature by the International Trust at its Publications Office 41, Queen's Gate, London, S.W.7
1957

Price Twelve Shillings

Issued 1st November, 1957

INTERNATIONAL COMMISSION ON ZOOLOGICAL NOMENCLATURE

COMPOSITION AT THE TIME OF THE ADOPTION OF THE RULING GIVEN IN OPINION 485

A. The Officers of the Commission

Honorary Life President : Dr. Karl JORDAN (*British Museum (Natural History), Zoological Museum, Tring, Herts., England*)

President : Professor James Chester BRADLEY (*Cornell University, Ithaca, N.Y., U.S.A*) (12th August 1953)

Vice-President : Senhor Dr. Afranio do AMARAL (*Sao Paulo, Brazil*) (12th August 1953)

Secretary : Mr. Francis HEMMING (*London, England*) (27th July 1948)

B. The Members of the Commission

(arranged in order of precedence by reference to date of election or of most recent re-election, as prescribed by the International Congress of Zoology)

Professor H. BOSCHMA (*Rijksmuseum van Natuurlijke Historie, Leiden, The Netherlands*) (1st January 1947)

Senor Dr. Angel CABRERA (*La Plata, Argentina*) (27th July 1948)

Mr. Francis HEMMING (*London, England*) (27th July 1948) (*Secretary*)

Dr. Henning LEMCHE (*Universitetets Zoologiske Museum, Copenhagen, Denmark*) (27th July 1948)

Professor Teiso ESAKI (*Kyushu University, Fukuoka, Japan*) (17th April 1950)

Professor Pierre BONNET (*Université de Toulouse, France*) (9th June 1950)

Mr. Norman Denbigh RILEY (*British Museum (Natural History), London*) (9th June 1950)

Professor Tadeusz JACZEWSKI (*Institute of Zoology, Polish Academy of Sciences, Warsaw, Poland*) (15th June 1950)

Professor Robert MERTENS (*Natur-Museum u. Forschungs-Institut Senckenberg, Frankfurt a.M., Germany*) (5th July 1950)

Professor Erich Martin HERING (*Zoologisches Museum der Humboldt-Universität zu Berlin, Germany*) (5th July 1950)

Senhor Dr. Afranio do AMARAL (*S. Paulo, Brazil*) (12th August 1953) (*Vice-President*)

Professor J. R. DYMOND (*University of Toronto, Toronto, Canada*) (12th August 1953)

Professor J. Chester BRADLEY (*Cornell University, Ithaca, N.Y., U.S.A.*) (12th August 1953) (*President*)

Professor Harold E. VOKES (*University of Tulane, Department of Geology, New Orleans, Louisiana, U.S.A.*) (12th August 1953)

Professor Béla HANKÓ (*Mezőgazdasági Muzeum, Budapest, Hungary*) (12th August 1953)

Dr. Norman R. STOLL (*Rockefeller Institute for Medical Research, New York, N.Y., U.S.A.*) (12th August 1953)

Mr. P. C. SYLVESTER-BRADLEY (*Sheffield University, Sheffield, England*) (12th August 1953)

Dr. L. B. HOLTHUIS (*Rijksmuseum van Natuurlijke Historie, Leiden, The Netherlands*) (12th August 1953)

Dr. K. H. L. KEY (*Commonwealth Scientific and Industrial Research Organisation, Canberra, A.C.T., Australia*) (15th October 1954)

Dr. Alden H. MILLER (*Museum of Vertebrate Zoology, University of California, U.S.A.*) (29th October 1954)

Doc. Dr. Ferdinand PRANTL (*Národni Museum V Praze, Prague, Czechoslovakia*) (30th October 1954)

Professor Dr. Wilhelm KÜHNELT (*Zoologisches Institut der Universität, Vienna, Austria*) (6th November 1954)

Professor F. S. BODENHEIMER (*The Hebrew University, Jerusalem, Israel*) (11th November 1954)

Professor Ernst MAYR (*Museum of Comparative Zoology at Harvard College, Cambridge, Massachusetts, U.S.A.*) (4th December 1954)

Professor Enrico TORTONESE (*Museo di Storia Naturale " G. Doria ", Genova, Italy*) (16th December 1954)

OPINION 485

DETERMINATION OF THE RELATIVE PRIORITY TO BE ASSIGNED TO THE NAMES " CHEIRODON AXELRODI " SCHULTZ (L.P.) AND " HYPHESSOBRYCON CARDINALIS " MYERS (G.S.) & WEITZMAN (S.H.) (CLASS PISCES), BOTH BEING NAMES PUBLISHED IN FEBRUARY 1956

RULING :—(1) It is hereby ruled that on the basis of the evidence submitted the Parts of the serial publications containing the names of the under-mentioned nominal species belonging to the Class Pisces were published on the dates severally specified below :—

(a) Part 4 of Volume 4 of the serial publication *Tropical Fish Hobbyist*, being a Part dated " April 1956 " on the cover and " February 20, 1956 " on the first page of the text (page [3]) ;

It is hereby ruled that on the evidence submitted the general mailing of the above Part of the serial publication *Tropical Fish Hobbyist*, being the Part containing the description of the new nominal species *Cheirodon axelrodi* Schultz (L.P.), commenced on 20th February 1956, on which date copies to a number estimated by the Editor at about 3,000 were distributed to subscribers

(b) Part 1 of Volume 7 of the serial publication *Stanford Ichthyological Bulletin*, being a Part dated " February 21, 1956 " :

It is hereby ruled that on the evidence submitted the general mailing of the above Part of the serial publication *Stanford Ichthyological Bulletin*, being the Part containing the description of the new nominal species *Hyphessobrycon cardinalis* Myers (G.S.) & Weitzman (S.H.), began on 21st February 1956, when 600 copies were mailed to subscribers.

(2) In the light of (1) above, it is hereby ruled that he name *Cheirodon axelrodi* Schultz (L.P.) is to be reated as having been published on 20th February 1956 nd the name *Hyphessobrycon cardinalis* Myers (G.S.) & Weitzman (S.H.) on 21st February 1956.

(3) It is hereby ruled that in the light of (2) above the pecific name *axelrodi* Schultz (L.P.), 20th February 1956, s published in the combination *Cheirodon axelrodi*, is to e accorded priority over the specific name *cardinalis* Myers (G.S.) & Weitzman (S.H.), 21st February 1956, as ublished in the combination *Hyphessobrycon cardinalis*.

(4) The under-mentioned specific name is hereby laced on the *Official List of Specific Names in Zoology*, vith the endorsement specified below and with the Name Number 1430 :—

> *axelrodi* Schultz (L.P.), 20th February 1956, as published in the combination *Cheirodon axelrodi* (a name ruled as possessing, on the basis of the evidence submitted, priority over the specific name *cardinalis* Myers (G.S.) & Weitzman (S.H.), 21st February 1956, as published in the combination *Hyphessobrycon cardinalis*).

I. THE STATEMENT OF THE CASE

In the period March-April 1956 enquiries were received by the Office of the Commission from various sources on the question f the relative priority to be assigned to the binomina *Cheirodon xelrodi* Schultz (L.P.) and *Hyphessobrycon cardinalis* Myers G.S.) & Weitzman (S.H.), both being names published in 'ebruary 1956 and both, in the view of the correspondents oncerned, being applicable to the same species. These enquiries ulminated on 14th May 1956 when Mr. L. W. Ashdown of the ditorial Department of the serial publication *Water Life*,

London, submitted the following formal request for th
determination by the International Commission on Zoologic<
Nomenclature of the relative priority to be assigned to th
foregoing names :—

Request for a Ruling as to the relative priority to be accorded to the name "Cheirodon axelrodi" Schultz, 1956, and "Hyphessobrycon cardinalis" Myers and Weitzman, 1956 (Class Pisces)

By L. W. ASHDOWN

(Editorial Department, " Water Life ", London)

I shall be grateful if the International Commission will give a rulin
on the question of which of two recently published names should b
applied to a newly described Characin. I should explain that what i
apparently the same species has been described by Dr. L. P. Schult
as *Cheirodon axelrodi* in the April 1956 number of the *Tropical Fis
Hobbyist* (pages 41/43) and, we understand, by George S. Myers an
S. H. Weitzman as *Hyphessobrycon cardinalis* in No. 1 of Vol. 7 of th
Stanford Ichthyological Bulletin. The same fish had been describe
in the February 1956 issue of *The Aquarium* by W. T. Innes, wher
it was stated that the fish had still to be classified, and it was given th
popular name of " Cardinal Tetra " pending the publication of
scientific name for it.

The issue of the *Tropical Fish Hobbyist* for April 1956 is date
on the first page (page 3) " February 20, 1956 ", while the issue of th
Stanford Ichthyological Bulletin referred to above is, we believe, date
" February 21, 1956 ". It is impossible without a ruling from th
Commission to determine which of the two names previously mentione
should take priority over the other since the Commission alone is in
position to obtain the relevant information.

This fish is likely to become widely used by aquarists, and it i
important therefore that the scientific name to be used for it shoul
be determined without delay. I accordingly ask the Internation<
Commission to look into this matter, and to give a ruling on it as soo
as possible.

**2. Particulars obtained from the parties concerned as to th
dates of publication of the names " Cheirodon axelrodi " Schult
and " Hyphessobrycon cardinalis " Myers & Weitzman res
pectively :** Upon the receipt of the communication from Mr

shdown reproduced in the preceding paragraph, Mr. Hemming s Secretary, took the view that no useful purpose would be rved by the submission of that communication to the ommission until evidence on the question of the dates of ublication of the relevant Parts of the serial publications in hich the names *Cheirodon axelrodi* Schultz (L.P.) and *Iyphessobrycon cardinalis* Myers (G.S.) & Weitzman (S.H.) had spectively been published had been obtained from the parties ho alone possessed first-hand evidence on this subject. ccordingly, on 16th May 1956 Mr. Hemming addressed letters f enquiry (i) as regards the name *Cheirodon axelrodi* Schultz,) to Dr. L. P. Schultz, the author of the above name and (b) to Ir. Herbert H. Axelrod, the Editor of the serial publication *ropical Fish Hobbyist*, in which the above name had been ublished, and (ii) as regards the name *Hyphessobrycon cardinalis* Iyers & Weitzman, (a) to Professor George S. Myers, the senior f the joint authors of the above name, and (b) to the Editor of the rial publication *Stanford Ichthyological Bulletin*, in which the bove name had been published. Upon receiving the information asked for, Mr. Hemming on 7th June 1956 prepared the llowing Report for the consideration of the International ommission to which he annexed copies of the replies which he ad received to the enquiries referred to above :—

rocedure adopted for dealing with Mr. L. W. Ashdown's request for a ruling as to the relative priority to be accorded to the names " Cheirodon axelrodi " Schultz, 1956, and " Hyphessobrycon cardinalis " Myers and Weitzman, 1956 (Class Pisces)

By FRANCIS HEMMING, C.M.G., C.B.E.

Secretary to the International Commission on Zoological Nomenclature)

Attention is drawn to the request submitted by Mr. L. W. Ashdown *Editorial Department, " Water Life ")* for a Ruling as to the relative riority to be accorded to two names for the same species of fish hich appear to have been published almost simultaneously in the arly part of 1956. The names concerned are (a) *Cheirodon axelrodi* chultz, published in Part 4 of volume 4 of the serial publication *ropical Fish Hobbyist*, a Part which on the wrapper bears the date April 1956 " and on the first page of the text (: [3]) the date February 20, 1956 " and (b) *Hyphessobrycon cardinalis* Myers and Veitzman, published in Part 1 of volume 7 of the serial publication

Stanford Ichthyological Bulletin (a serial publication published by the Natural History Museum of Stanford University) a Part bearing the date " February 21, 1956 ".

2. The answer to be returned to the question submitted in this case will depend on the evidence furnished by the parties concerned as to the dates on which the Parts of these serial publications referred to above were respectively " published ", the term " published " being interpreted in the manner prescribed by the International Congress of Zoology, Paris, 1948 (1950, *Bull. zool. Nomencl.* **4** : 223—225).

3. As both the names concerned are new and neither has as yet established itself in the literature, special priority for publication in the *Bulletin of Zoological Nomenclature* has been accorded to Mr Ashdown's application in order that the International Commission may be in a position to give a Ruling in this matter at the earliest possible date.

4. In order to assist the International Commission in arriving at a decision on this question a request for full information as to the date of publication, as defined by the International Congress of Zoology, of the respective Parts of the serial publications concerned was addressed as a matter of urgency to the Editor of the *Tropical Fish Hobbyist* and to the Editor of the *Stanford Ichthyological Bulletin*. The replies received are given in Annexes 1 and 2 to the present note.

ANNEXE 1

Reports on the date of publication of the name " Cheirodon Axelrodi " Schultz, 1956

(a) Letter dated 23rd May 1956 from Leonard P. Schultz, Smithsonian Institution, U.S. National Museum, Washington, D.C., U.S.A.

Thanks for your letter of May 16, 1956 (Z.N.(S.) 1082) concerning relative priority of *Cheirodon axelrodi* Schultz and *Hyphessobrycon cardinalis* Myers and Weitzman.

Mr. Axelrod sent to me on March 6, 1956 the U.S. Post Office receipt for the mailing of the March-April issue of *Tropical Fish Hobbyist* and it is in my files, a photographic copy of which I could furnish if needed by the Commission. It contains the following information which I quote :—

> " Jersey City, N.J.
> Tropical Fish Hobbyist
> 2/20—24/56 and 3/2—3—5/56
> Mar.-April-1956
> Total pounds mailed 1514
> Computed by T. Falconer "

The first date of mailing was on February 20, 1956 as shown by the above receipt. This is verified by the postmark on the folder in which my copy of the April issue of T.F.H. arrived. I quote : " Jersey City, N.J., February 20, 1956, P.B. Meter 333294, U.S. Postage 05 ".

Mr. Axelrod mailed to me on February 18th a printed tear sheet from the T.F.H. magazine of the description of *Cheirodon axelrodi* Schultz, which I received at 9.00 a.m. on February 20 1956.

I received a letter from Dr. George S. Myers which bore the date of February 16, 1956, as originally typed, but which had been re-dated as February 21, 1956 by Professor Myers in his hand-writing. He stated in long hand which I quote : " Dear Leonard : Copies of our latest Stan. Ichth. Bulletin just came in so I am enclosing your copy with this. There is a new aquarium tetra in it, GSM ". " P.S. I didn't get back to the office for several days to sign this. Thus change in date ". The rest of the letter was typed but about other matters. Enclosed in the letter was the printed description of *Hyphessobrycon cardinalis* Myers and Weitzman, also dated February 21, 1956. The envelope in which the letter and Stanf. Ichth. Bull. Vol. 7, no. 1 were enclosed were postmarked " Stanford, Calif., Feb. 21, 1956, 12.30 p.m.", which I have in my files. It was received February 23, 1956.

(b) Letter dated 23rd May 1956 from Herbert R. Axelrod, Editor Tropical Fish Hobbyist Magazine

This will acknowledge receipt of your letter dated May 16 relative to the priority of the names *Cheirodon axelrodi* Schultz and *Hyphessobrycon cardinalis* Myers & Weitzman.

I shall answer your queries according to (a), (b) and (c) as outlined in your letter.[1]

(a) The magazine *Tropical Fish Hobbyist* which bears the cover date April 1956 was printed on February 17th and 18th. Some copies were distributed on that date to pet shops in our neighbourhood. General mailing started on February 20th and continued for a week or so. This information was verified by Myers, Innes and Dr. Schultz. I am enclosing the story which appeared in the next issue of our magazine explaining this procedure.

---

[1] The queries here referred to by Mr. Axelrod are those contained in my letter to him of 16th May 1956 which were as follows :—
  (a) The date on which were available the first copy or copies of the issue of the *Tropical Fish Hobbyist* which bears the date " April, 1956 " on the cover and the date " February 20, 1956 " on page 3 ;
  (b) The date on which the first copies of the above number were distributed to subscribers and the number of copies so distributed ;
  (c) If not all subscribers' copies were distributed on the date referred to in (b) above, the date on which the remaining copies were distributed and the number of such copies. (intld. F.H. 6th June 1956.)

(b) First copies went to the post office on February 20th. There were about 3,000 copies mailed on this date.

(c) 6,718 copies were distributed between February 20th and May 4th.

Verification of this information is available from the Postmaster, Jersey City 2, N.J. He has the records of mailing this issue.

Enclosure to letter dated 23rd May, 1956 from Herbert R. Axelrod

Extract from pp. 16 and 17 of the issue of the serial publication " Tropical Fish Hobbyist " for May—June, 1956

In the last issue of T.F.H., Dr. Schultz kindly named this beautiful fish *Cheirodon axelrodi* in my honor. I am, naturally, quite proud of this fact, especially since it is one of the most beautiful fishes I've ever seen. The story behind the scenes is a very interesting one and as a matter of record I'll tell you about it.

On February 10th or 11th the beautiful Scarlet Characins were brought to my attention by several of my friends. Sol Kessler, a fish dealer in nearby New Jersey town, was kind enough to give Bill Vorderwinkler a few specimens. I had Timmerman take a few color pictures of them, then sent them down to Dr. Schultz for identification. While this was going on, I held up printing T.F.H. until I heard from Schultz. I called him in Washington nearly every day until finally he said that he thought it was a new species and was naming it after me. He said it would take another day or two to write it up but he would send the manuscript up special delivery. On the morning of February 16th I received the manuscript . . . three hours later I had the pages set in type and the proofs were in the mail to Dr. Schultz. We received Dr. Schultz's corrections back the next day but by that time we were printing the magazine already, so we made the corrections as best we could on the plate. We mailed the first copies of the magazine on February 20th, as the records of the post office will verify (Innes and Myers both checked them !).

Now Dr. Schultz is a very finicky guy ! When I sent him the fish he wanted an exact location for the " type locality ". He doesn't believe in general areas . . . he wants THE place. I knew that Fred Cochu and his father-in-law, Herr Schnelle of Paramount Aquarium, were probably the only two white men to know the exact locale and

I further know that they wouldn't be fools enough to tell me or anyone else ! This fish was worth thousands of dollars and when others found out where they were getting the Neons from, the market was killed and the Neons were and still are selling for a price lower than that of White Clouds ! They didn't want the same thing to happen to this fish.

I asked a very good friend of mine, Mr. Mervin Roberts, to ask Schnelle where the fish comes from. Schnelle and Roberts are close associates. Roberts could not get a specific locale from Schnelle. Then I remembered a man who used to collect fish in that region.

I told him the story . . . he told me where the fish come from (north of Porto Velho on the Rio Madiera). He knew the exact area . . . even told me how to get there by plane. Take a four engine plane to Manaos, then a small seaplane to Porto Velho. Later I learned that Schnelle had reported to Myers that the fish came from near Manaos. Myers should have known better than to believe that for two reasons :—

1. Paramount Aquarium make their living selling tropical fish. They don't want every importer to have the fish that they now have exclusively.

2. The waters near Manaos have been combed for many years for lots of fishes. Why hadn't this beautiful species turned up before ?

Myers wrote to Kessler and others trying to get information that he should have written to me or Schultz about . . . Innes did the same thing ! WHY ?

Anyway, the fish I sent to Schultz were all females. The balance I sent to Tutwiler in Florida and to Bill Vordewinkler to see if they could spawn them. I am trying to spawn them myself . . . nothing yet.

The fish are very hardy and healthy. They are not easily killed by diseases, nor do they succumb to the ich very readily (other fishes in the same aquarium got the ich, but not these beauties !) Schultz, who hasn't seen a male yet, suggests that males might have the characin hook on their anal fins. I looked and couldn't find any on the specimens I have . . . maybe they are all females ? In the interests of ichthyology and tropical fishkeeping, I am offering, through T.F.H., a reward of $50.00 for the exclusive rights to the publication of the first detailed spawning report of *Cheirodon axelrodi*. The report must be verified by three people or a month old baby fish must be sent along as proof. If photographs of the spawning sequence can be taken, we'll pay an additional $10 for each reproducible photograph.

ANNEXE 2

Report on the date of publication of the name " Hyphessobrycon cardinalis " Myers and Weitzman, 1956

Letter dated 23rd May, 1956 from Margaret H. Storey, Associate Editor, Stanford Ichthyological Bulletin

In reply to your letter of 16th May, 1956[2], may I state that Prof. G. S. Myers is Editor of the *Stanford Ichthyological Bulletin*. However, as Associate Editor, my duties include direct dealing with the printers (Stanford University Press) and with the posting of each number of this serial. It is my responsibility that the greater part of each issue be in the mails on or before the publication date, which invariably appears just below the masthead of each number.

I followed my usual procedure when I addressed and mailed volume 7 no. 1 of the *Stanford Ichthyological Bulletin*, dated February 21, 1956 and hereby affirm :

1. That the entire edition of this number was delivered to me by the Stanford University Press on the morning of February 21, 1956.

2. That, envelopes having been addressed while the issue was in press, approximately 600 copies in individual envelopes were mailed by me at Stanford Post Office, at approximately 11.30 a.m. on February 21, 1956 by regular second class mail, and that six or seven additional copies were mailed by me at the same time by first-class airmail, in individual envelopes provided by Professor Myers.

3. That this mailing included all current names and addresses on the regular mailing list maintained by the Natural History Museum for S.I.B. and that the mailing list had been brought up to date between November 1955 and February 1956 by means of reply-paid return post cards—regular U.S. double post cards to the United States, and Universal Postal Union Reply Paid Return Post Cards to other countries. Copies of vol. 7, no. 1 were sent only to those who had replied.

4. That this mailing list included the principal zoological, ichthyological, or natural history museum libraries in Ann Arbor, Berkeley, Cambridge, Mass., Chicago, Honolulu, New Haven, New York, Philadelphia, San Francisco, Washington, Berlin, Calcutta, Cape Town, Copenhagen, La Plata, Leningrad, London, Paris, Rio de Janeiro and Sydney, and many other cities in a total of 58 countries

---

[2] The letter here referred to by Miss Storey contained the same questions as those set out in Mr. Hemming's letter to Mr. Axelrod of the same date. These have been given in Footnote 1 above.

throughout the world, the Editors of " Science " and " Nature ", numbering in all, 258 ; and approximately 335 individual ichthyologists throughout the world.

5. That this number was available through public sale from the Director of this Museum, upon the morning of February 21, 1956.

6. That approximately 350 additional copies of this number were delivered to the Gift and Exchange Department of the Stanford University Library on February 21, 1956, to be used by them for exchanges with 282 libraries of institutions, in 52 countries, with which the Natural History Museum Library does not directly exchange. The Stanford Library distributed 282 copies during the month of March.

7. That a number of post card receipt notices have been received by us from institutions and individuals, showing that this number of the Bulletin was received without undue delay in many widely scattered parts of the world. (Unfortunately, almost no persons or institutions in North America or Western Europe commonly send us such receipts.)

8. That February 21, 1956 fell on a Tuesday, followed by a legal national holiday (Washington's Birthday, Feb. 22), so that no copies sent to any great distance and delivered by the United States mails could have been delivered until February 23. (I am told by Professor Myers that several persons on the Atlantic Seaboard, approximately 3,000 miles from Stanford, received airmail copies on February 23.)

I trust that the above will be satisfactory.

II.　THE SUBSEQUENT HISTORY OF THE CASE

3. Registration of the present application : Upon the receipt in the Office of the Commission of the preliminary enquiries referred to in paragraph 1 above, the question of the relative priority to be accorded to the names *Cheirodon axelrodi* Schultz and *Hyphessobrycon cardinalis* Myers & Weitzman was allotted the Registered Number Z.N.(S.) 1082.

4. Publication of the present application : The documents relating to the present case were sent to the printer on 7th June 1956 and were published on 24th August 1956 (Ashdown [request for Ruling by the International Commission], 1956, *Bull. zool. Nomencl.* **12** : 184 ; Hemming [Report as Secretary], 1956, *ibid.*

12 : 185 ; Schultz [letter dated 23rd May 1956], 1956, *ibid.* 12 : 186 ; Axelrod [letter with enclosure dated 23rd May 1956], 1956, *ibid.* 12 : 187—188 ; Storey (Margaret H.) [letter dated 23rd May 1956], 1956, *ibid.* 12 : 189—190).

5. Comment received from Denys W. Tucker (British Museum (Natural History), London : On 19th September 1956 Mr. Denys W. Tucker (*British Museum* (*Natural History*), *London*) communicated the following comment to the Office of the Commission (Tucker, 1956, *Bull. zool. Nomencl.* **12 :** 317) :—

Support for " Hyphessobrycon cardinalis " Myers & Weitzman versus " Cheirodon axelrodi " Schultz

The ordinary question of date priority for one or other of these names will be decided by the International Commission on the basis of the evidence provided in *Bull. zool. Nomencl.* **12 :** 184—190. I can add nothing further to this aspect of the problem, except the expression of a certain curiosity as to why Vol. 4, No. 4 of the *Tropical Fish Hobbyist* should carry the precise date 20th February 1956, whereas the preceding issue is merely dated January—February 1956, and the succeeding one reverts to the similar form May—June 1956. I feel that the Commission should carefully weigh all the possible implications of this phenomenon.

A factor that I would emphasize in favour of *Hyphessobrycon cardinalis* Myers & Weitzman is that this name was clearly published as a voluntary act of publication by these authors and in a journal normally serving as a vehicle of taxonomic publication. *Cheirodon axelrodi* Schultz, on the other hand, does not appear to have been deliberately published by its author.

Dr. Schultz sent a personal letter to Mr. H. R. Axelrod which the latter apparently published on his own responsibility in the *Tropical Fish Hobbyist* (4(4) : 41—43) a lay journal. The letter contains no indication that Dr. Schultz was anticipating immediate publication in that form and, in fact, his concluding paragraph may be construed as a statement that he intended further study before undertaking definitive publication. This interpretation of his intentions is further supported by Mr. Axelrod's statement in *Tropical Fish Hobbyist* (4(5) : 16) that the magazine was already printing before Dr. Schultz's corrected galley proofs were returned.

6. Report submitted to the Commission by the Secretary at the close of the Prescribed Six-Month Waiting Period following the publication of the present case in the " Bulletin of Zoological

Nomenclature " :   At the close of the Prescribed Waiting Period following the publication of the present case in the *Bulletin of Zoological Nomenclature*, Mr. Hemming submitted the following brief Report to the International Commission on 28th February 1957 as part of the arrangements for the taking by the Commission of a vote on the issue raised in the present case :—

The situation created by the virtually simultaneous publication of scientific names (a) by Schultz (L.P.) and (b) by Myers (G.S.) & Weitzman (S.H.) respectively for the same species of Characin fish

By FRANCIS HEMMING, C.M.G., C.B.E.

(Secretary to the International Commission on Zoological Nomenclature)

The time has come when it is due to submit to the International Commission for decision the question as to which of the following names, which it is agreed apply to the same previously undescribed species of Characin fish, was the first to be published :—

(a) *Cheirodon axelrodi* Schultz (L.P.), 1956, *The Tropical Fish Hobbyist* 4 (No. 4) : 41—43 ;

(b) *Hyphessobrycon cardinalis* Myers (G.S.), & Weitzman (S.H.) 1956, *Stanford Ichthyol. Bull.* 7(1) : 1—4.

2. The application now before the International Commission was submitted on 14th May 1956 by Mr. L. W. Ashdown (*Editorial Department, " Water Life ", London*), who asked for a Ruling as to which of the foregoing names should be accepted in preference to the other (Ashdown, 1956, *Bull. zool. Nomencl.* 12 : 184).

3. In order to assist the International Commission in dealing with the present case, I addressed formal invitations to those concerned in the publication of these names to furnish such evidence as might be available regarding the date of mailing of the Parts of the serials in which the names concerned were respectively published. The following information was received in response to the above request :—

(a) **Letters relating to the publication of the name " Cheirodon axelrodi " Schultz**

(i) Letter dated 23rd May 1956 from Leonard P. Schultz

(ii) Letter with enclosure, dated 23rd May 1956 from Herbert R. Axelrod, Editor, " The Tropical Fish Hobbyist "

(b) Letter relating to the publication of the name " Hyphessobrycon cardinalis " Myers & Weitzman

Letter dated 23rd May 1956 from Margaret H. Storey, Assistant Editor, " Stanford Ichthyological Bulletin ".

4. The above letters were published in the *Bulletin of Zoological Nomenclature* concurrently with the publication of the application submitted by Mr. Ashdown. The references are as follows : (1) Schultz, 1956, *Bull. zool. Nomencl.* **12** : 186 ; (2) Axelrod, 1956, *ibid.* **12** : 187—188 ; (3) Storey, 1956, *ibid.* **12** : 189—190. These letters contain a wealth of detail in regard to the subjects with which they deal. I do not propose to summarise them here, for I consider that they should be studied carefully *in extenso*.

5. *Comments received* : A comment was received from Denys W. Tucker (*British Museum* (*Natural History*), *London*) who expressed certain criticism in regard to the circumstances in which the name *Cheirodon axelrodi* Schultz was published and indicated a preference for the name *Hyphessobrycon cardinalis* Myers & Weitzman. The text of this letter has been published on page 317 of volume 12 of the *Bulletin*. It had been hoped that the Nomenclature Committee of the American Society of Ichthology and Herpetology might have been able to assist the Commission in the consideration of this case, but no response has been received to the invitation issued to that body.

6. It will be apparent to any reader of the papers relating to the present case that the circumstances surrounding it have excited strong feelings. It is particularly necessary therefore that in considering this matter the Commission should address itself solely to the issue before it, namely the question as to which of the two names concerned was the first to be published.

7. The specific name of whichever of the nominal species the Commission decides was the first to be established will need to be placed on the *Official List of Specific Names in Zoology*. It will not, however, be possible to place on the *Official Index of Rejected and Invalid Specific Names in Zoology* the specific name of the nominal species which the Commission decides was the later established of the two nominal species concerned, for, although it is agreed that the two names concerned apply to the same taxon, the names being based upon different specimens are subjective and not objective synonyms of one another and both are therefore nomenclatorially available names. Accordingly, in order to place formally on record the decision now to be taken by the Commission it will be necessary, when the proposed entry is made on the *Official List of Specific Names in Zoology*, to adopt the procedure followed in analogous cases by endorsing the entry in question to the effect that by a Ruling given by the Commission the name so placed on the *Official List* is to be treated as having been published prior to the other of the two names concerned.

III. THE DECISION TAKEN BY THE INTERNATIONAL COMMISSION ON ZOOLOGICAL NOMENCLATURE

7. Issue of Voting Paper V.P.(57)22 : On 28th February 1957 a Voting Paper (V.P.(57)22) in the following terms was issued to the Members of the International Commission on Zoological Nomenclature :—

VOTING PAPER

Having carefully weighed the evidence submitted by the parties concerned (1956, *Bull. zool. Nomencl.* **12** : 186—190) regarding the dates on which were published the relevant Parts of the serial publications *The Tropical Fish Hobbyist* and the *Stanford Ichthyological Bulletin* respectively, I am of the opinion that of the two names concerned

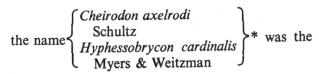

first to be published and I accordingly vote in favour of the specific name of the nominal species in question being placed on the *Official List of Specific Names in Zoology*, the entry so made to be endorsed in the manner specified in paragraph 7 of the Report bearing the Registered Number Z.N.(S.) 1082 submitted by the Secretary[3] simultaneously with the present Voting Paper.

Signature of Commissioner..

Date of Signature..

* Delete whichever name is considered inappropriate.

8. The Prescribed Voting Period : As the foregoing Voting Paper was issued under the Three-Month Rule, the Prescribed Voting Period closed on 28th May 1957.

---

[3] The text of the Report here referred to has been reproduced in paragraph 6 of the present *Opinion*.

9. Particulars of the Voting on Voting Paper V.P.(57)22 : A
the close of the Prescribed Voting Period, the state of the voting
on Voting Paper V.P.(57)22 was as follows :—

   (a) *In favour of the acceptance of the name " Cheirodon*
     axelrodi " Schultz as having been published before the name
     " Hyphessobrycon cardinalis " Myers & Weitzman, nine-
     teen (19) *votes :*

     Lemche ; Holthuis ; Hering ; Mayr ; Bonnet ; Vokes ;
     Key ; Boschma ; Riley ; Dymond ; Esaki ; do Amaral ;
     Bradley (J.C.) ; Cabrera ; Hemming ; Sylvester-Bradley ;
     Tortonese ; Stoll ; Miller ;

   (b) *In favour of the acceptance of the name " Hyphessobrycon*
     cardinalis " Myers & Weitzman as having been published
     before the name " Cheirodon axelrodi " Schultz, five (5)
     votes :

     Mertens ; Prantl ; Bodenheimer ; Jaczewski ; Kühnelt ;

   (c) *Voting Papers not returned, one* (1) :

     Hankó.

10. Declaration of Result of Vote : On 29th May 1957, Mr.
Hemming, Secretary to the International Commission, acting as
Returning Officer for the Vote taken on Voting Paper V.P.(57)22,
signed a Certificate that the Votes cast were as set out in paragraph
9 above and declaring that the proposal submitted in the foregoing
Voting Paper had been duly adopted and that the decision so
taken was the decision of the International Commission in the
matter aforesaid.

11. Preparation of the Ruling given in the present " Opinion " :
On 24th June 1957 Mr. Hemming prepared the Ruling given in

the present *Opinion* and at the same time signed a Certificate that the terms of that Ruling were in complete accord with those of the proposal approved by the International Commission in its Vote on Voting Paper V.P.(57)22.

12. Original Reference : the following is the original reference for the specific name placed on the *Official List of Specific Names in Zoology* by the Ruling given in the present *Opinion* :—

axelrodi, *Cheirodon*, Schultz (L.P.), 20th February 1956, *Tropical Fish Hobbyist* **4** (No. 4) : 42

13. The prescribed procedures were duly complied with by the International Commission on Zoological Nomenclature in dealing with the present case, and the present *Opinion* is accordingly hereby rendered in the name of the said International Commission by the under-signed Francis Hemming, Secretary to the International Commission on Zoological Nomenclature, in virtue of all and every the powers conferred upon him in that behalf.

14. The present *Opinion* shall be known as *Opinion* Four Hundred and Eighty-Five (485) of the International Commission on Zoological Nomenclature.

DONE in London, this Twenty-Fourth day of June, Nineteen Hundred and Fifty-Seven.

*Secretary to the International Commission
on Zoological Nomenclature*

FRANCIS HEMMING

Back to the Rio Negro

Therefore when in the fall of 1975 I found myself in Manaus once again, I thought it might be nice to take the same trip up to Tapurucuara to see if the priest was still alive, almost 20 years later!

Willi Schwartz of Acuario Rio Negro was ready, as usual, to lend me a boat and a good crew, and we soon departed for Tapurucuara, a 3- to 4-day journey running 24 hours a day. Since I was on my way to the home of the real *Symphysodon discus* and searching for the missing link in the angelfish story, it was worth going to Tapurucuara, perhaps only another day's journey. Can you imagine the thoughts crashing through my head as I waited, hour by hour and day by day, until we reached the area? Willi told me the priest was still alive and twice as fat as he was when I had last seen him. But he was still a fully dedicated servant of God. On our way we stopped at a few houses to drop off some freeloaders we had picked up in Manaus. In talking with them (by this time, 20 years later, I could manage to get by with *lingua geral*) I found out that the priest was indeed alive and well, but he wasn't in the area. He had gone away on holiday. So I continued in my efforts to collect the missing link angelfish and also to find some of the real blue discus.

The night after we found all the cichlids we wanted (angelfish and discus are cichlids, of course), I told Silas (Selia) Fonte, the skipper of the boat, that I had originally planned on going to Tapurucuara to see the priest and to catch some *"cardinais,"* as they called them in *lingua geral*.

"Eo ten cardinas aqui..." (I have cardinal tetras here), said Fonte.

"But the water is so deep, almost 30 feet above normal...how would we ever catch them?" I asked.

"Let's go see the fishermen who normally collect

them for Willi. Perhaps they can help us. After all, you want only a few thousand anyway."

We left Igarape Anapichi at about 7 A.M. and took two dugout canoes through the very dense jungle that was not completely inundated. It's a spooky feeling to pull your way through the tops of trees that are 20-40 feet high, sharing the security with screeching monkeys and fluttering parrots. The monkeys could be called by kissing the inside of your palm loudly and repeatedly making the same noise they do.

How lucky we were not to have mosquitoes or any other biting insects that fly...but I did get very nicely bitten by some fire ants that had climbed high into the trees to get out of the water. I pulled a beautiful flowering orchid from its tenacious grip on the top of some tree only to be showered by biting red ants that left huge welts which eventually turned into pus-punctuated sores that itched and burned. It seemed as if the jungle were advising me to leave its beauty alone.

Paddling and pulling our way through the jungle for more than an hour, we eventually found some high ground. I quietly stepped from the canoe into the coffee-black water and waited...sure enough, in a few minutes the first cardinal tetra crossed my sneakers (the same sneakers, by the way, as those I wore in 1952...but not the same shirt. My shirt was a beautiful hand-painted gift from Rodney Jonklaas which featured a clown triggerfish, *Balistoides conspicillum*.). In a few minutes, using both our metal-framed dip nets and the most effective butterfly nets of the professional cardinal catcher, we had a few thousand cardinals.

The butterfly nets are worth describing. They are three feet long and half as wide. They have a wooden frame and are shaped like a bullet. They have very fine soft netting, and they have a stick across the one flat end so the collector can get a grip on it. The collector uses two hands and two nets, slowly using one net to guide the fish into the other, which is gently lifted with about 10 to 20 cardinals in every try. The bottom of the stream is a soft cushion of an accumulation of leaves that have fallen over thousands of years. This is obviously the source of the color of the Rio Negro. Plants and other obstructions impede the progress of a seine, and only dipnets are effective in collecting cardinal tetras.

Also protecting the cardinals was a type of thorny bush that made a rose bush seem like a featherbed. The thorns were sharp and extremely fine-pointed. I had been pierced several times and therefore was most careful not to force my body against anything when I suddenly felt a piercing pain in my right foot. I involuntarily jerked my foot in the air and saw something large and black scamper away. I had stepped on either an alligator (caiman) about 18 inches long or a very spiny black catfish. The spines or teeth went through my old sneaker and dug into the bottom of my foot at least an inch. I guess I was more frightened than hurt; in a few minutes, when I saw the Indians were ignoring my problem, I continued fishing with them.

When we filled all of the boxes we had with cardinals, we headed back to the large boat for lunch. On the way Manoel Nena suggested that we stop at a fisherman's house and see if he had anything interesting in his floating fish trap. The "trap" is merely a large piece of netting about 5 x 10 feet which is held in the form of a rectangle by six poles, one at each edge and two in the middle. He had some cardinal tetras and was most pleased to sell them all (about 5,000) for 100 cruzeiros. This breaks down to 4 for a penny. He also had some leaf fish, a mottled *Epicyrtus* and some tetras that looked like rosy tetras. By the time we got to the boat, my foot was throbbing. I still wanted to go to Tapurucuara, though, but since we were all tired we decided a siesta was in order. After eating my usual spaghetti lunch, I fell asleep in my hammock.

The sound of Silas Fonte changing the water in the plastic trays woke me, and as I tried to swing out of the hammock, an intense pain shot through my foot. Red streaks were running up the side of my leg, and I knew I was in trouble. Fortunately we had lots of salt, and I soaked my foot continuously, imploring Silas to get me back to Manaus as quickly as possible. We sailed down-river day and night for two days while my foot turned blue and my body temperature rose to 103°F. I made it to the hospital just in time...and while I was in the trance that usually accompanies high body temperatures, I dreamt of swimming with all my beautiful relatives, the cardinal tetras...their last name is Axelrod, too.

My Most Successful Expedition—Cardinals in Colombia (1965)

I was tingling with excitement as our Avianca plane began to lose altitude over the high Andes Mountains preparatory to landing in Bogota, Colombia. This rainy capital city, 8,000 feet up in the Andes, contains no fish which might ever adorn an aquarium, but it does represent the western gateway to the huge Amazon River system. It was from here that I was to take a breathtaking ride through the Andes, by taxi, to the first city on the llanos (plains), east of Bogota.

With me on this expedition was William "Bill" Riese, of Aquatic Fisheries, New York City. Bill, my constant travelling companion, made valuable contributions to the T.F.H. expeditions. His sense of humor, even at a time when my spirits were at a low ebb, never failed to brighten even the most discouraging situation...and his knowledge of imported tropical fishes is almost legendary. Bill's losses from imported fish run less than 20% of his entire gross. There isn't another importer in the world who approaches that figure!

But back to Bill's sense of humor for a moment. The first night we were in Bogota, we stayed at the Steve's Hotel. This isn't the swankiest hotel in Bogota, but Steve is an American, he flies his own C-47, he has holding facilities for 250,000 neons in his hotel, and he hauls tropical fish from Colombia to Tampa on a bi-weekly basis. We were waiting for Steve to make arrangements for hauling the fish we hoped to catch back to Florida. Bogota in November is anything but a paradise. The temperature fluctuates from 75 to 45° in a matter of minutes; it is almost constantly raining; and the air is so thin at 8,000 feet that we were plagued with spells of breathlessness and constant headaches. Rather than eat every meal at Steve's Hotel, we decided to experiment with the local chow, and we took one meal at the "best" hotel in town.

Now everybody knows that Colombia is famous for its coffee, and I love strong black coffee and drink it without sugar (while most South Americans drink it with five or six spoonfuls to the cup). After finishing a very uneventful meal of a steak that dared you to chew it, I looked forward to my hot, strong coffee. I almost quivered with delight when we were served in cups that were a bit larger than the 2 ounce coffee cups for which Colombians are noted. After the first mouthful, I noticed a decidedly peculiar taste and I said to Bill: "Even the coffee tastes bad here. Let's get rolling to Villavicencio; Steve will catch up to us."

Bill just sat there and stared into space.

"I had to let you talk me into coming here, when I could be in Belem (Brazil) catching discus?" he said, rather despondently.

276

Suddenly I broke the lethargy, and said, "Come on Bill, let's go. Let's take the first taxi to Villavicencio. This place is awful." With that, I picked up my coffee cup and drained the cup dry. Almost instantly I spat out the mouthful of coffee, for in the bottom of the cup was a huge 1 1/2 inch cockroach...and as I spat it out, its spiny legs caught on my tongue and the side of my mouth, making the whole effort an awkward, sloppy splatter that decorated everyone within spraying distance.

Bill was unimpressed. He merely looked at his stained jungle jacket, shrugged, and said, "What are you getting excited about; he was dead, wasn't he?"

I tasted that dead cockroach for weeks afterward. (By the way, I took the insect with me, preserved it in formalin and donated it to the Smithsonian Institution along with my collection of fishes. Wouldn't it have been a riot if it turned out to be a new species...and we named it *coffeeiensis!*)

I finally convinced Bill that we should head for Villavicencio the next morning, and thus began the most beautiful automobile ride I have ever taken. The road from Bogota to Villavicencio is a first class road most of the way. It goes through mountains and valleys that defy description...and I have ridden through the Alps in Switzerland, the Burma Pass, the Khyber Pass, the Canadian Rockies and the mountains north of San Francisco, California. Nothing compares with this ride for sheer beauty. The trip takes about four hours, and almost exactly halfway there is a roadside rest which serves the traveler. It is manned by the local Indians, and the food is unbelievably tasty. Our luncheon snack was about two quarts of the sweetest freshly squeezed orange juice I ever tasted (marred only by thousands of flies and dirty hands doing the squeezing) and potatoes boiled and then deep fried (whole) in the fat of some kind of animal I have never seen cooked before. Perhaps it was llama. From that experience on, Bill and I always took the cab ride of four hours from Villavicencio to Bogota, even though the airplane made it in 20 minutes and cost the same.

Arriving in Villavicencio, we went immediately to the Hotel Meta where we were greeted by Capt. Emilio Saiz. Our whole experience with Capt. Saiz is so different that I must describe some of the details of this visit. First of all, the Hotel Meta (named for the Meta River) is a beautiful tropical hotel. Here, only 75 miles from Bogota, the climate was better than Miami Beach...and the hotel *almost* as comfortable. In the center of the hotel is a huge, clean swimming pool with filtered water; a very comfortable bar is to be found in the hotel, in a room 100 feet wide and 300 feet long. The restaurant is clean and neat, except for the huge rats which scampered about every few minutes, distracting you with their scratching sound as they moved quickly from one side of the room to the other. The meals were enjoyable except for the beef, which was so tough it defied chewing.

Capt. Saiz, trained as an accountant, is a university graduate and retired from the Colombian Army. He served for many years in Leticia, the southeastern-most tip of Colombia, at the Peruvian-Brazilian border. It was here that Saiz learned about fishes and fishing, and it was here that he started in business after he retired from the military to enter the business world. What was the most striking about Capt. Saiz was his command of English and his immaculate appearance. The compound he maintains is also immaculate, and no small engineering feat either. In order to get running water, Capt. Saiz ran an aqueduct from a clear fresh stream in the mountains through a 16-inch pipe to his compound half a mile away and a thousand feet lower. The cool, fresh water is a tonic for the fishes, and the outdoor pools need never be shaded, for the running water keeps the pools sweet and the fishes cool. The water from the stream has a pH of 6.8 and is 74°F. Ideal for handling fishes!

The very next morning, after a restful night at the Hotel Meta, we went to the river and started our fishing. In the shallow, rapid parts of the river close to the compound (which is near the airport about five miles outside of town), we used various types of nets to catch the beautiful *Corydoras metae* and *Hypostomus plecostomus*. Also in the same stream were colorless silver tetras and the magnificent green-gold variety of *Corydoras aeneus*. This variety is extremely beautiful and very valuable because the fish don't lose the reddish yellow glow to their bodies and lower fins. They are different from the Trinidad *aeneus* in other respects, too. First, they are more "friendly" and don't spend so much of the daylight hours lying motionless on the bottom. Secondly, they are very peaceful and even when kept with a tankful of newborn guppies, they didn't bother them. Thirdly, and most importantly, they are strong and hardy and live for many months in the home aquarium where they are subject to many abuses. The green-gold *Corydoras* is worth the few extra pennies it might cost. It is a very colorful scavenger.

Assisting us in this fishing were two Indian boys. One of them, named Inuma, was from Leticia and was extremely capable, hardworking and uncomplaining. What a refreshing difference from the white-skinned campesiños of South America. Inuma knew how to fish and together we collected several hundred *Corydoras* and *Hypostomus* in five or six hours.

After completely investigating the fishes in the Villavicencio area, we chartered a small Norseman plane and flew northeast to what looked like a promising area in the llanos (plains) separating the Amazon jungle from the Andes mountains. This plain is a hundred miles wide and is infamous for its bandits. As a matter of fact, when we arrived at one small city on the Rio Meta, we were met by Sgt. Tomas Galan, Batallon de Infanteria, No. 21 "Vargas," of the Colombian Army. The Sergeant was extremely cooperative, and merely for a 55-gallon drum of gasoline he provided us with military transportation and an armed guard. We needed a guard, too, for only a short time before we arrived, and at the exact same place in which we fished, a most cruel and inhumane murder took place.

The bandits approached the thatched hut of a cowboy living on the plains to steal his cows. They herded the entire family into the one large room of the house and bound all the children and their mother together, leaving them to lie helplessly on the floor. They took the cowboy, stripped him and slammed a drawer shut on his genitals, nailing the drawer locked after they finished. Then they nailed one of the cowboy's hands to a post in the house, threw a very old, dull knife on the table and set fire to the house. Even after the cowboy sacrificed himself to save his family, they murdered his wife and children and left the cowboy to die slowly in the hot sun. (He didn't die, having been saved by a chance visit from a neighbor.)

It felt comfortable to have the army, with loaded and cocked rifles, assisting us.

We drove out into the llanos for many miles, stopping only to dip a net experimentally into the water now and then. Suddenly I gasped, for ahead of us on the horizon I could make out the familiar buriti-palm tree. This is the palm tree that is always found where cardinal tetras are found. I wondered...

I could hardly wait as the truck drove slowly across the plains to the swampy land adjacent to the palms.

This was the rainy season and everything was muddy. Even as we rode, the insects were eating us alive. But I forgot about the bugs now. This beautiful sight—buriti-palms in the middle of the plains—was overpowering. It's almost like finding banana trees in Central Park, New York.

When the truck had to stop about a mile from the water, I quickly jumped off, grabbed Inuma and Bill Riese, and we headed for the stream which was nourishing the buriti-palms. The water was cool (73°F.), perfectly clear, pH 6.4, and very deep. Though only ten feet or so in width, the stream was 20 feet deep in some places, and the local Indians who watched me fish refused to go in the water for fear of the large snakes that drag you down and drown you before you are eaten.

The sides of the stream went straight down and were lush with the most beautiful water plants. There wasn't an inch that wasn't bright green with plants I had never seen before. The scene was hypnotizing, and Inuma, Bill and I were standing there for at least ten minutes before the rest of the crew caught up to us.

Inuma and I went into the water immediately, and when I brought up the first net, we screamed with delight! Every fish in the net was a prize! Magnificent *Microgeophagus ramirezi*, not the grubby washed out specimens that result from years of inbreeding, but yellows, blues and reds that defy the imagination. In the same net we found the paradoxical *Hyphessobrycon stictus*. In nature, this fish has a bright cardinal red caudal peduncle. This soon fades if the fish is not kept in water which has a pH of around 5. We also found marble hatchetfish and a beautiful new *Apistogramma*. The second netful of fish brought up beautiful *Copella* and one lone specimen of the cardinal tetra. Imagine finding cardinals thousands of miles from the Rio Negro! We also found along with them the red phantom, *Megalamphodus sweglesi*. I have never found so many commercially valuable fish in one small stream as I did there—but this is not the end of the story.

As I fished for more and more cardinals, in water over my head most of the time, while the Indians gleefully watched expecting me to gobbled up by a 30-foot long boa, Bill went along with Inuma looking for other fish. Suddenly I heard a scream and could only picture Billy being dragged down by the snake monster the Indians were bragging about. Then, Billy's voice rang loud and clear.

"Herb, come here, I found a solid red cardinal!"

It didn't take me long to reach Bill and I gasped at what I saw.

His hands at first looked red with blood, but on closer examination I noticed that he had a fist full of tiny red fish less than an inch long. Only their caudal peduncle sported a small black spot. What a fish paradise this was!

Well, any further excitement would be anti-climatic, but Capt. Saiz was no slouch either, and he came up with a magnificent catfish we call the angelicus *Pimelodella*. This is not the real scientific name, but only a nickname we are giving the fish because its silver body and contrasting black spots remind us of the African *Synodontis angelicus* in reverse. (That African fish has white spots on black; this one has black spots on a silver field.) We were very fortunate in bringing back all of the fishes alive, thanks to Capt. Saiz, who maintained them for us until we were ready to return.

After consulting with Dr. Jacques Gery, we discovered that our all-red fish, which we called the "red ruby," was not only a new species, but also a new genus! Quite a find. It was eventually named *Axelrodia riesei*.

A pair of cardinal tetras, *Paracheirodon axelrodi*, in brilliant color. The heavy-bodied female is above the more slender male. Photo by M. Chvojka.

In the nighttime, we fished several rivers that were shallower and caught many *Exodon paradoxus*, green *Pimelodella*, giant 5″ headstanders, *Caenotropus labyrinthicus*, as well as more *Corydoras metae* and other interesting forms.

All in all, because of the great people I fished with and the accumulation of such beautiful fishes in one small area, I consider this to be the most successful expedition I have ever been on.

INDEX

Abramites hypselonotus, 129
Acanthodoras spinosissimus, 144
Acanthophthalmus anguillaris, 145
Acanthophthalmus javanicus, 145
Acanthophthalmus kuhli, 123, 145
Acanthophthalmus myersi, 123, 145
Acanthophthalmus semicinctus, 123, 145
Acanthophthalmus shelfordi, 123, 145
Acanthopsis choirorhynchus, 145
Aequidens curviceps, 85
Aequidens maronii, 82
Aequidens portalegrensis, 74, 85
Aequidens pulcher, 85
African Knifefish, 160
African water frogs, 173
Air pumps, 183
Algae, 170
Amazon sword, 97
Ameca splendens, 73
American flagfish, 153
Ampullaria cuprina, 126
Anabantoids, 49
Anableps anableps, 72
Anacharis, 155, 158, 159, 163
Ancistrus species, 140
Angelfish, 59, 66, 81, 94, 173
Angelicus catfish, 144
Anguillula silusiae, 175
Anostomus anostomus, 132
Antibiotics, 168
Aphanius mento, 153
Aphyocharax anisitsi, 129
Aphyosemion arnoldi, 130
Aphyosemion australe, 149
Aphyosemion bivittatum "loennbergi", 149
Aphyosemion cinnamomeum, 149
Aphyosemion occidentale, 130
Aphyosemion sjoestedti, 130, 149
Apistogramma agassizi, 85
Apistogramma bitaeniata, 85
Aplocheilus lineatus, 152
Aplocheilus panchax, 152
Apple snail, 126
Arapaima gigas, 157
Argentine pearlfish, 152
Artemia, 170
Asian weatherfish, 148
Astronotus ocellatus, 64, 81, , 83, 125
Astyanax fasciatus mexicanus, 96
Aulonocara "night", 89
Axelrodia riesei, 282
Bacterial infections, 168
Badis badis, 156
Bala shark, 137
Balantiocheilos melanopterus, 137
Balistoides conspicillum, 273
Banded loach, 148
Banded snakehead, 157
Banjo catfish, 144
Barbodes everetti, 133
Barbodes lateristriga, 133
Barbodes schwanenfeldi, 133

Barbs, 113
Bedotia geayi, 156
Beef heart, 176
Belonesox belizanus, 72
Belontia signata, 80, 240
Betta macrostoma, 76
Betta splendens, 51, 76
Bettas, 173
Big-spot rasbora, 136
Bitterling, 137
Black molly, 43, 65
Black neon tetra, 96, 110
Black ruby barb, 116, 133
Black shark, 137
Black tetra, 96, 110
Black-finned celebes halfbeak, 73
Black-finned rummy-nose tetra, 93
Black-lined tetra, 96
Black-winged hatchetfish, 129
Bladderworts, 164
Bleeding heart tetra, 96
Bleeding-heart platy, 192
Blind cave tetra, "Anoptichthys", 96
Bloodfin tetra, 129
Blue acara, 85
Blue gourami, 49, 56
Blue gularis, 149
Blue panchax, 152
Blue-eyed livebearer, 73
Bluefin killifish, 153
Boehlke's penguin, 96
Botia hymenophysa, 148
Botia lecontei, 148
Botia macracantha, 148
Botia sidthimunki, 148
Brachydanio albolineatus, 136
Brachydanio frankei, 113, 136
Brachydanio rerio, 111, 136,
Brachygobius nunus, 157
Brine shrimp, 31, 74, 100, 109, 170
Bristlenose pleco, 140
Broad-banded coolie loach, 145
Brochis splendens, 141,
Broken-banded loach, 148
Bronze corydoras, 121, 141
Brown discus, 81
Brown-lined labido, 89
Brunei beauty, 76
Brycinus longipinnis, 132
Bubble-nest, 51, 163
Buenos Aires tetra, 93
Bunocephalus coracoideus, 144
Butterfly goodeid, 73
Butterfly siamese fighting fish, 76
C. fasciata, 56
C. labiosa, 56
Cabomba caroliniana, 159
Cabomba, 30, 170
Caenotropus labyrinthicus, 283
Callichthyidae, 120
Capoeta oligolepis, 133
Capoeta tetrazona, 114, 133
Carassius auratus, 137,
Carbon dioxide, 17, 71, 138, 139

ardinal tetra, 93, 107, 239, 273
arnegiella marthae, 129
arnegiella stritgata, 129
atfish, 119
atoprion mento, 132
audo, 72
elestial goldfish, 137
halceus macrolepidotus, 129
handa ranga, 157
hanna striatus, 157
haracins, 106
harales, 150, 162
hecker barb, 133
heckerboard lyretail cichlid, 85
heirodon axelrodi, 245,
hinese algae-eater, 123, 145
hloramines, 22
hlorella algae, 45
hlorine, 22, 169
hocolate cichlid, 84
hocolate gourami, 77
hopped lettuce, 35
ichlasoma coryphaenoides, 84
ichlasoma cyanoguttatum, 78
ichlasoma dovii, 83
ichlasoma festivum, 66, 84
ichlasoma labiatum, 83
ichlasoma meeki, 78, 84
ichlasoma nigrofasciatum, 84
ichlasoma octofasciatum, 79, 84
ichlasoma salvini, 84
ichlasoma severum, 79, 84
ichlids, 59
innamon panchax, 149
lams, 123
lown barb, 133
lown loach, 148
lown pleco, 140
olisa chuna, 77
olisa fasciata, 77
olisa labiosa, 77
olisa lalia, 55, 77
olossoma brachypomum, 132
ompressed cichlid, 91
ongo Ctenopoma, 80
ongo tetra, 110, 132
onvict cichlid, 84
opeina guttata, 129
opella, 281
orydoras adolfoi, 141
orydoras aeneus, 121, 141, 279
orydoras agassizi, 122
orydoras julii, 121
orydoras metae, 279, 283
orydoras paleatus, 120, 141
orydoras robineae, 141
orydoras cf. trilineatus, 141
osby blue gourami, 80
renicara filamentosa, 85
rowding 165
ryptocoryne, 118, 163
tenobrycon spilurus, 129
tenopoma congicum, 80
uban rivulus, 153
ynolebias bellotti, 152
ynolebias whitei, 152
yphotilapia frontosa, 88
yprinidae 111
anio aequipinnatus, 136
anios, 111
aphnia, 31, 59, 74, 87, 100, 171
atnioides microlepis, 157

Dawn tetra, 111
Day's paradise fish, 76
Dermogenys pusillus, 49, 73
Diet, 167
Discus, 99
Double-banded dwarf cichlid, 85
Dried tubifex, 173
Drosophila, 174
Duckweed, 170
Dwarf banded gourami, 55, 77
Dwarf cichlids, 102
Dwarf loach, 148
Earthworms, 174
Echinodorus, 162
Egg yolk, 59
Egglayers, 27
Egyptian mouthbrooder, 59, 66, 86
Eigenmannia virescens, 160
Eight-banded leporinus, 132
Enchytraeids, 171
Epicyrtus, 274
Epiplatys dageti, 152
Epiplatys fasciolatus, 152
Eretmodus cyanostictus, 92
Etroplus maculatus, 82, 88
Exodon paradoxus, 283
False neon tetra, 93
Fanwort, 159
Farlowella species, 140
Feeding, 169
Fenestratus hap, 89
Festivum, 66
Filters, 185
Firemouth cichlid, 78, 84
Five-spotted archer fish, 156
Flag cichlid, 84
Flame tetra, 96, 110
Flatworms, 166
Floating plants, 163
Fluorescent lights, 17
Freeze-dried tropical fish foods, 35
Freshwater butterfly fish, 157
Freshwater clams, 124
Frontosa, 88
Fruitflies, 174
Fuelleborn's lab, 89
Fundulus chrysotus, 153
Fungus, 63, 71, 98
Gambusia, 45, 46, 72
Garmanella pulchra, 153
Garnet tetra, 93
Gasterosteus aculeatus, 160
Geisha girl, 116
Geophagus balzani, 88
Giant danio, 136
Giant gourami, 77
Girardinus metallicus, 73
Glass catfish, 122, 144
Glossolepis incisus, 156
Glowlight tetra, 93, 111
Gnathonemus petersii, 160
Gold swordtail, 69
Golden blue gourami, 80
Golden Convict cichlid, 84
Golden dwarf cichlid, 85
Golden European weatherfish, 148
Golden nyasa (Malawi) cichlid, 90
Golden orange chromide, 88
Golden pheasant, 149
Golden-eared killie, 153
Golden-sided victoria hap, 88
Golden-spotted panchax, 152

Goldfish, 113
Gold-naped corydoras, 141
Gonopodium, 26
Gordon's formula, 40, 47, 177
Gravel, 21
Gravid spot, 30
Green knifefish, 160
Guppy, 32, 68, 94, 170
Gymnocorymbus ternetzi, 96, 110
Gyrinocheilus aymonieri, 123, 145
Gyrodactylids, 166
Half-banded coolie loach, 145
Halfbeaks, 49
Haplochromis brownae, 88
Haplochromis fenestratus, 89
Harlequin rasbora, 136
Harrison's pencilfish, 129
Head and tail lights tetra, 93
Headstander, 129
Heater, 19, 181
Heckel's discus, 81
Helostoma temmincki, 57, 77
Hemichromis bimaculatus "lifalili", 88
Hemichromis bimaculatus, 66, 75
Hemigrammus caudovittatus, 93
Hemigrammus erythrozonus, 93, 111
Hemigrammus ocellifer, 93
Hemigrammus pulcher, 93
Herotilapia multispinosa, 81
Heterandria formosa, 47, 73
Hifin platy, 38
Hi-fin tuxedo platy, 68
Hi-fin wagtail platy, 68
Honey gourami, 77
Hooded bumblebee goby, 157
Hoplosternum thoracatum, 141
Hormones, 37
Horse-faced loach, 145
Humpbacked limia, 72
Hydras, 57
Hygrophila, 161
Hygrophila polysperma, 161
Hyphessobrycon bifasciatus, 111
Hyphessobrycon cardinalis, 245
Hyphessobrycon eos, 111
Hyphessobrycon erythrostigma, 96
Hyphessobrycon flammeus, 96, 110
Hyphessobrycon herbertaxelrodi, 96, 110
Hyphessobrycon scholzei, 96
Hyphessobrycon simulans, 245
Hyphessobrycon stictus, 281
Hypoptopoma inexpectatum, 140
Hypostomus plecostomus, 279
Hypostomus cf. *punctatus*, 140
Ich, 19
Ichthyophthirius, 167
Indian glassfish, 157
Infusoria, 53, 87, 171
Iridescent plated catfish, 141
Iridescent shark catfish, 144
Jack Dempsey, 79, 84
Japanese livebearing snail, 125
Javan ricefish, 153
Jewel fish, 66, 75
Jordanella floridae, 153
Julidochromis marlieri, 92
Julidochromis ornatus, 92
Julie, 92
Keyhole cichlid, 82
Killifishes, 134
Kissing Gourami, 57, 77
Korthaus's notho, 149

Krib, 104
Kryptopterus bicirrhus, 122, 144
Kuhli loaches, 123, 240
Labeo bicolor, 137
Labeo erythrurus, 137
Labeotropheus fuelleborni, 89
Labeotropheus trewavasae, 89, 91
Labeotropheus, 90
Labidochromis exasperatus, 89
Labidochromis cf. *mathothoi*, 89
Labyrinth fish, 27
Lamprologus brichardi, 92
Lamprologus compressiceps, 91
Lamprologus leleupi, 91, 92
Lancer upside-down catfish, 144
Latipinna, 44
Leaf fish, 156
Least Killifish, 47, 73
Lemna minor, 164
Lemon cichlid, 91, 92
Leopard corydoras, 121
Leopard danio, 113, 136
Leporinus octofasciatus, 132
Libby betta, 54
Lifalili jewel cichlid, 88
Light, 16, 166
Live food, 170
Livebearers, 27, 173
Livingstone's mbuna, 92
Long-finned African tetra, 132
Long-finned spot-tail, 73
Long-finned white cloud, 137
Long-finned zebra danio, 136
Lucania goodei, 153
Ludwigia, 163
Ludwig's aquarium, 99
Lymnaea, 127
Lyretail Lamprologus, 92
Lyretail molly, 44
Lyretail sailfin molly, 65
Lyretailed panchax, 149
Macropodus opercularis, 54, 76
Madagascar rainbowfish, 156
Magdalena spot-finned killie, 152
Malawi cichlids (Mbunas), 90
Malawi golden cichlid, 89
Malayan halfbeak, 73
Marbled hatchetfish, 129
Marigold variatus platy, 72
Marlier's julie, 92
Maroni River, 82
Mastacembelus armatus, 160
Medaka, 116
Megalamphodus sweglesi, 96
Melanochromis auratus, 89, 90
Melanotaenia splendida, 156
Merry widow, 72
Metabolic waste products, 167
Methylene blue, 98, 104
Metynnis hypsauchen, 132
Mexican swordtail, 35
Mickey mouse platy, 68
Microgeophagus, 102
Microgeophagus ramirezi, 85, 103, 104, 281
Microworms, 74, 175
Milfoil, 158
Misgurnus anguillicaudatus, 148
Misgurnus fossilis, 148
Mollienesia, 41
Mollies, 41, 170
Mono, 157
Monocirrhus polyacanthus, 156

Monodactylus argenteus, 157
Moonfish, 37, 38
Moonlight gourami, 80
Morulius chrysophekadion, 137
Mosquito larvae, 174
Mosquitofish, 45, 72
Mudpussers, 42
Mussels, 123, 124
Myers's hillstream loach, 148
Myriophyllum spicatum, 158
Mystery snail, 126
Mystus micracanthus, 144
Nannacara anomala, 85
Nannostomus harrisoni, 129
Nemacheilus botia, 148
Neon tetra, 93, 107
New Guinea red rainbowfish, 156
Night peacock cichlid, 89
Nitella, 29, 106, 107, 114, 115, 117, 150, 154
Nomorhamphus liemi, 73
Nothobranchius korthausae, 149
Nothobranchius palmqvesti, 149
Nothobranchius rachovi, 149
Orange chromide, 82, 88
Oryzias javanicus, 153
Oryzias latipes, 116, 193
Oscars, 83
Osphronemus goramy, 77
Otocinclus flexilis, 140
Overcrowding, 17
Overfeeding, 17, 18
Oxygen, 63, 138, 139
Pachypanchax, 150
Palmqvest's notho, 149
Panaque sp., 140
Pangasius sutchi, 144
Pantodon buchholzi, 157
Paracheirodon axelrodi, 93, 107, 239
Paracheirodon innesi, 93, 107
Paracheirodon simulans, 93, 107
Paracheirodon, 107, 245
Paradise fish, 49, 54, 76
Paraguay mouthbrooder, 88
Paramecia, 53, 70, 171
Parasites, 167
Pearl danio, 136
Pearl gourami, 57, 58
Pelvicachromis pulcher, 88, 104
Pelvicachromis, 102
Peppered corydoras, 141
Peppered sucking catfish, 140
Perch, 78
Persian minnow, 153
Peter's elephantnose, 160
Petitella georgiae, 93
Phallichthys amates, 72
Phalloceros caudimaculatus, 72
Phenacogrammus interruptus, 110, 132
Photosynthesis, 154
Pike livebearer, 72
Pimelodella, 283
Pimelodus pictus, 144
Pink kribensis cichlid, 88
Pink-eyed albinos, 220
Pink-tailed chalceus, 129
Pirarucu, giant arowana, 157
Plain coolie loach, 145
Plain metynnis, 132
Plain-fin popondetta rainbowfish, 156
Plane-head sucking catfish, 140
Planorbis corneus, 126
Planting tongs and snips, 190

Plants, 170
Platy, 37, 38
Poecilia latipinna, 43, 65,
Poecilia nigrofasciata, 72
Poecilia reticulata, 32, 65, 68, 193
Poecilia sphenops, 43, 65
Poecilia velifera X latipinna, 65
Polka-dot upside-down catfish, 144
Polycentrus schomburgki, 156
Pomacea bridgesi, 126
Pond snails, 127
Popondetta connieae, 156
Port acara, 85
Port Hoplo, 141
Power filters, 186
Prepared foods and formulas, 176
Priapella intermedia, 73
Prickly pleco, 140
Procatopus gracilis, 153
Pseudacanthicus spinosus, 140
Pseudocrenilabrus multicolor, 86, 88
Pseudogastromyzon myersi, 148
Pseudosphromenus cupanus dayi, 76
Pseudotropheus livingstoni, 92
Pseudotropheus tropheops, 92
Pseudotropheus zebra, 90, 92
Pseudoxiphophorus bimaculata, 73
Pterolebias longipinnis, 152
Pterophyllum dumerilii, 94
Pterophyllum scalare altum, 94
Pterophyllum scalare, 66, 81, , 94
Puntius conchonius, 116
Puntius lineatus, 133
Puntius nigrofasciatus, 116, 133
Puntius ticto, 116
pH test kits, 189
ph of the water, 166
Rachovia brevis, 152
Rachow's fire killie, 149
Rainbow cichlid, 81
Rainbow fish, 32
Rainbow shark, 137
Ram, 85
Rasbora heteromorpha "hengeli", 136
Rasbora heteromorpha, 117, 240
Rasbora kalochroma, 136
Rasbora trilineata, 118, 136
Rasboras, 117
Red devils, 83
Red phantom tetra, 96
Red ramshorn snail, 126
Red-bellied piranha, 132
Red-breasted pacu, 132
Red-chinned panchax, 152
Red-lined Australian rainbowfish, 156
Red-spotted Copeina, 129
Red-tailed black shark, 137
Red-tailed goodeid, 73
Red-top trewavasae, 89
Rhodeus sericeus, 137
Riccia, 164
Rice fish, 116
Rineloricaria cf. hasemani, 140
Rivulus cylindraceus, 153
Rosy barb, 116, 133
Round-spotted puffer, 160
Sagittaria, 161
Sagittaria graminea, 161
Sailfin platy, 38
Salt, 108
Salvinia, 164
Scat, 157, 170

287

Scatophagus argus, 157
Scavengers, 17, 27, 122
Schomburgk's leaf fish, 156
Scissortail rasbora, 136
Serrasalmus cf. nattereri, 132
Severum, 84
Short-bodied labido, 89
Shrimp, 123, 176
Siamese fighting fish, 51, 76
Siamese tiger fish, 157
Silver needlefish, 160
Silver tetra, 129
Siphoning tubes, 188
Snails, 123, 124, 125
Snakes, 130
Snakeskin gourami, 80
Spade-tailed dwarf cichlid, 85
Spanner barb, 133
Specific gravity of the water, 166
Sphaerichthys osphromenoides, 77
Spirodela polyrhiza, 164
Spot-banded coolie loach, 145
Spotted pleco, 140
Sternopygus macrurus, 160
Stoneworts, 150
Striped barb, 133
Striped goby cichlid, 92
Striped gourami, 56
Striped green panchax, 152
Striped headstander, 132
Stripe-tailed corydoras, 141
Sunset honey gourami, 77
Surface area, 17
Swordtail, 35, 192
Symphysodon aequifasciata aequifasciata, 100
Symphysodon aequifasciata axelrodi, 81, 100
Symphysodon aequifasciata haraldi, 100
Symphysodon aequifasciata, 81
Symphysodon discus discus 100
Symphysodon discus willischwartzi 100
Symphysodon discus, 81
Synodontis alberti, 144
Synodontis angelicus, 144, 282
Tanganyika cichlids, 94
Tanichthys albonubes, 117, 137
Tape Grass, 159
Temperature change, 17
Temperature 165
Tetraodon fluviatilis, 160
Tetras, 106, 173
Texas cichlid, 78
Thayeria boehlkei, 96
Thermometers, 23, 178

Thermostat, 23, 180
Thick-lipped gourami, 56, 77
Three-lined corydoras, 141
Three-spined stickleback, 160
Three-spot gourami, 56
Tic-tac-toe barb, 116
Tiger barb, 114, 133
Tinfoil barb, 133
Topsail platy, 38
Toxotes jaculator, 156
Trewavas nyasa (Malawi) cichlid, 91
Trichogaster leeri, 58, 80
Trichogaster microlepis, 80
Trichogaster pectoralis, 80
Trichogaster trichopterus, 56, 80,
Tropheops mbuna, 92
Tubifex, 59, 86, 172
Turtles, 130
Tuxedo platy, 68
Twig catfish, 140
Two-spot catfish, 144
Two-striped panchax, 149
Underfeeding, 18
Vallisneria americana, 159, 170
Variable ghost knifefish, 160
Variegated green swordtail, 69
Variety of food, 169
Veil angelfish, 99
Viviparus, 125
Water changers, 187
Water hyacinth, 164
Whiptailed catfish, 140
White cloud mountain minnow, 117
White spot disease, 19
White's pearlfish, 152
White-spotted spiny eel, 160
White-striped spiny catfish, 144
Whiteworms, 97, 100
Wimple piranha, 132
Wingless fruitflies, 49
Xenentodon cancila, 160
Xenomystus nigri, 160
Xenotoca eiseni, 73
Xiphophorus helleri, 26, 33, 35, 69
Xiphophorus helleri X maculatus, 69
Xiphophorus maculatus, 37, 68, 193
Xiphophorus variatus, 37, 72,
Yellow tetra, 111
Yellow-belly cichlid, 84
Yellow-finned loach, 148
Yolk sac, 70
Yucatan pupfish, 153
Zebra danio, 111, 120, 136
Zebra nyasa (Malawi) cichlid, 90